INFLATION MATTERS

Inflationary Wave Theory,
its impact on inflation past and present ...
and the deflation yet to come

Pete Comley

Copyright

Copyright 2015. All rights reserved.
Version 1.0 Paperback, July 2015.
Published by Pete Comley.

No part of this publication may be reproduced in any material form whether by photocopying or storing in any medium by electronic means whether or not transiently or incidentally to some other use for this publication without the prior written consent of the copyright owner except in accordance with the provisions of the Copyright, Designs and Patents Act 1988 or under the terms of a licence issued by the Copyright Licensing Agency Limited of 90 Tottenham Court Road, London WIP 0LP.

Many of the product names contained in this publication are registered trademarks, and the copyright owner has made every effort to print them with the capitalisation and punctuation used by the trademark owner. For reasons of textual clarity, the use of symbols for Trade Mark, Copyright and Registered, etc. has been omitted. However, the absence of such symbols should not be taken to indicate absence of trademark protection; anyone wishing to use product names in the public domain should first clear such use with the product owner.

ISBN: 978-1515090991

Contents

INTRODUCTION v

PART I: INFLATION FACT AND FICTION 1
1 What is inflation? 3
2 Inflation and the money supply theory 9
3 Other theories about inflation 19
4 Deflation and why it is regarded as a problem 29
5 UK inflation measures 43
6 Inflation measurement issues 51

PART II: INFLATION PAST 67
7 Inflationary Wave Theory 69
8 World War I and learning about hyperinflation 79
9 The 1930s depression and the deflation bogeyman 91
10 World War II, debts and the low inflation world 99
11 The 1970s inflation crisis and fiat currencies 109

PART III: INFLATION PRESENT 117
12 The Great Moderation and the Great Recession 119
13 Japan and deflation 127
14 Governments and inflation 137
15 The era of inflation targeting 149
16 The impact of current inflation 161

PART IV: DEFLATION YET TO COME 175
17 The big picture: a century of more stable prices 177
18 The transition period and near-term inflation 189
19 Price stability and the consolidation period 209
20 Managing wealth as we head towards near-zero inflation 221

EPILOGUE 235
GLOSSARY OF TERMS 236
INDEX 238
ABOUT THE AUTHOR 241
ACKNOWLEDGEMENTS 243

Q. Why are you reading this book?

A — I want to know why inflation is so low

B — I want to understand what causes inflation

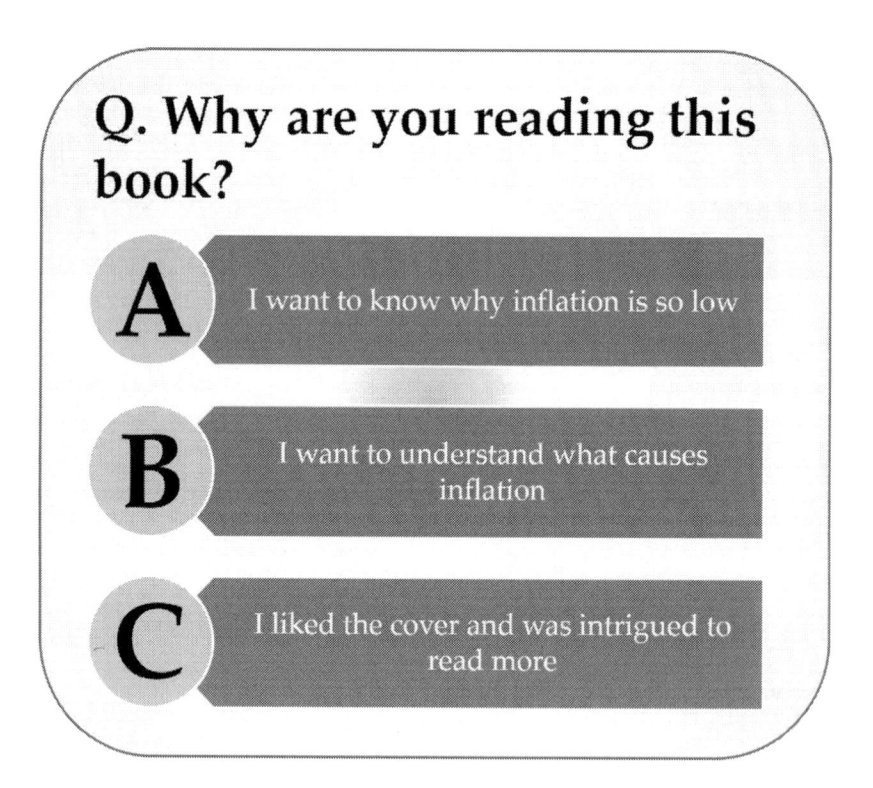

C — I liked the cover and was intrigued to read more

Quiz answers can be found at the end of each chapter.

INTRODUCTION

Before we start, I have a confession to make.

I'm not an economist by trade. I do not have an economics degree. Indeed I have no formal economics training. So why should you read this book about inflation and the coming deflation from someone who appears to know very little about the subject?

Who wrote this?

My name is Pete Comley. My day job is actually market intelligence and I'm an insight consultant[1]. I founded a company called *Join the Dots*, which now employs around 100 people. The objective of the consultancy is to understand our clients' issues, synthesise data from a vast array of sources to answer them and then succinctly convey what it all means back to our clients. We are very successful at what we do and our client base is growing strongly. That is because we do exactly what it says on the tin: we join the dots.

When we approach our clients' problems we objectively collect data and review the evidence. We do not just look at the facts as seen through the normal lens but we're happy to use other disciplines, like history and psychology where appropriate. We look for the big picture and try to link it into trends we see around the world. We seek out the story and our aim is convey it as creatively as we can to engage our audience.

Most existing books on inflation are at the other extreme. Indeed some people[2] have argued that inflation is one of the most boring subjects out there. I have sympathy with them. The problem with most of the information you read about inflation and deflation is that it is written by macro-economists for other macro-economists. It is full of jargon, formulas and complex theories.

This book takes the opposite tack. It is written in plain English for the average person. It tries to avoid economics speak wherever possible and aims to bring the subject alive. As you'll see, the subject is actually far from dull and could have profound implications for us all over the coming decades.

Why this book on inflation?

My interest in inflation started a few years ago whilst writing *Monkey with a Pin*[3]. Inflation is one of the most important variables affecting the real returns of private investors. However I then started thinking more broadly over why we have inflation. That research led me to write *Inflation Tax: The Plan To Deal With The Debts*[4] in 2013. That book highlighted how inflation had only really become a serious problem in the UK following World War II. It looked at the key role that politicians appeared to have played in fostering it to help deal with governmental debts.

Since then, I have continued my research into inflation. My thinking has moved on somewhat, hence the desire to write this book. It builds on that earlier work and incorporates much more data. It was sparked by looking further back into history and finding that inflation is more usual across the world than I realised. The relative price stability seen in the Victorian period appears to be the exception in a bigger trend of ever higher prices. These increases seems to follow a wave-like pattern; hence my decision to call this *Inflationary Wave Theory*.

Inflationary Wave Theory

The driving force behind this inflation appears to be the long-term growth in the world population and the competition that it creates for resources.

Inflationary Wave Theory

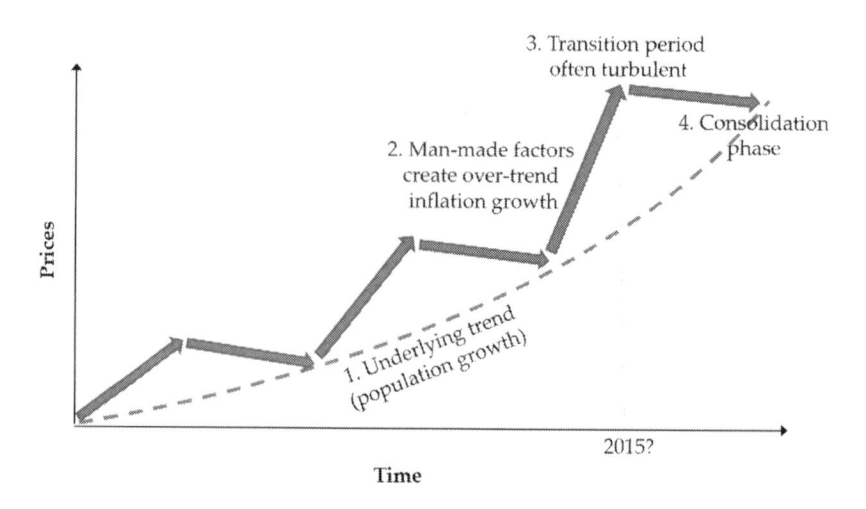

Man-made factors then interact with this trend over the medium-term, ranging from governments sanctioning increases of the money supply through to those seeking to exploit the situation for personal gain. These can be further exacerbated by short-term surges in inflation caused by commodity price rises and devaluations. These all cause a strong rise in inflation where prices get too far ahead of the primary force. This upward part of the inflationary wave typically lasts for around a century or more. We are approaching the end of one soon.

Prices eventually crash into a phase of relative calm surf and the world enters the consolidation part of the wave of more stable or declining prices for a long period of time. However, the transition between the two phases is often a turbulent one and is usually accompanied by a temporary sharp fall in prices and a significant destruction of wealth.

The consolidation phase usually fosters prosperity and with it, eventually, the seeds of its own demise. The improved quality of life and fortune spur people to procreate and this starts to put pressure on resources again and the whole cycle starts over again. This is the basis of Inflationary Wave Theory.

Implications for inequality

The other motivation for writing a new book was a concern about the rising inequality in the world. My previous book highlighted how recent inflation has caused declining living standards for many. This issue has become more mainstream post Thomas Piketty's *Capital in the 21st Century*[5]. However by largely concentrating on data since the 19th Century, what Piketty failed to highlight was the cyclicality of inequality over the very long-term.

The wave peaks of inflation (that occur every two hundred years or so) are also associated with massive transfers of wealth. These enrich governments and already wealthy individuals at the cost of the general public who are largely unaware of the real cause of their difficulties. Historically these periods have been associated with misery, poverty, death and revolutions.

Piketty however is right that these inequalities are probably set to increase. This is because we have yet to reach the crest of the present inflation wave. Thankfully, this time, modern systems of welfare will protect most from the worst of these ills. Nevertheless ordinary people will suffer until this latest inflation wave finally crashes and

INFLATION MATTERS

we enter another century of relative price stability and more equal prosperity. Inflation is at the heart of rising inequality.
Inflation matters.

inflationmatters.com
#inflationmatters
@petecomley

QUIZ ANSWER:
A, B or C.

---

[1] In the old days we used to be called market researchers.

[2] The first people to whom I mentioned that I was writing this book on inflation told me clearly not to bother as it was a boring subject that nobody wanted to hear about. I hope that you find that they were wrong.

[3] Comley, P., 2012, "Monkey with a Pin: Why You May Be Missing 6% a Year From Your Investment Returns", Self-published.

[4] Comley, P., 2013, " Inflation Tax: The Plan To Deal With The Debts", Self-published.

[5] Piketty, T., 2014, "Capital in the 21st Century", *Harvard University Press*.

PART I

INFLATION FACT AND FICTION

Q1. What is inflation?

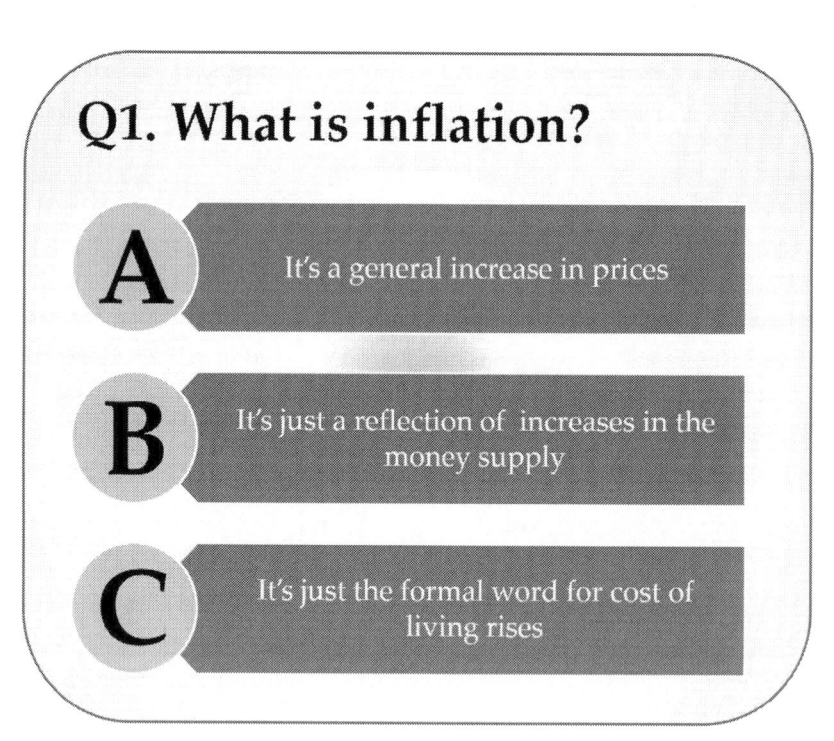

A — It's a general increase in prices

B — It's just a reflection of increases in the money supply

C — It's just the formal word for cost of living rises

1

What is inflation?

It is important to understand what inflation is. It is not as easily defined as many people might imagine. There are in fact a number of accepted definitions and this can result in misunderstandings, particularly if you start trying to comprehend the economics behind it.

Definitions of inflation

If you look online or in the glossary of most modern economics books[1], you'll see inflation defined as:

"A sustained increase in the general price level of goods and services in an economy over a period of time."

If you ask the average man in the street to define inflation they'll probably describe it as being a general increase in the price of things. This is largely framed by the way that the media portray it every month when the latest inflation data are announced. These all focus on the annual percentage change in prices.

Many people also regard it as synonymous with the *cost of living* and think inflation is merely a technical term for it. Indeed this causes confusion as measures often used to quantify inflation, such as CPI in the UK, were not designed as cost of living indices. (See: "6-Inflation measurement issues.")

However, if you look up inflation in other current dictionaries, you'll often find a definition such as:

"A persistent increase in the level of consumer prices or a persistent decline in the purchasing power of money."[2]

What is interesting from this definition is that although most people would recognise the first part, they generally do not understand the second part, which highlights the effects of inflation i.e. the decline in purchasing power[3]. Indeed it is the second aspect of inflation that has been key in increasing inequality in recent times. (See: "16-The impact of current inflation.")

But these are all modern definitions of inflation. Fifty or more years ago, if you looked in a dictionary you would have found inflation defined in a completely different way. It was usually described in terms of the amount of money in circulation. For example, the definition in the first dictionary I purchased as a student in the 1970s said inflation was:

"An increase in the amount of fiduciary (paper or token) money issued beyond what is justified by the country's tangible resources."[4]

This definition is much closer to that used by a group of economists called the Monetarists. However as we will see, although inflation is influenced by the money supply, it is more complicated than this as other factors can and do affect prices. (See: "2-Inflation and the money supply theory.")

The evolving definitions of inflation

Current layman's:
- *An increase in prices (or the cost of living)*

Recent dictionary:
- *An increase in the level of consumer prices or a decline in the purchasing power of money*

Older dictionary:
- *An increase in the amount of money issued beyond what is justified by the country's tangible resources*

Economists' many definitions

Confusingly there is no single accepted definition of inflation used by all economists. If you ask a group of them to define it, most would probably describe it in terms of an increase in prices and/or the money supply in some way. However they would be at pains to point out that the answer to the question is much more complex than this since they measure more than one type of inflation:

WHAT IS INFLATION?

1. **Goods and services inflation (or price inflation).** This is the inflation that the average layman thinks of when they talk about inflation. It includes everything the consumer buys and is well represented by measures such as the CPI.
2. **Asset price inflation.** This includes assets such as housing, shares, commodities and other non-cash assets. The prices of such assets seem particularly sensitive to changes in the money supply.
3. **Wage inflation.** This refers to the average increase in workers' wages. Some argue this might be a better measure for central banks to monitor when setting interest rates, as it perhaps more accurately reflects the slack in the economy. It is also a key determinant of government tax revenue.
4. **Producer price inflation.** This refers to the change in output prices of goods/services created in a country. It is often regarded as a leading indicator of future changes in consumer price indices like CPI.
5. **Core inflation.** This is price inflation but excluding volatile items such as food and energy prices. It is created to try to measure the long-term trend in prices. This is the measure used by some central banks (e.g. the US Federal Reserve) to assess inflation.

For clarity in the rest of this book when I refer to *inflation*, I mean the standard layman's definition (i.e. rising prices), unless specified otherwise.

KEY LEARNING POINTS:
- The current layman's definition of inflation is an increase in prices.
- Monetarist economists define inflation as an increase in the money supply.
- Economists now often distinguish between different types of inflation, e.g. price inflation, asset inflation, wage inflation, producer price inflation and core inflation.

QUIZ ANSWER:
A.

[1] Blanchard, O., 2000, "Macroeconomics (2nd ed.)", *Prentice Hall*.
[2] The American Heritage Dictionary
(http://www.ahdictionary.com/word/search.html?q=inflation, accessed 1/6/2013).
[3] Some of this is due to a phenomenon called the "money illusion". This term refers to the fact that people focus much more on the numerical value of money than on its real purchasing power (after you have factored in inflation). It is not a surprising fact. Who has the inclination or mathematical brain to keep doing those complex calculations?
[4] Source: Collins Dictionary published in 1970.

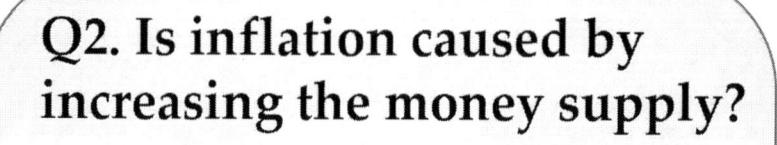

Q2. Is inflation caused by increasing the money supply?

A — No, it is created by central banks

B — Yes, as money is created, prices go up directly

C — Ultimately yes, but the relationship is weak short-term

2

Inflation and the money supply theory

This chapter looks at the most common explanation of inflation i.e. that it is related to the expansion of the money supply. It reviews the evidence for the theory and explains exactly how it is supposed to work.

If you ask most economists what causes inflation, they'll probably mention that it is linked to the amount of money in circulation. As an example, they might ask you to imagine a simple world of bakers and brewers.

The effect of a money supply increase on prices

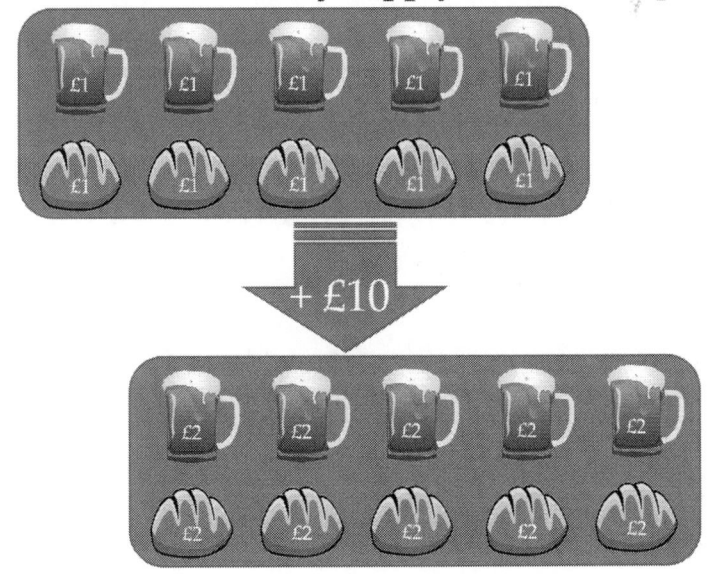

There might be five bakers and five brewers each selling a loaf and a pint of beer to each other every day. Each costs £1 in gold coins. The total wealth of the world is £10. Now imagine what would happen if another £10 in gold coins is found and everyone gets a share of them.

The amount of money in the world has suddenly doubled to £20 but there are still only 5 loaves and 5 pints of beer being made each day. Everyone feels a bit richer but the only thing they can buy is bread and beer. As people think they have more money, they all try and outbid each other to get extra provisions. Very quickly the prices of all the bread and beer will increase until they cost around £2 and a new equilibrium is reached again. £1 in gold coins now only buys half a loaf or half a pint of beer.

That is a simple example of the theory behind the link between the money supply and inflation. In real life, it is a lot more complex and it can take a long time for prices to rise to the new equilibrium and hence the relationship is not always as visible as the theory suggests it should be. However, there is strong evidence that the theory holds over the medium-term as you'll see below.

History of the theory

Sharp increases in prices have been observed in many periods of ancient history from ancient Babylonia to the Roman Empire. A particularly prolonged period of rising prices throughout the globe was seen in the 16th and early 17th Centuries. (See: "7-Inflationary Wave Theory.")

At that time, money was defined in Europe in terms of precious metals. Silver and gold coins were issued as the primary medium of exchange. That era was the time of Christopher Columbus and the great discovery of the Americas. The key thing plundered from the New World and brought back to Europe was vast quantities of gold and silver. This made certain countries and financiers much richer as wealth was defined in terms of precious metals. The amount of money circulating in Europe therefore increased.

At the same time prices were rising in Europe and many scholars started to suggest reasons why this was happening. Amongst them was the famous astronomer Copernicus. He was one of the first people to propose the theory that the price increases seen were in fact related to the increases in the money supply.

INFLATION AND THE MONEY SUPPLY THEORY

Copernicus - one of the first theorists on inflation
Source: "Nikolaus Kopernikus" - http://www.frombork.art.pl/Ang10.htm.
Licensed under Public domain via Wikimedia Commons

The key formula

In its most simplified form, scholars such as Copernicus stated that Prices (P) vary in proportion to the supply of money (M) i.e. $P \propto M$.

This simple discovery was to have major implications for centuries to come. Indeed, as we've seen in the previous chapter, it became part of the very definition of inflation for a long time.

Quantity theory of money

Many developments and variants of Copernicus's theory have been put forward since. Probably the most notable was in 1848, when John Stewart Mill[1] formally proposed the "quantity theory of money" and produced the "equation of exchange". He showed that the simple formula is only applicable if both the size of the economy is stable (i.e. GDP is constant) and there has been no change in the number of times money is spent during that period by people i.e. people's saving levels and spending levels haven't gone up or down. The full formula he proposed was thus: MV=PQ.

I will try and translate this jargon into words that might make some more sense. It is saying that at any period of time, the money supply (M) multiplied by the number of times people use that money (V) is equal to the average prices (P) multiplied by the total value of all the goods we produce in that time i.e. GDP (Q).

$$MV = PQ$$

Money supply × Velocity of money = Average prices × Value of goods/GDP

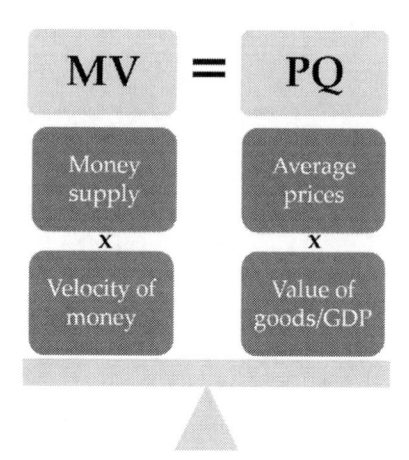

The difficult aspect of this is the number of times people use money, or the "velocity of money", as it is known. This is to do with saving and spending levels. The basic idea behind this qualification is that if lots of people save money, fewer people will be buying goods. For a while at least, too many goods will be being made relative to buyers. Sellers therefore will be forced to drop prices as they compete for what business is left. The reverse situation also occurs when saving decreases and spending levels go up in an economy i.e. prices rise.

Evidence for the theory

Proponents of the theory (called Monetarists) can point to many more recent examples than the 16th and 17th Centuries where excessive money printing appears directly linked to rising levels of inflation. The most infamous of these was during the Weimar Republic in Germany in the early 1920s. (See: "8-World War I and learning about hyperinflation.")

Indeed if you examine the long-term rise in inflation in the UK since 1900, it is strongly correlated to the growth in the money supply. The graph below shows an index of UK prices from 1900 and compares this with an index of the UK money supply. (In order to satisfy the equation of exchange, a deduction from the money supply has been made for the extra money required because of our expanding economy, i.e. the index is money supply less GDP[2].)

The graph shows that over the last century inflation has fairly closely followed the money supply. However there have been quite long periods when one of the two was slightly higher. Indeed for the last couple of decades, consumer price inflation has been lagging behind increases in the money supply in the UK and this situation must be resolved at some point. (See: "18-The transition period and near-term inflation".)

The link between UK prices and the money supply

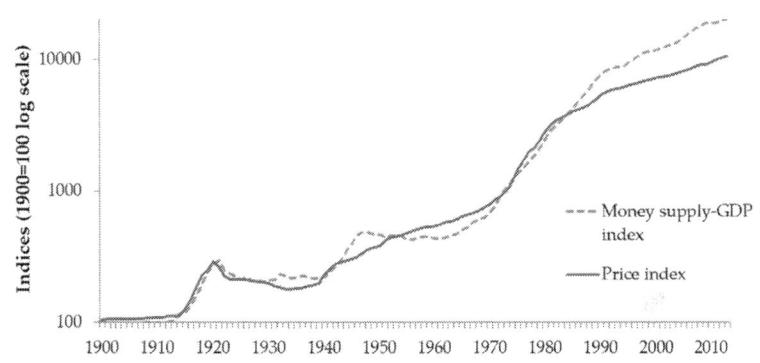

Sources: Price index - ONS longitudinal series. Money supply - The Bank of England's preferred measure (M3/M4/M4x). GDP - measuringworth.com.

Some issues with the theory

What the above chart also illustrates is that changes in the money supply are not always directly reflected in the prices of goods and services. Indeed the two can go for many years or even decades in opposite directions. This is partly because of changes in people's desire to save/spend (i.e. the velocity of money) and partly because the newly created money does not always flow directly into goods and services - see below.

No one tells the population that the money supply has increased. The very first response to an increase in money supply is often for people to save, and so effectively they keep the amount of money in circulation the same. Therefore prices do not immediately change either. As that money spreads further around the economy, more and more gets into circulation. Prices then rise. Furthermore, money supply and velocity of money are often correlated. As money supply increases, velocity of money goes up (and vice versa in a recession) and so the price changes can be bigger than the money supply calculations alone might predict.

To further complicate matters, this process is very much dependent on where the increases in money supply have gone (i.e.

into retail prices or into asset prices) and more generally on consumer sentiment and the state of the business climate and cycle. It is therefore not surprising that there is often little short-term synchronicity between the money supply and inflation. This is clearly illustrated in the data from the UK in recent years.

There has been little correlation between the money supply and inflation in the last 20 years

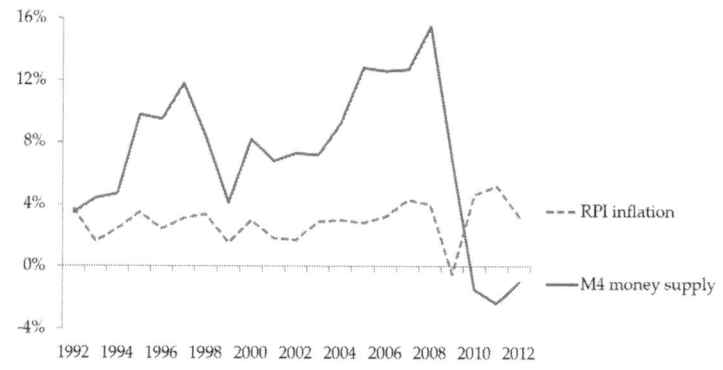

Sources: Bank of England, 12-month change in money supply M4 and ONS annual RPI inflation.

As the above chart shows, there has been little correlation[3] between increases in the money supply in the UK and retail inflation in the twenty years between 1992 and 2012.

Many economists now acknowledge that changes in the money supply are not predictive of retail inflation over short-term periods or in low-inflation environments.[4] In a recent paper[5] examining the real world correlation between money supply and inflation of all countries between 1969 and 1999, the following conclusion was reached:

"This strong link between inflation and money growth is almost wholly due to the presence of high-inflation or hyperinflation countries in the sample. The relation between inflation and money growth for low-inflation countries (on average less than 10 per cent per year over 30 years) is weak, if not absent."

Money supply and asset price inflation

But what these simplistic analyses of monetary theory miss out is the complexity of inflation. To comprehend this, you need to understand exactly how the money supply is expanded. Money is normally

INFLATION AND THE MONEY SUPPLY THEORY

created in an economy when private banks make loans to individuals or companies. (See box below: "How money is created.") Typically this money is first used for speculation or to purchase assets e.g. houses, companies/shares, bonds, commodities (or more complex derivatives of them). It is not normally created to spend directly in the economy on goods and services, although typically it ends up there.

Therefore when the money supply is expanded, as happened markedly during the 80s and the following decades in the UK, it creates inflation in the assets that the money is first used for. This so-called "asset price inflation" is clearly illustrated in the chart below with data from the UK.

Asset price inflation and the money supply

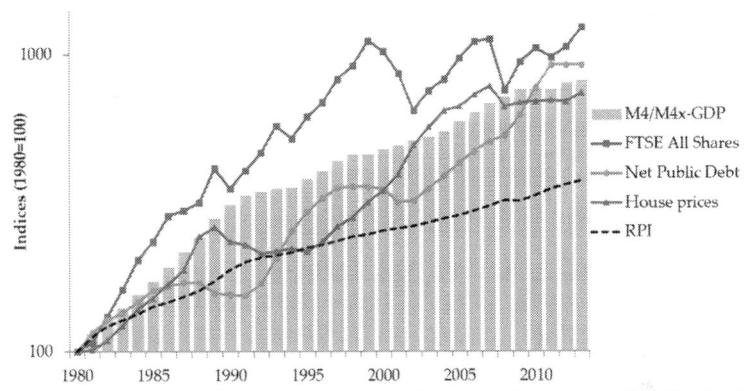

Sources: Price index - ONS longitudinal series. Money supply - *Bank of England* (M3/M4/M4x). GDP - measuringworth.com. FTSE - Finfacts and SwallowPark. Net Public Debt - ukpublicspending.co.uk . House prices - ONS.

The solid bars on the chart show an index of the money supply (M4/M4x) less GDP growth, i.e. the net increase in the money supply over and above that required by the UK economy during this time. The lines show where that money then flowed to. These depict the index prices of key asset classes such as shares (i.e. FTSE All Share Index), bonds (i.e. Net Public Debt) and house prices. It shows that a series of bubbles were created over this period in these assets. The prices of all of them have kept up with or exceeded the overall increase in the money supply.

The dotted line on the chart shows an index of goods and services prices (RPI) and how the expanded money supply since 1980 has yet to have its full impact in this area. The gap between the two and the implications of this are discussed more in later chapters. (See: "18-The transition period and near-term inflation".)

Two separate money supplies? Two separate inflations?

What is key to understand about the quantity theory of money concerning inflation and the money supply is that it affects two separate economies: wealth (i.e. asset prices) and consumer spending (i.e. goods and service prices). Money flows between these two economies. For example when someone sells a house and spends the proceeds in the real economy on goods/services like holidays or health care, they are transferring money from one economy to the other. Similarly when they save their salary in a pension, money is transferred in the opposite direction.

It has been argued that the two sectors obey the quantity theory separately (and over the medium-term in totality too). However economists rarely highlight this issue. This is probably because it is difficult to demonstrate as countries do not normally publish data separately for the money supply in the two areas.

HOW MONEY IS CREATED

Although many people talk about the money supply in the context of Monetarist theories, comparatively few really understand how money is actually created and how the money supply is increased.

Contrary to popular conception, very little of the money that exists in the UK has been created by the government. Our money is not usually created by the Bank of England (except recently during Quantitative Easing). Very little is in the form of coins and notes.[6] Instead 97 per cent of our money has been literally created from nothing by commercial banks when people or companies have sought loans. Mervyn King, the ex-governor of the Bank of England, made this very clear in an article he wrote back in 1994:

"In the United Kingdom...money is created by the banking system."[7]

Moreover in 2014, the Bank of England published a paper[8] clearly outlining exactly how private banks create the money in our economy and debunking the commonplace misconception that people deposit money first and then banks lend it out.

What really determines the money supply is the willingness of commercial banks to lend money. This is in part a reflection of their ability to lend within the constraints of their assets and the need to have a certain amount of reserve capital covering those loans (a concept called "fractional reserve banking"). This was why they did not lend as much after the 2008 recession, as their assets had been reduced by bad loans and at the same time regulation demanded that they hold higher reserves.

INFLATION AND THE MONEY SUPPLY THEORY

KEY LEARNING POINTS:
- The quantity theory of money states that: MV=PQ, i.e. the money supply multiplied by the velocity of money is equal to average prices (P) multiplied by GDP (Q).
- There is evidence that increases in money supply create price rises medium-term, but the relationship is poor in the short-term.
- This is primarily because most new money goes into a separate money supply related to assets and not into the economy of goods and services. It is further complicated by changes in the velocity of money that are difficult to measure.

QUIZ ANSWER:
C.

---

[1] Mill, J., 1848, "Principles of Political Economy", *John W. Parker*.

[2] The logic for deducting GDP from the money supply index is a direct application of the theory of exchange which states: change in money supply + change in velocity = change in prices + change in quantity of goods produced i.e. GDP. The graph ignores the effect of velocity of money, as this cannot be measured independently of the other variables. See: Laidler, D., 1985, "The Demand for Money: Theories, Evidence, and Problems", 3rd edition, *Harper and Row*. The consumer pricing data was the ONS longitudinal series, which largely mirrors RPI and its predecessor the UK Cost of Living Index. The money supply index used a broad measure of money supply and the one that is the *Bank of England's* preferred measure. This was originally M3, then became M4 and is now M4x.

[3] The relationship over the last 20 years is slightly negative, $r^2 = -0.09$.

[4] For example, see: LK, 2010, "The Quantity Theory of Money: A Critique", *Social Democracy for the 21st Century blog*, 18 July 2010.

[5] De Grauwe, P. and Polan, M., 2005, "Inflation Always and Everywhere a Monetary Phenomenon?", *Scandinavian Journal of Economics*, 107.

[6] Less than 3% is cash according to Jackson, A. & Dyson, B. (2013), "Modernising Money", *Positive Money*.

[7] King, M. (1994), "The Transmission Mechanism of Monetary Policy", *Bank of England Quarterly Bulletin*, August.

[8] McLeay, M., Radia, A. and Ryland, T. (2014), " Money creation in the modern economy", *Bank of England Quarterly Bulletin*, March

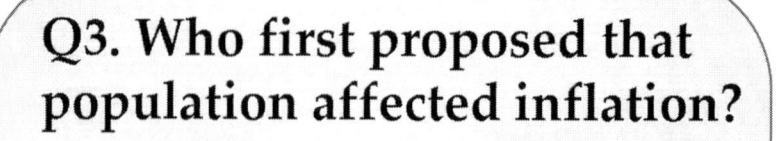

Q3. Who first proposed that population affected inflation?

A Ben Bernanke in 1995

B Reverend (Thomas) Robert Malthus in 1794

C John Maynard Keynes in 1937

3

Other theories about inflation

In addition to monetarism, there are two main other theories about the causes of inflation which have been proposed by leading economists of the past:

1. John Maynard Keynes: That inflation is a combination of demand-pull factors (e.g. when demand outstrips supply due to wars, population growth or government policy) and cost-push factors (e.g. when higher prices are forced upon us due to tax rises, devaluations, or commodity price rises).
2. Reverend (Thomas) Robert Malthus: That the long-term increase in prices is a result of the ever increasing world population and competition for resources that this creates.

All three of the theories discussed in this and the previous chapter probably influence inflation rates but over different time scales. Over the short-term, Keynes's theory explains the daily gyrations of price indices best (e.g. in response to commodity price changes and governmental policies). Over the medium-term, money supply is important. Over the very long-term, it is population growth and demographics that most impacts inflation.

Keynes's cost-push and demand-pull inflation theory

The eminent economist John Maynard Keynes theorised a lot about inflation. He postulated that the money supply had an influence on inflation in a much more complex way than the strict monetarists suggested.

John Maynard Keynes
Source: Reproduced with permission of the IMF

Instead Keynes proposed that inflation was caused in number of different ways:
- By demand outstripping supply and pulling inflation higher
- By inflation being built into the system
- By higher costs pushing inflation higher.

Examples of Keynesian view of inflation

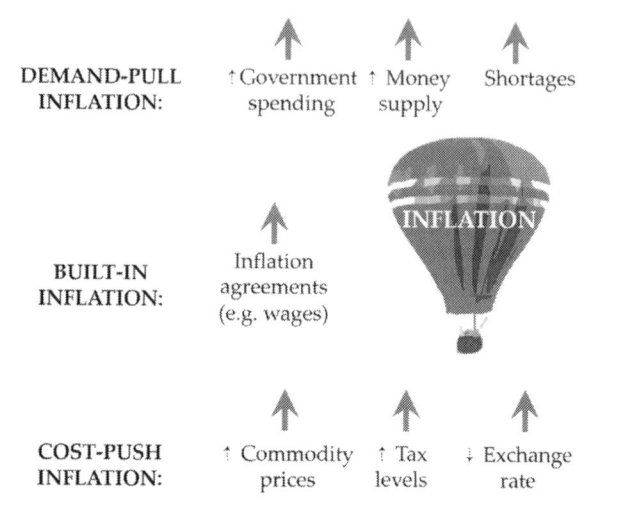

DEMAND-PULL INFLATION: ↑ Government spending ↑ Money supply Shortages

BUILT-IN INFLATION: Inflation agreements (e.g. wages)

COST-PUSH INFLATION: ↑ Commodity prices ↑ Tax levels ↓ Exchange rate

OTHER THEORIES ABOUT INFLATION

It was also Keynes's view that inflation expectations were important. They impact the wage settlements that workers seek and affect other inflation agreements that are created. These can have a marked effect on future inflation rates[1].

Furthermore Keynes and his followers have argued that governments face a trade-off between unemployment and inflation – i.e. if you want full employment you may need to tolerate higher inflation.[2] Indeed, as Keynes was writing during the Great Depression, he not surprisingly gave great importance to reducing unemployment. This thinking paved the way for post-war governments that were less concerned about creating inflation than their predecessors, as they saw it as a necessary trade-off to create full employment. (See: "10-World War II, debts and the low inflation world.")

It is interesting that the Keynesian theory of inflation has gone out of fashion. This is probably related to the rejection of Keynesian thinking in general which started in the 1970s. However Keynesian ideas have had something of a renaissance following the Great Recession of 2008 as governments seek alternative solutions to the problems we now face.

Evidence for the Keynesian theory

In order to examine the merits of the theory, it is instructive to look at the periods of inflation greater than 4 per cent in the UK since the last war and their probable causes – see chart on next page.

This analysis shows that Keynes's theory does explain the majority of the inflation spikes witnessed in the UK since the 1940s. Some are demand-pull factors e.g. war shortages and increases in the money supply. However cost-push factors have been particularly important i.e. increases in the price of oil, sterling devaluations (which have increased the prices of our imports) and tax rises.

Monetarists might say that the money supply is at the root of most of these factors. For example, it could be argued that the gradual devaluation of the pound against a basket of world currencies over the last century has had much to do with increasing UK money supply. Global money supply increases in the 1970s and following decades could well have significantly contributed to the trend of higher commodity prices—although clearly the short-term spikes in prices were often related to wars restricting supplies.

Probable causes of UK inflation peaks since 1940

Period of inflation (when RPI>4% pa)	Peak year	Peak inflation (%)	Probable main causes
1940–1942	1940	17.2	Decline of the pound in 1939/1940 by 22%. War shortages.
1947–1948	1947	7.4	Expansion of money supply (16% in 1947).
1951–1952	1951	9.5	Devaluation of pound in 1950 by 30%.
1956	1956	4.7	Petrol price rise/rationing in 1956 (Suez Crisis).
1965	1965	4.9	Various price/tax rises.
1968–1985	1975	24.2	Devaluation of pound in 1967 by 14%. Expansion of money supply (20%+ in 1972/3). Oil price rise in 1974 (OPEC restrictions).
	1980	18.0	Expansion of money supply (19% in 1978). Oil price rise in 1979 (Iranian revolution).
1987–1991	1990	9.5	Expansion of money supply (18% in 1988). Oil price rise in 1990 (invasion of Kuwait).
2007–2008	2007	4.3	Oil price rise in 2007. Pound slides 30% in two years.
2010–2011	2011	5.2	Oil price rise in 2011. VAT increase.

Note also that this analysis only looks at the spikes in inflation. Inflation has been increasing at low levels almost continuously since the war and the causes of that could be related to the overall steady increase in the money supply, both directly and indirectly.

Keynes's theory of inflation is therefore useful in explaining more short-term changes in the rate of inflation and probably much more so than Monetarist doctrine. This has implications for central banks, which usually adopt a Monetarist approach in controlling short-term inflation rates with macroeconomic tools such as the money supply and interest rates. (See: "15-The era of inflation targeting.")

Keynes and current inflation drivers

Although Keynes's model is useful for describing changes in inflation that we see today, it does not provide any measure of the relative importance of the many factors he describes. Keynes might have argued that he didn't do so as they can all be important in different circumstances, and that is probably correct. However, for us in the early 21st Century, some of the above factors do seem to more frequently affect the inflation rate than others. In particular the most important determinants of short-term UK inflation rates currently are governmental policy and commodity prices.

Governments control or influence many prices. In the UK this includes everything from energy to education to transport. Moreover they can and do ensure that many of them rise. Governments also set sales taxes and these can have a simple direct effect on inflation rates. This is clearly demonstrated by Japan which used such tax increases in 2014 to help foster inflation.

Most important drivers of current inflation

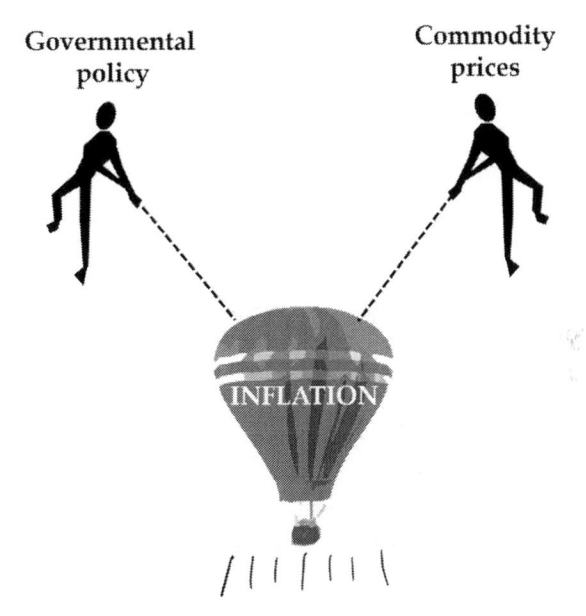

Commodity prices, including oil and foodstuffs, are also particularly important in affecting short-term inflation rates, as the spikes in UK inflation since 1940 clearly illustrates (see chart previously). This is because there are still many items in cost of living indices that are closely linked to these raw commodities e.g. petrol prices and crude oil prices. For example in 2014, oil prices declined by a half in a matter of months and this led to inflation rates in many countries declining towards near-zero levels.

Malthusianism

Let us now look back in time again at a different theory of inflation and one that pertains not to the short or medium-term but the longer-term.

Keynes took his influence from many sources. One of these was a late 18th Century economist, the Reverend (Thomas) Robert Malthus. Malthus proposed that long-term inflation was a result of the ever-increasing population[3].

INFLATION MATTERS

The Reverend (Thomas) Robert Malthus
Source: "Thomas Robert Malthus" by John Linnell
Licensed under Public domain via Wikimedia Commons

He suggested that the human population had the potential to grow exponentially. A key problem with this according to Malthus was that the increased supply of commodities used for our basic needs tended to grow only arithmetically. This mismatch created competition for resources, which caused prices to rise, especially in times of rapid population increases.

> It's the ~~economy~~ population, stupid!
>
> Thomas Malthus, 1798
> ~~James Carville, 1992~~

Malthus was writing at just one of those times in history. His theory fitted well with the previous waves of price increases in the 13th and 16th Centuries prior to that. Both of these were associated with marked rises in populations. Following Malthus's death, the 20th century witnessed an enormous surge in the world's population. From 1950 until 2013 the population almost trebled, from 2.5 billion to 7.2 billion. This period also saw the world's largest increases in prices ever recorded.

OTHER THEORIES ABOUT INFLATION

The influence of population size on inflation

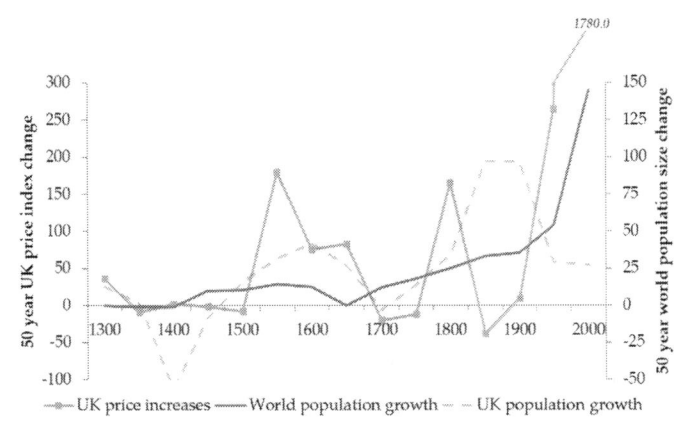

Source of population statistics: 1300-1950: McEvedy, C., and Jones, R., 1978, "Atlas of World Population History" and 2000-2100: Sanyal, S., 2013, "The Wide Angle Predictions of a Rogue Demographer". Source of prices: Phelps-Brown and Hopkins, 1956, and ONS.

But correlation does not infer causality. In addition, the fit with population increase is not precise. It does not explain why in the 19th Century, when populations continued to rise, prices were so stable. One explanation is that the pressure on prices in the UK was less during the 19th Century due to expanding resources provided by the Empires. Another factor was that during that time the UK owned the world's reserve currency and this may well have helped keep prices in check, relative to population.

The theory that inflation is related to demographics has had something of a renaissance in recent years. For example Harry Dent, the US economist and author, has written a number of books[4] proposing that the demographic profile of a country is strongly correlated with its economic prosperity. The main thrust of his argument is that people's expenditure increases through their lives until the late 40s and then declines. Therefore when there is a rise in the number of younger people in a population it leads to inflation and, similarly, when the average age of the population rises significantly, you get deflation as the net expenditure declines.

Average weekly UK household expenditure by age

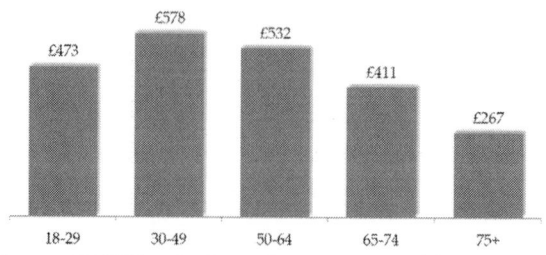

Age	Expenditure
18-29	£473
30-49	£578
50-64	£532
65-74	£411
75+	£267

Source: ONS Family Spending Survey, published 2013.

In addition, other factors beyond population, such as the money supply, have undoubtedly contributed significantly to price rises, especially in the short to medium-term. However Malthus was probably right that population growth can be a contributing factor to long-term inflation and, as we will see later, is often the trigger for the start of a new secular wave of inflation. (See: "7-Inflationary Wave Theory".)

Different theories. Different time frames

Recapping all these theories leads to an interesting conclusion. Maybe all the theories are right to some extent. It is just the time frame of their influence that distinguishes them.

Theories of inflation and their impact

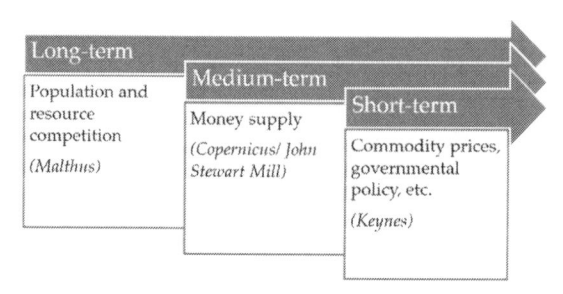

Long-term	Medium-term	Short-term
Population and resource competition (*Malthus*)	Money supply (*Copernicus/ John Stewart Mill*)	Commodity prices, governmental policy, etc. (*Keynes*)

Malthus's theory about demographics, population growth and competition resource probably have an impact over the very long-term inflation rate. Medium-term rates are influenced by money supply. Latent inflation created by printing money must be rectified at some point, but this might be delayed for decades. Short-term it seems to be factors expounded by Keynes that best explain the

OTHER THEORIES ABOUT INFLATION

gyrations of price indices on a daily basis, e.g. commodity price rises and government-regulated price increases.

KEY LEARNING POINTS:
- John Maynard Keynes proposed that inflation primarily results from a combination of demand-pull factors (e.g. when demand outstrips supply due to wars, population growth or government policy) and cost-push factors (e.g. when higher prices are forced upon us due to tax rises, devaluations, or commodity price rises).
- The most important influences on the short-term inflation rate currently are governmental policy and commodity prices. Therefore the Keynesian theory explains shorter term changes in inflation better than monetary theory (which explains medium-term changes better).
- Longer term inflation rates might also be more affected by demographics and population change, i.e. the theory proposed by the Reverend (Thomas) Robert Malthus.

QUIZ ANSWER:
B.

---

[1] Much research has been done on the subject of inflation expectations by economists and it shows that they are primarily influenced by observations of past inflation together with perceptions of likely future inflation proposed by experts e.g. in the media.

[2] Economists have created graphs to illustrate this relationship, called the Phillips Curve (see Phillips, A., 1958, "The Relationship between Unemployment and the Rate of Change of Money Wages in the United Kingdom 1861–1957", *Economica,* 25(100), pp 283–99.)

[3] Malthus T.R., 1798, "An Essay on the Principle of Population", *Oxford World's Classics.*

[4] Dent, H., 2014, "The Demographic Cliff: How to Survive and Prosper During the Great Deflation of 2014-2019", *Portfolio.*

Q4. What is the main effect of deflation?

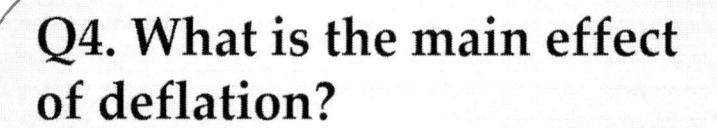

A It makes the average person worse off

B It stops people buying goods

C It increases the real value of debts

4

Deflation and why it is regarded as a problem

The experience of deflation in 1930s America has left a legacy of thinking that is extremely negative towards lower prices. (See: "9-The 1930s depression and the deflation bogeyman."). Economic opinion seems very one-sidedly against deflation. It often fails to even distinguish between the concepts of good, bad, or even benign deflation.

This chapter examines the evidence for all the arguments normally put forward for why deflation is supposedly a problem. It shows that deflation is indeed often bad for certain influential groups (i.e. governments, bankers, speculators and debtors). However for the vast majority of the population, steadily declining prices are actually a benefit most of the time.

Deflation vs lowflation

It is important first to distinguish between deflation and a world of low inflation or near-zero price rises, which is now becoming known as "lowflation". Many media commentators use the D word to refer to the current state of many world economies.

D *deflation* is for ~~dog~~

L *lowflation* is for ~~lamb~~

This is incorrect for a number of reasons. Firstly, in the developed nations in Europe there has not really been deflation in 2014. There has just been something called "disinflation" i.e. a slowing of the speed of price rises. Only in two of the worst affected European economies (Greece and Ireland) were the price indices lower in 2014 than pre-crisis levels and then by only 2-3 per cent. This is hardly falling prices as the man on the street would know it.

Even in Japan where nearly all commentators use the D word, prices did not decline at all in the 1990s and then largely moved sideways in the noughties. Following recent Quantitative Easing, they are now in late 2014 at all-time highs. Again this is not deflation.

We currently mostly live in a world of "lowflation". Most of the standard economic arguments against deflation assume we are talking of significant declines in prices like those witnessed in the 1930s depression i.e. 25 per cent or more. It is therefore important to remember when we look at the arguments below that none are applicable to the current state of inflation anywhere (even in Japan or Greece).

The negative economic wisdom

Negativity in economic thinking about deflation primarily originated in the 1930s and in the analysis of that event thereafter. This has fostered an economic consensus that deflation is a bad thing. For example, the *Economist* magazine has run a number of negative stories about deflation over the last few years. On 9th November 2013 it headlined the magazine with an article entitled the "*Perils of falling inflation*"[1]. On 25th October 2014 it ran another story about deflation called "*The world's biggest economic problem*". In this the *Economist* stated that low inflation is the biggest problem facing the rich world today and talked of declining inflation being "depressing", "scary" and a "pernicious threat".

Other economists have likened deflation to an ailment. A country with a low inflation rate is described as having the "Japanese disease". (See: "13-Japan and deflation.") A BBC website commentary[2] even went as far as saying: *"Deflation is like diabetes. Just like diabetes, deflation induces other complications and makes it worse."*

However like many things in economics, the reality is not quite as simple as the theory.

Reasons for deflation

There are many arguments put forward for why deflation is bad. However before we examine them, it is useful to understand what can cause deflation of prices. Economists sometimes distinguish between good and bad deflation.

1. **Bad deflation.** This is caused by decreased demand and is usually related to severe contractions in the money supply and/or reductions in the velocity of money. Normally contractions of the money supply occur in conjunction with financial crises and especially banking ones. In these events, banks restrict the amount of credit, interest rates often rise and money is destroyed either through defaults or net paying back of credit. These usually lead to asset price deflation (i.e. reductions in house prices, shares etc.) and sometimes to goods and service deflation (e.g. CPI/RPI). These situations are also normally accompanied by people saving more, coupled with simultaneous reductions in the velocity of money which amplify the effect caused by the shrinking money supply.
2. **Good deflation.** This is caused by reductions in the cost of goods. This can come about for a number of reasons. The main ones seen recently include: technological improvements (think computers), the digital revolution (which has reduced prices across many sectors), globalisation of production (e.g. outsourcing production to cheaper countries), reductions in labour costs (due to reduced trade union power, privatisations etc.), reductions in the costs of raw commodities (think of the recent declines in the oil price) and finally by appreciation of the local currency versus other producer nations.

The distinction is arguably more complicated than this, as there are different causes of decreased demand for goods and they should not all be grouped under the bad deflation banner. The most frequently experienced reason for decreased demand is related to financial crises and this does deserve the term bad deflation. However demand can also be lower due to population changes as we have witnessed in Japan. Here the working population has shrunk and this has caused a decline in economic production. The ageing population also consumes less. Both of these have been a downward force on prices. However it is unhelpful and somewhat misleading to group this type of decrease in demand into the bad deflation category. Perhaps a better description would be to add a third category of **benign deflation**.

Types of deflation

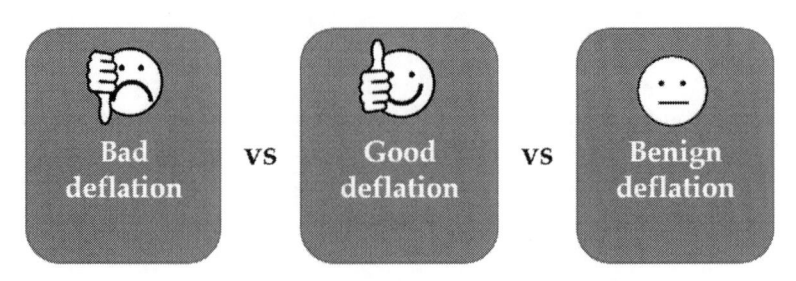

| Bad deflation | vs | Good deflation | vs | Benign deflation |

Given all this, you might think that whether deflation is regarded as a problem must depend on its cause and your perspective i.e. whether you own assets like shares or property or not. Despite this, most economists still argue that deflation is bad for the following five reasons.

Argument 1: Deflation is bad for the economy

The main argument is that deflationary periods are associated with bad times economically. This is because, as noted above, deflation is a typical side effect of financial and banking crises.

A bank run in Berlin in 1931
Source: Reproduced with permission from Bundesarchiv (*Bild* 102-12023/Georg Pahl/CC-BY-SA)

However what is usually missing from such arguments is the causality. In the Great Depression, it was the financial crisis that caused the problems. The results of this then included problems for

DEFLATION AND WHY IT IS REGARDED AS A PROBLEM

the economy and resulted in deflation. (See: "9-The 1930s depression and the deflation bogeyman.")

In addition to the 1930s, another example often quoted is that of the *Great Deflation* of the 1870s - 1890s. During this time prices in many countries around the world declined due to improvements in productivity and trade. For example in the UK, prices declined 15 per cent over the two decades from 1868. Many traditional businesses suffered due to the effects of technological changes and improvements in transport and communications; hence many historians regard it as another great depression.

However the consumer did not suffer. Analysis has shown that average incomes in the UK increased not only in actual terms but significantly also in inflation-adjusted ones. This increased purchasing power was so great that there was a marked shift in consumption from necessities to luxury goods.[3]

The last example usually quoted in the context of the problems of deflation is that of Japan. Here the financial crisis struck in 1990. It has been argued that the country then suffered two "lost decades" of deflation and poor economic growth. However as we'll see later, the reality is slightly different. It is debatable how badly the economy has suffered. It has been pointed out that standards of living[4], the strength of the yen[5] and trade surpluses have all increased[6]. Moreover GDP, when looked at on a per worker basis, has increased at a higher rate than in most developed European economies over the same period. (See: "13-Japan and deflation.")

A more recent example is Spain. In 2014, Spain was the only major EU economy to have deflation[7] (albeit at a low level). However it also topped the EU economic growth table that year with around 2 per cent. Deflation does not have to lead to problems for the economy.

CONCLUSION: Financial crises create asset price reductions which then can create reductions in consumer prices. Deflation of goods and service prices per se, does not have negative effects on the economy. They are a symptom but the not the cause of the problem.

Argument 2: Deflation is bad for debtors

The argument here is simpler. If deflation occurs, the real cost of servicing debts increases. This is because income declines (be it wages, company profits or taxation), yet the repayment costs remain the same. This also increases the risk of the debtor defaulting and being unable to repay the loan.

The effects of deflation on debts

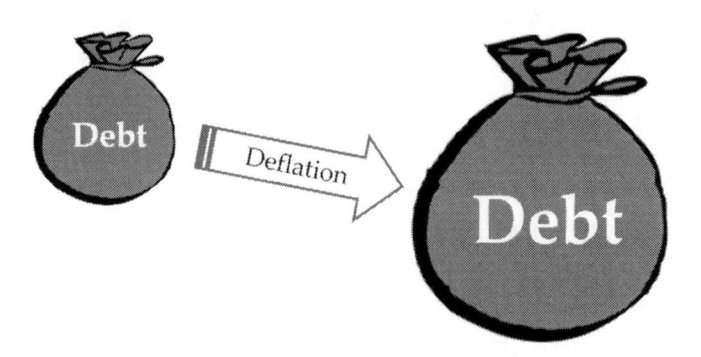

The effects of this depends on the debtor. For individuals it potentially means being made bankrupt or losing the security for the loan (e.g. a house). For companies, it means either cutting back on other business expenditure, reducing costs (e.g. laying off staff) or in the worst case, closing down. Both of these have implications for the banking sector, which then suffers losses on the loans that are defaulted on.

The impact on government debts is somewhat different though. It should mean that reductions in expenditure are required to balance the budget. However in practice nowadays, governments do not normally cut back expenditure. They run a bigger deficit during crises/deflationary periods and add to their total debt pile.

The knock-on effects of all the above directly impact GDP. If individual debtors have to use more money to service debts, they spend less money elsewhere in the economy. Reductions in spending by companies and governments also have the potential to reduce GDP.

However this theory does not match up with the facts, as evidenced by the 1980s and 1990s. This was a period of falling inflation rates. They dropped in most highly developed economies from about 20 per cent to nearly zero by the year 2000. During this time, there was no marked increase in the number of defaults amongst individuals or companies. In other words the higher debt burden of near-zero inflation rates at the end of this time in many economies did not appear to harm GDP growth.

Another issue with the argument that deflation increases the burden for debtors is that deflation causes an equal and opposite gain for savers and creditors. They see the real value of their purchasing power increase in deflationary periods. Those that acknowledge this counter that the spending habits of debtors are greater than those of savers, so it is better for the economy to have more inflation. Even if this is true, the economy has many more savers than debtors i.e. just over a third of UK households have a mortgage, whilst three quarters have savings and a similar number have additional pension wealth[8].

Linked to this is another factor that during all periods of inflation, there is a slow but incessant transfer of wealth taking place from savers to debtors. In periods of near-zero inflation it stops. During periods of deflation this flow is reversed. The argument against deflation might therefore be better framed as a moral one over whether creditors should be allowed to stop subsidising loans to borrowers and speculators. (See: "16-The impact of current inflation.")

CONCLUSION: *Deflation makes debts harder to pay and in theory this can have a knock-on impact on economic growth. However near-zero inflation rates appear not to have this effect.*

Argument 3: Deflation is bad for companies

Deflation is bad for companies as virtually all corporates nowadays are financed with significant amounts of debt. The sheer size of these debts is enormous.

Take Tesco, a retailer and FTSE 100 company, as an example. The company was in trouble in 2014 and its revenues were declining. This was mainly due to the lower prices it was charging, brought about by competition and decreased commodity prices. Deflation was sometimes blamed for its problems.

However the main problem for Tesco, like most listed companies, was actually debt. In late 2014, its market capitalisation was around £14bn but its total debts were also about £14bn[9]. When deflation happens revenues decline, but the size of the debt repayments remain the same. The free subsidy provided by creditors during periods of inflation is effectively removed when deflation happens. Therefore company profits suffer. The amount of money for investment also declines and this has a knock-on effect on other businesses' turnover and the whole economy.

In addition, in order to remain competitive during deflation, companies might seek to decrease wages in periods of deflation (just as they offer cost of living rises in periods of inflation). However reducing wages is difficult to do. It is far easier for a company to regain competitiveness by not offering a cost of living rise in a period of 2 per cent inflation than it is to cut wages by 2 per cent when there is zero inflation. It is therefore argued that company profits suffer during periods of deflation.

The impact of the inability to cut real wages is undoubtedly less than it used it to be in times of greater trade union power. In the recent recession, some companies cut back on wages effectively by reducing working hours. Moreover markets are now much more competitive in many areas. Contract workers are easier to replace with lower-paid ones. Despite this, there is still some evidence that companies are less likely to reduce wages than they are to award a zero pay rise in the current economic environment[10].

CONCLUSION: *Deflation decreases company profits primarily because modern business is founded on debt-based finance. That finance relies on inflation to help reduce its cost by transferring wealth from savers. Again there is a moral question on whether this hidden subsidy should exist for business.*

Argument 4: Deflation stops people spending

The argument goes something like this. If people realise that prices are gradually going down they behave logically and decide that it would be more efficient to delay their spending until items have become cheaper. This therefore slows down consumer expenditure and GDP declines as the velocity of money declines.

This is a nice economic theory, but evidence does not always support it. Indeed as some analysis[11] by an M&G Investments analyst recently concluded: "The argument that deflation stops purchases does not hold up in the real world." Moreover, it is also contrary to another very established economic theory that suggests that for every 10 per cent drop in prices, unit sales go up by approximately 10 per cent.

During the first decade of this millennium, the west was flooded with cheaper goods from China and discount retailers such as Poundland sprung up. Those retailers have been remarkably successful in encouraging impulse purchasing of cheaper stuff that arguably people do not need. There is no evidence from them that offering lower prices causes a decrease in unit sales.

Another example is electrical goods. As technological improvements have been made over the last 50 years, the prices of everything from TVs to phones have declined. There is no indication that people have cut back their purchasing in the hope that prices will become cheaper. Indeed sales of most electronics are increasing as their prices decline[12].

It is possible that the economists who proposed this theory were not fully factoring in declines in the velocity of money i.e. when people decide to save more and spend less. The uncertainty brought on by a financial crisis affects people's psyche. The fear it brings causes people to save more of what they have as they don't know what the future might hold and whether they still might have a source of income in the future. Seen this way it is not the lower prices in the shops that causes a slow-down in consumer spending but the impact of greater uncertainty brought on by a banking crisis.

CONCLUSION: *The evidence does not support the theory that decreased prices stop people spending. In fact, the opposite often happens and sales can increase. Decreased spending only occurs when accompanied by a banking crisis which affects consumer confidence.*

Argument 5: Deflation makes it difficult to control the economy

Central banks are primarily tasked with controlling monetary policy to aid the economy growing at a consistent and positive rate. The main lever they have for doing this is by controlling interest rates. The logic of this is as follows. If inflation takes off (above say the 2 per cent target in the UK), the central bank increases interest rates, so private banks tend to lend less money and reduce the money supply. As less money is chasing the same amount of goods being sold, prices should decline. When they do, interest rates can then be reduced.

The system also works the other way and when an economy is in recession, reducing interest rates helps stimulate the economy. This is carried on until demand picks up and prices start to rise.

Central banks' model of controlling inflation

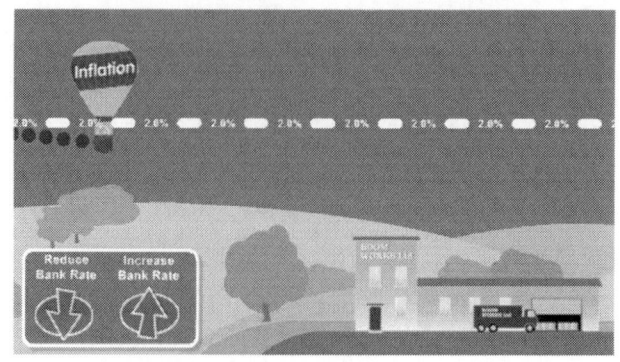

Source: "The Monetary Policy Balloon Game" - Bank of England

Therefore, in general, interest rates are usually highly correlated with inflation rates. However should deflation happen in an economy, central banks cannot easily decrease interest rates and make them negative. They therefore lose one of their most important tools to control monetary policy and it is argued that downturns in the economy become more prolonged because of it.

The counter argument to this is that the model of the way the economy works which central banks are using is a bit simplistic and that things often do not quite work the way they proclaim. Monetary policy often has an impact on asset price inflation (e.g. share prices) but the link with consumer prices is much less clear in the short-term. For example, when the Bank of England drastically reduced base rates from 5 to 0.5 per cent in the second half of 2008, CPI inflation remained high over the following several years.

Finally it should be remembered that central bankers have become powerful and influential and any scenario of inflation in which this power is reduced is not going to be welcomed by them. Perhaps it is not surprising we often used to see headlines about Ben Bernanke fighting against the threat of deflation[13].

CONCLUSION: *In periods of deflation, traditional monetary policy implemented by central banks will not work. However it is debateable how much this matters for society as those interest rate policies have a limited direct impact on consumer inflation anyway.*

The winners and losers with deflation

The above arguments clearly highlight that the main groups negatively affected by deflation are: companies, banks, central banks, governments, mortgage holders and speculators. These include the most influential groups in society. Balanced against these groups is the key winner with deflation—the general public.

The effects of deflation

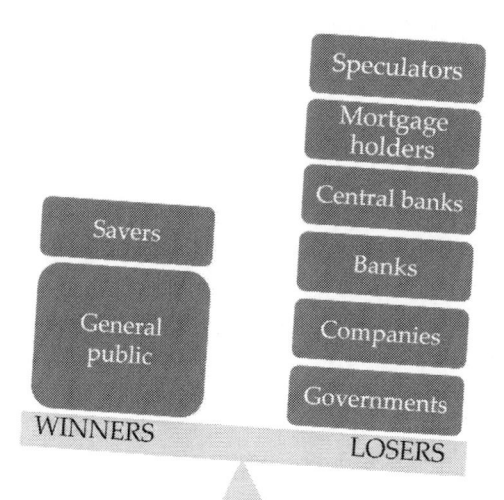

WINNERS: Savers, General public

LOSERS: Speculators, Mortgage holders, Central banks, Banks, Companies, Governments

Living in a world of near-zero inflation can be positive for many individuals. This is particularly so when it is so-called "good deflation" when the costs to produce goods and services genuinely reduce. As in the period of the Great Deflation of the 1870s-1890s, this means that most individuals become better off. The money in their pocket buys more goods as its purchasing power increases.

In addition, individuals with cash in their pockets and the three quarters of the population with some form of savings in banks see them retain their value over time. As interest rates will more than likely be very low in that circumstance, they are also subject to less tax.

In conclusion for general public, deflation is not the bogeyman it is commonly portrayed to be.

KEY LEARNING POINTS:
- Most economists regard deflation very negatively. Many fail to distinguish between the concepts of good deflation, benign deflation and bad deflation.
- Some of their arguments against deflation have some support. Deflation makes real debt repayments higher. This is bad for

debtors such as governments and particularly for most corporates which are highly indebted. It also makes it more difficult for central banks to enact policy (although the monetarist model that policy is based on has debatable efficacy over the short-term).
- However, a number of anti-deflation arguments are not supported by the facts. Decreasing the price of goods does not cause purchasing to be postponed in today's society. Good deflation, when prices decline because things are cheaper to produce, is not bad for the economy or the general public either.

QUIZ ANSWER:
C.

---

[1] Economist Editorial, 2013, "The perils of falling inflation", *The Economist*, 9 November 2013.

[22] Takeshita, S., 2009, "Japan's economic battle with deflation", *BBC News*, 23 March 2009.

[3] Selgin, G., 1997, "Less Than Zero: The Case for a Falling Price Level in a Growing Economy", *Institute of Economic Affairs*.

[4] Woolnough, R., 2014, "The lesson the Japanese economy has for the developed world", *M&G Investments Blog*, 7 October 2014.

[5] Exchange rates increased until the period of Abenomics started in 2013.

[6] Fingleton, E., 2012, "The Myth of Japan's Failure". *The New York Times*, 6 January 2012.

[7] Flanders, S., 2014, "In the next act of the Eurozone's economic drama, keep a close eye on Spain", *FT*, 21 December 2014.

[8] Source: *Save Our Savers*.

[9] Source: *Yahoo Finance*.

[10] Cardoso Lecourtois, M., 2014, "Improvements in competitiveness and reduction of imbalances in Spain", *Spanish Economic and Financial Outlook* Vol 3, No 5, September 2014.

[11] Woolnough, R., 2014, "Deflating the deflation myth", *Bond Vigilantes Blog*, 7 February 2014.

[12] A recent example of this is impact of declining mobile phone prices. See: Hamblen, M., 2014, "Smartphone prices are dropping, and will continue to dip through '18", *Computerworld*, 29 May 2014.

[13] For example: Caryl, C., 2008, "Bernanke's Fight Against Deflation", *Newsweek*, 19 December 2008.

Q5. Why was CPI invented in the UK?

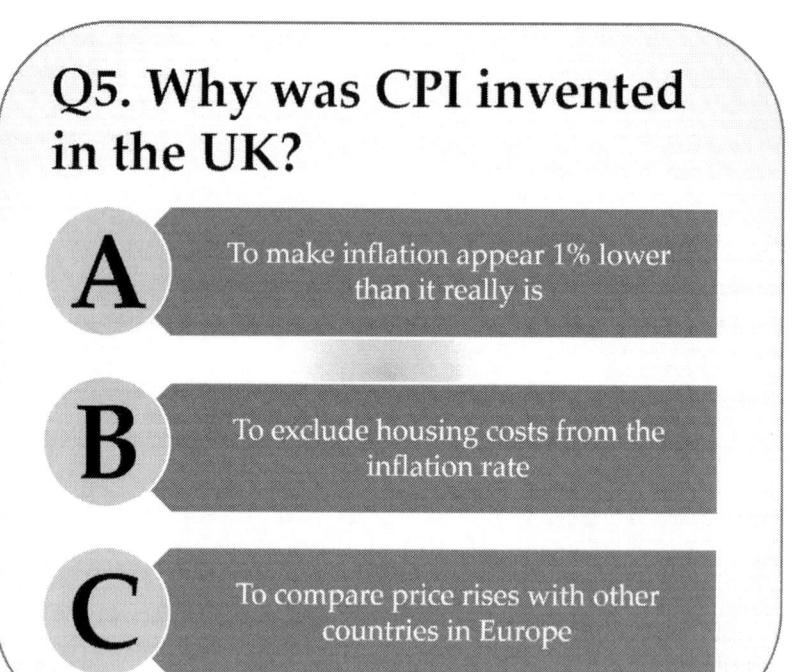

A — To make inflation appear 1% lower than it really is

B — To exclude housing costs from the inflation rate

C — To compare price rises with other countries in Europe

5

UK inflation measures

This chapter looks at the main inflation measures that are quoted in the UK, why they exist and what the differences between them are. The two key measures are:

- RPI - Retail Prices Index
- CPI - Consumer Prices Index.

RPI is the original UK index with history dating back to World War I. CPI is an EU invention which was not intended to measure cost of living and was created for a completely different purpose. CPI's method of calculation ensures it is usually around 1 per cent lower than RPI.

The history of price indices in the UK and the birth of RPI

The first cost of living index in the UK was published in 1914 and covered food alone. It was quickly expanded in 1916 to include clothing, fuel and some other items. Its main function was to help ordinary workers argue for fair cost of living rises – especially given the effects of the price rises that ensued due to World War I. The coverage of the index was very limited. It was purely meant to include working class people's expenditure (though, bizarrely, it excluded things like beer) and was largely based on a 1904 survey of urban working class households' expenditure.

This index and its antiquated construction continued until 1947, when it was relaunched as an "Index of Retail Prices" on the basis of a new survey. It was again radically overhauled in 1956 into the first Retail Prices Index (RPI). This index expanded the coverage to include many more products and services and, more importantly, most people's expenditure. However, it excluded the top wage earners and certain low-earning households such as state pensioners – and still does to this day[1].

Since then, the RPI has continually evolved with changes to the method and coverage. Its basket of items that are surveyed every month is updated annually on the basis of household expenditure surveys.

What is CPI and why was it created

The Consumer Prices Index (CPI), on the other hand, was first collected in this country in 1996. When originally created, we used to know it more correctly by its original and more descriptive name: the Harmonised Index of Consumer Prices (HICP). It was so-called because it was developed by the EU with the sole purpose of allowing European comparisons to be made for the requirements of the Maastricht Treaty. The terms of this treaty determined whether you had a government that was fiscally responsible enough to be able to join the Euro.

CPI was invented as part of the Maastricht Treaty

Included among the six key criteria of the Treaty was that a country's inflation rate had to be low and no more than 1.5 per cent higher than the three states with the lowest inflation rate. This caused a problem for the EU, because: (i) everybody had been using different inflation rate calculations; and (ii) inflation rates historically were volatile and often very high in some countries. They therefore came up with a new statistic that they asked members to calculate alongside their existing measures. It was recognised that it was not a cost of living index, and that it excluded some things that nations normally monitored, but at least it would allow comparisons.

Why CPI is now the preferred UK measure of inflation

In most European countries, HICP is not used as the preferred inflation measure by governments. For example, Germany continues to use its own bespoke CPI measure as its main indicator and only uses HICP for international comparisons.[2]

So how has the UK government's "preferred measure of inflation" become HICP (or CPI as we now call it), instead of the UK's own measure (RPI)?

The answer could be quite simple. According to a report by the government's own Office for Budget Responsibility,[3] CPI is usually around 1 per cent lower than RPI. Therefore, merely by utilising the European CPI rather than the old UK RPI measure, inflation appears significantly lower. More recently the Office for National Statistics (ONS) has gone as far as declassifying RPI as a "national statistic" apparently justified on the grounds that its method of calculation is not internationally acceptable.

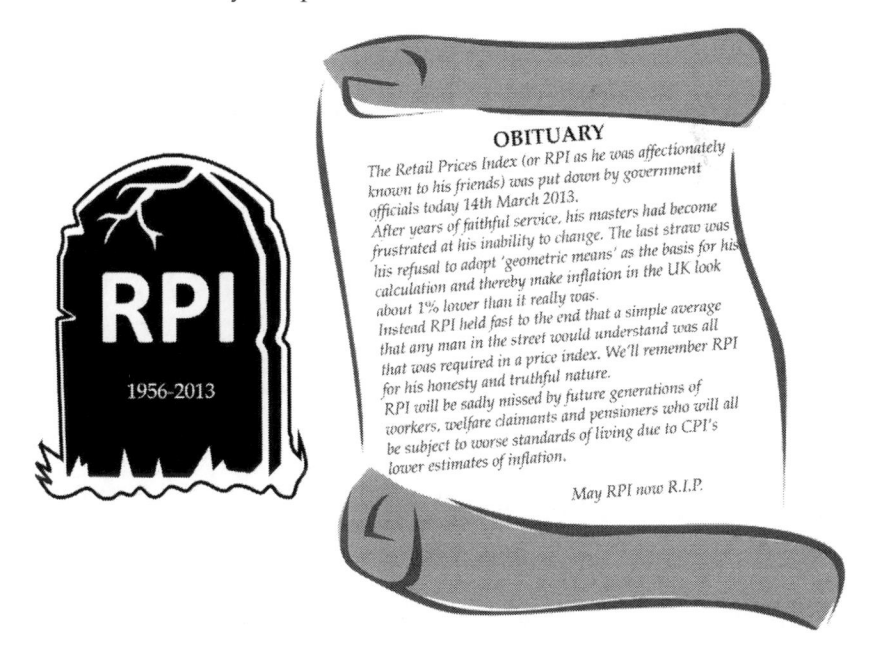

RPI
1956-2013

OBITUARY

The Retail Prices Index (or RPI as he was affectionately known to his friends) was put down by government officials today 14th March 2013.

After years of faithful service, his masters had become frustrated at his inability to change. The last straw was his refusal to adopt 'geometric means' as the basis for his calculation and thereby make inflation in the UK look about 1% lower than it really was.

Instead RPI held fast to the end that a simple average that any man in the street would understand was all that was required in a price index. We'll remember RPI for his honesty and truthful nature.

RPI will be sadly missed by future generations of workers, welfare claimants and pensioners who will all be subject to worse standards of living due to CPI's lower estimates of inflation.

May RPI now R.I.P.

INFLATION MATTERS

The main take-out of this is that the way inflation is calculated affects the result. Inflation is a key statistic. Unfortunately because of this, it may be subject to political pressure to ensure methods are used that help it look low. (See: "6-Inflation measurement issues.")

The differences between CPI and RPI

The table below summarises all the key differences between these two measures. They vary not only in the items included in the indices and their weightings but more importantly the method of calculation. CPI is almost always going to be lower than RPI because it uses a method of calculation called a geometric mean. It also leaves out a number of housing-related costs that often have a significant impact on the cost of living and the RPI index. (For a more detailed discussion, see: "6-Inflation measurement issues.")

Key differences between CPI and RPI

	CPI	RPI
Origins	EU in 1996	UK in 1956
Purpose	To compare euro countries for compliance with Maastricht Treaty	To monitor cost of living for government planning and the basis of many agreements (e.g. wages)
Main exclusions (compared with household expenditure)	Council tax Mortgage interest payments House prices (depreciation) House purchase costs (e.g. stamp duty) Buildings insurance Ground rent Holiday spending abroad Income tax/National insurance	Income tax/National Insurance Life insurance and pension charges
But includes	Foreign students tuition fees Forex commission for tourists	Spending when abroad on holiday
How data averaged	Mainly geometric means Some normal ratio of averages	Mix of ratios of averages (i.e. normal average of all prices checked) and average of the relatives (i.e. work out the price change at each store and then average these)
Data source for weights	Household monetary consumption expenditure component of the national accounts (-> weighted towards consumption of the rich)	ONS's Living Costs and Food Survey
Population for weighting	All UK residents	Excludes the wealthy and pensioners on state benefits (i.e. 13% of population)
Used to index	Benefits Tax credits Public service pensions	Government debt payments Most pay negotiations Most private sector pensions

What are RPIJ, CPIH and TPI?
In response to criticisms of the large difference between CPI and RPI, in 2013 the ONS created some additional measures.

- **CPIH** is similar to the CPI index but it includes household rents. Importantly it does not include any measure of house prices nor the cost of mortgages. It therefore typically creates an estimate of inflation that is lower than CPI. The H stands for Housing.
- **RPIJ** is similar to RPI but instead of using ordinary mean scores to combine the prices it uses the geometric means which CPI uses. This ensures it will always produce a lower apparent level of inflation. The J stands for Jevons who was a statistician who promoted the use of geometric means.
- **TPI** is similar to RPI but includes the effects of taxation changes on the cost of living. It was intended to show the change in gross taxable income needed for taxpayers to maintain their purchasing power. T stands for Tax.

Other measures of inflation
In addition to the above there are a number of other measures of UK inflation not directly related to the consumer:

- **PPI** - The Producer Price Index, which measures changes in the cost of goods and services made in the UK
- **GDP deflator** - which is deduced having calculated the actual value of GDP and compared with a similar volume measure from the previous period. In recent years, the GDP deflator has been significantly lower than even CPI. The reasons for this are complex and I have discussed them elsewhere[4].

More technical details on inflation measures
Measures such as CPI include over 600 individual items which aim to represent the typical household budget. The items covered are updated annually. Each month ONS either checks the prices of them directly (in the case of nationally listed prices e.g. newspapers, utilities, train fares, etc.), or sends out its team of researchers to look for them in around 150 locations spread around the UK.

The ONS publish detailed information on how they do this and the items checked - see http://www.ons.gov.uk/ons/guide-method/user-guidance/prices/cpi-and-rpi/consumer-price-indices--a-brief-guide.pdf.

KEY LEARNING POINTS:
- Britain's price indices date back to World War I. In 1956 this measure was revised into the Retail Prices Index (RPI). This index comprises over 600 items which are updated annually.
- The Consumer Prices Index (CPI) is the UK name for an EU statistic called the Harmonised Index of Consumer Prices (HICP). It was invented in 1996 not as a cost of living index but solely as a way to determine eligibility to join the euro under the Maastricht Treaty. It excludes a number of items included in a normal price index (e.g. housing costs) and also adopts a statistical technique that will ensure that the index is always about 1 per cent lower than measures such as RPI.
- The UK government subsequently made CPI its preferred measure of inflation. RPI is still published but the UK authorities have now declassified it as an official "national statistic".

QUIZ ANSWER:
C.

---

[1] The reason for this exclusion is unclear. Officially it was argued that their purchasing was atypical. An alternative explanation could be that the very wealthy and elderly were two groups that were difficult to interview in market research surveys and so were just missing from the dataset that was being used for the calculations.

[2] https://www.destatis.de/EN/Meta/abisz/VPI_e.html (accessed 1/6/2013).

[3] Chote, R., Nickell, S. & Parker, G., 2011, "Economic and fiscal outlook", *H.M. Treasury*, March 2011.

[4] Comley, P., 2013, "Even Mark Carney does not believe ONS data now", *Inflation tax book blog*, 27 November 2013.

Q6. What is the best estimate of UK inflation?

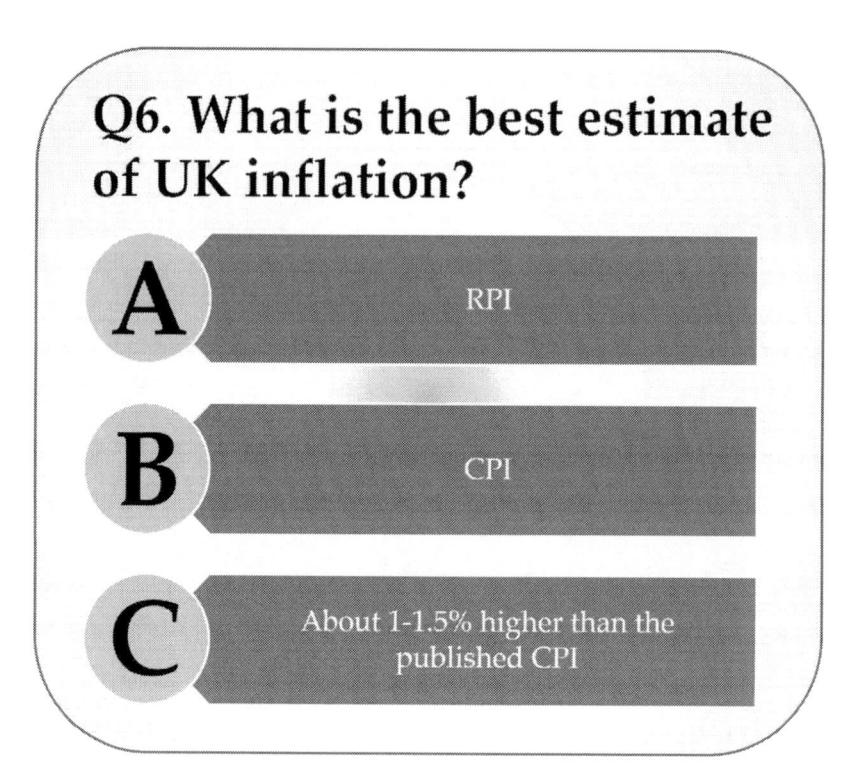

A   RPI

B   CPI

C   About 1-1.5% higher than the published CPI

6
Inflation measurement issues

Trying to create a reliable and valid measure of inflation is not easy. You can get very different results by changing the elements in the shopping basket, by deciding different rules on how you keep the basket up to date, by altering the way you weight those items together, and even by changing the way you mathematically average the prices. All of these decisions can have a significant impact on the reported levels of inflation.

This chapter examines the four key issues that affect published inflation rates. It compares the ideal index with reality and makes particular reference to the UK's price indices.

Inflation measurement issues

Issue	Main features of issue	Ideal
1. Politics	Influence is often subtle but persists in all countries	Free from any influence and political bias
2. Coverage	Selection of items to be checked and the expenditure that they represent	Index should reflect typical expenditure of all the population equally weighted
3. Calculation	There are many ways to calculate a price index and they give different numbers	Should be an easily understood calculation that reflects the real increases
4. Substitution	Indices need to deal with new products and baskets must evolve over time	Baskets should be updated every few years and there have to be systems to deal with new products

1. The politics of inflation measures

Measurement of inflation is usually performed by government authorities—in the UK by the Office of National Statistics (ONS). The indices are normally created by supposedly independent statisticians. However inflation indices are key measures of the political performance of governments both internally and externally in comparison to other countries. Governments therefore have an incentive to portray their country's inflation in the best possible light, usually taken to mean low but not negative. Moreover the lower the apparent inflation rate, the higher the growth of the economy appears to be, because inflation is deducted from the raw figures before GDP growth rates are calculated.

As the *Economist*[1] recently noted: "Statistical offices vary in their ability to resist political pressure" to manipulate both these key numbers (inflation and GDP). Therefore, when statistical authorities make changes to the system, especially ones that tend to result in lower levels of apparent inflation, there will always be calls of foul play, and often with some justification.

For example, most economists believe that the official rate of inflation in Argentina is now more than double that published by the government due to persistent changes[2]. Economist John Williams set up a website called *ShadowStats* to not only chronicle such statistical adjustments in the US but also produce an alternative set of data (including inflation). His data suggest that had the US continued to use the same methods of CPI calculation employed in the 1980s, current inflation might be up to 8 per cent higher than officially reported.

Another alternative system to the US government stats was created by academics at MIT and is called the *Billion Prices Project*. Since 2008, they have been automatically collecting online prices every day from major retailers in the US. The inflation measure so created (now called the *Price Stat Index*) covers a wide variety of items, from food to clothing to electronics, furniture and energy[3]. Although initially it seemed to follow the official stats quite well, in recent years it has been indicating that inflation may well be quite a lot higher than the official figures. For example at the beginning of 2014, *Price Stats* estimated inflation to be around 3 per cent, whilst the US government had a level of just half that, at 1.5 per cent[4].

In the UK, there is evidence of similar adjustment of the reported inflation level, but the abuse is on a smaller scale. Measures such as

RPI only slightly under-report its true level. CPI on the other hand has a number of issues as you will see below. It does markedly underestimate the true inflation level.

2a. Item coverage

This issue may come as a surprise. In theory, it would be expected that price indices cover everything that the population spends its money on. However in most cases they do not. Many indices leave out expenditure related to taxation and nearly all omit direct taxation costs such as income tax. They usually do not include elements related to savings and investments. The only exception sometimes is when that investment is housing; and most people would probably feel that is correct.

Indeed housing is one of the most important areas in which the two main UK indices differ. Unlike RPI, CPI excludes mortgage interest payments, house price rises and rents.[5] Also omitted are buildings insurance (but not contents insurance, bizarrely), ground rents and council tax. Housing accounts for over 25% of the RPI and so these are significant omissions from what most would regard as an ideal index.

What is fascinating is that their exclusion was not due to their lack of importance; it was merely that EU officials could not agree on a standardised way to measure them. Therefore, they left them out. This may have been a sensible decision for international comparisons, but it was not a good thing if you wanted to rely on it as a comprehensive cost of living measure, as we have now done in the UK.

These missing housing components do have an impact on CPI. The amount depends of course on what is happening to the cost of mortgages and house prices. Generally, it lowers the apparent CPI inflation figures when house prices and/or interest rates are increasing (which is most of the time). In August 2014, the exclusion of mortgages and houses from the CPI list reduced it by about 0.6 per cent, i.e. from 2.1 per cent to 1.5 per cent.

ONS decided in March 2013 to start producing a version of CPI that includes the effects of housing: CPIH. However few realise that the only housing component they added into CPIH was an estimate for rents. This has had the paradoxical effect of actually lowering inflation still further. It remains to be seen if this will become the government's preferred measure of inflation in the future.

2b. Population coverage and weighting issues

An ideal price index should cover the expenditure of the whole population and give each member of it an equal weight. In the UK, there are issues for CPI and RPI in this respect but for different reasons.

The RPI index weights are based on the "Living Costs and Food Survey" that covers the complete household expenditure of over 6,000 households. However, two groups are excluded from these weights: (i) the 4 per cent of the population who are the wealthiest; and (ii) pensioners for whom three quarters of their income comes from state pensions and benefits. Between them these two groups account for 13 per cent of all spending.

The sample exclusions from RPI

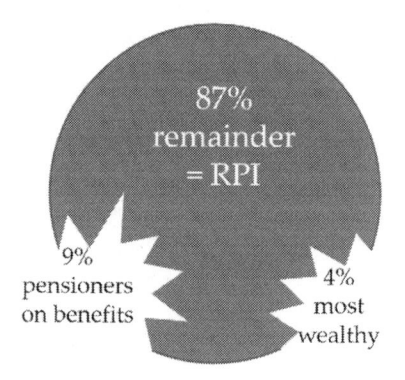

87% remainder = RPI

9% pensioners on benefits

4% most wealthy

The logic behind the above exclusions is that such households are likely to spend their money on atypical items and including them might distort the overall average. Some argue that RPI therefore reflects the "average household" better.

It is difficult to ascertain the precise effect of such exclusions. The rich undoubtedly have a different spending profile; pensioners who are mainly on benefits will spend a larger proportion of what little money they have on fuel and food. The impact of the latter can to some extent be measured by the pensioner versions of RPI that the ONS publishes monthly. These show that single person pensioners have experienced an average inflation rate 0.8 per cent above the rest of the population every year over the decade[6]. Given the proportion of pensioners in the population (and missing from RPI), this has lowered the overall RPI index by just under 0.1 per cent[7] e.g. from 2.5 per cent to 2.4 per cent in August 2014.

INFLATION MEASUREMENT ISSUES

The issue for CPI is different. Its weights are not survey based. Instead they are based largely on the "black box" (i.e. not published) of the government's own calculations of GDP (and more specifically the Household Final Monetary Consumption Expenditure component of it). This means also that they have a different structure, which makes comparisons between the two difficult.

However one key issue with the GDP data is that it is value weighted. This means that the expenditure of the wealthy counts more. You can see the impact of this in the importance of items such as alcoholic drinks. They account for 2 per cent of the CPI index but over 6 per cent of RPI, as the poor spend relatively more of their income on drink. In contrast, 10 per cent of CPI is based on expenditure in restaurants and eating out, whilst less than 5 per cent of RPI is. Therefore RPI more accurately portrays the prices of the average person not only because it uses verifiable survey data but because it is not biased towards the expenditure of the more wealthy. The total impact of this on the CPI index is not simple to calculate.

3a. Calculation issues - the historical background

An ideal index is worked out using a simple method that is easy for all to understand and accurately portrays the price rises actually experienced by the total population.

It might be thought that the solution to this is simple. You just measure the price rise each month for each item and compute the index. Indeed the very first price indices created in the 18th Century did just this. A French economist called Dutot suggested that the best way to calculate a price index was to take an average of the prices and compare it to the average seen in the same places in the period before. This method called the *"ratio of the averages"* is also sometimes referred to as the *Dutot index*.

At a similar time (1764), an Italian economist Giovanni Carli published what is believed to be the first historical price index based on three key commodities: grain, wine and oil[8]. He used a slightly different method. Instead of taking the average each month across the shops, he worked out the change in price for each location and then averaged those. This method has become known as the *"average of the relatives"* or the *Carli index*.

Either of these would satisfy being a method that would be easy to understand. However it might be argued that Carli's average change for each shop better represents what would happen to the population, assuming a good sampling frame of stores is adopted.

However as statisticians started to use these formulae they became aware of differences between them. Dutot's simple averages gave more weight to locations where items cost more and this could distort the data if prices of an item varied a lot. However other theorists pointed out that Carli's method of averaging the changes could create strange results over a period of time too[9]. If prices reverted to their original levels the sum of all the monthly changes might be greater than zero[10] — this phenomenon is known as the *price reversibility* problem or the *price bouncing* issue.

Many alternatives were proposed to get around these issues. The one that gained most attention was suggested by an English economist, William Jevons, in 1863. He suggested a similar approach to Dutot but, instead of taking a simple average of the store prices, he suggested taking a *"geometric mean"* of them (also known as the *Jevons index*). Geometric means are calculated by multiplying all the numbers together and then taking the nth root of them — hardly what most would describe as a simple to understand calculation.

It too had some issues; for instance, it was impossible to average prices which included free products. However it did fix the issue identified with the Carli method of price reversibility over time. But this came with a side effect. The resulting average also had the property of always being lower than Carli's simpler average. Moreover if there was a wide range in the price increases seen between different stores the reducing effect could be very large. Compared with the Dutot method, the Jevons scores were also normally lower too, but the effect was more variable and it was possible for Jevons to be higher.

Statisticians favouring the Jevons approach justified the lower price rises the method created on the basis that they were taking account substitution effects. They argued that if the prices of an item went up people would not experience that price rise fully as some would switch to cheaper products. They said that was why the Jevons was lower and why it was more accurate.

As we will see later in this chapter, substitution is already covered elsewhere in price index calculations and does not need further adjustment. But, more importantly, if the price of a product goes up, then the prices have gone up and this should be reflected in a cost of living index. If people then decide to cut back their spending by buying an inferior quality product, that is their decision, but the item

INFLATION MEASUREMENT ISSUES

they used to buy is now indisputably more expensive. Furthermore, how the psychological dilemma of substitution could be estimated by taking a mathematical nth root was never explained.

In addition, in the recent debate about switching to Jevons in the UK in 2012, the Institute of Fiscal Studies[11] pointed out the supposed advantage of Jevons over Carli on reversibility grounds was actually not that important as *any* price index in totality is not reversible (because of the way it is made up of a weighted average of many different items). Despite this, the Jevons method has become very popular as you will see.

3b. Calculation issues – the world today

When it created RPI in the UK, the ONS took a pragmatic view and used a combination of simple averages (Dutot) where price variability was not that great and used the average of the relatives (Carli) when it was greater (e.g. for clothes and food). In contrast, CPI primarily uses geometric means (Jevons).

The main types of average used in UK price indices

Ordinary name	Statistical name	How calculated	Where used
Ratio of the averages	Dutot index	Averages the prices across shops and compares waves in the way any ordinary person might expect	RPI (a few CPI items)
Average of the price relatives	Carli index	The change in price is calculated for each store and the average of the changes is taken	RPI
Geometric means	Jevons index	Like 'ratio of averages' but the initial average uses a geometric mean not an arithmetic mean	CPI

Other methods of calculation are also used in CPI and RPI for a few items such as the Laspeyres Index and straight averages.

Note, ONS will not divulge the exact which method they use for each item or even the total numbers of items being averaged using each method[12].

Some other countries, such as Germany and Japan, use just the simple Dutot method to calculate inflation. Unlike the UK, they tend to be very specific over the items selected by their price checkers and so face less price variability than the ONS (which can tell the checkers to just find things like "any ladies' blouse").

INFLATION MATTERS

Indeed, until the 1990s, most countries used Dutot or a combination of the Dutot and Carli methods, but many have now switched to the Jevons method. It can only be speculated whether this was part of a desire to appear to be bringing inflation down following its peak in the early 1980s. The switch was given a further impetus by the EU in 1996 when it sanctioned the use of only the Dutot and Jevons methods when compiling its harmonised inflation measure (HICP).

Most countries have justified their switch to Jevons either on the grounds of it dealing with substitution better (e.g. France), the reversibility issues of Carli (e.g. Canada) or that it is now the internationally accepted method (which was ONS's main argument in 2012)[13]. Outside the UK, relatively little work has been published on the effects of switching to Jevons. However some estimate that it helped reduce US inflation rates by 0.3 per cent after their switch from Dutot and in other countries by up to 0.2 per cent.[14]

Jevons has a larger impact than this in the UK. The so called "formula effect" of using Jevons in CPI (as opposed to Carli and Dutot in RPI) has been around 1 per cent from 2011-2014[15]. To demonstrate the impact, if inflation in the UK was 3 per cent, it would have been reported as only being 2 per cent if you use the Jevons geometric mean as CPI does.

How much UK CPI underestimates inflation

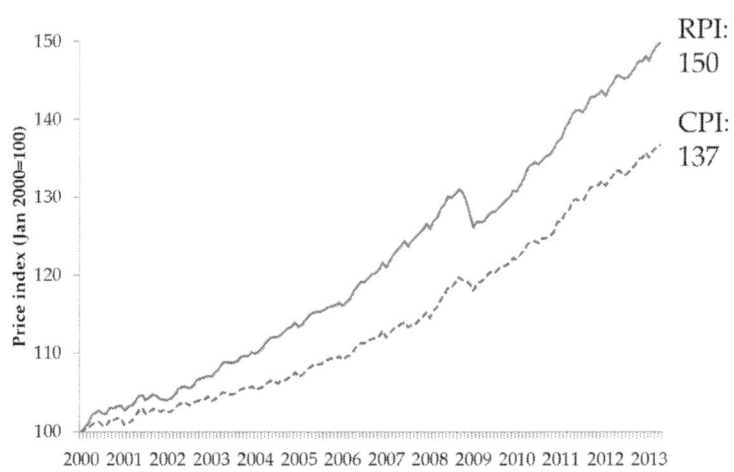

Source: ONS (Jan 2000–Apr 2013)

This may not seem much, but of bigger concern is the cumulative impact of this adjustment. For example, from January 2000 to April 2013 RPI inflation was recorded as increasing prices by a half. With CPI, prices went up by only just over a third. To make this clear, if your income had been indexed by the CPI instead of the RPI over that period, you would now be around 10 per cent worse off (i.e. 137/150).

4a. Substitution issues

An ideal price index must make some provision for changing purchasing habits and expenditure levels as people switch to new and different products. The average shopping basket and what people choose to spend their money on today is very different from that of fifty years ago. An index also has to have a method for dealing with items that cease to be sold. Inevitably, the approaches taken to deal with these issues can have an impact on the resulting index – often lowering it.

In the UK, the ONS reviews the items on the shopping list every year. It then has one overlap period where it monitors both the old and new list and then "chain links" the two datasets together with statistical wizardry. In the US the review takes place every two years (it used to be every ten) and in Germany every five years.

That process seems sensible on the face of it. However it creates a few issues. Say the price of something goes up a lot, so much that many people choose not to buy it. People have indeed suffered inflation and the new prices are higher than before. Under the ONS system of annual changes, these items will quickly stop being checked and instead are substituted with cheaper items potentially of inferior quality that are not necessarily rising in price.

It is difficult to determine the effects of this. However, if you do look at the constant items in the index (or more specifically some of the food items where ONS publishes the backdata[16]) and then compare them with the overall RPI food index, you see clear evidence of the increases of the average individual items being greater than the increase in the apparent total index, which adopts the substitutions.

INFLATION MATTERS

Increase in some specific food prices from 2000-2013

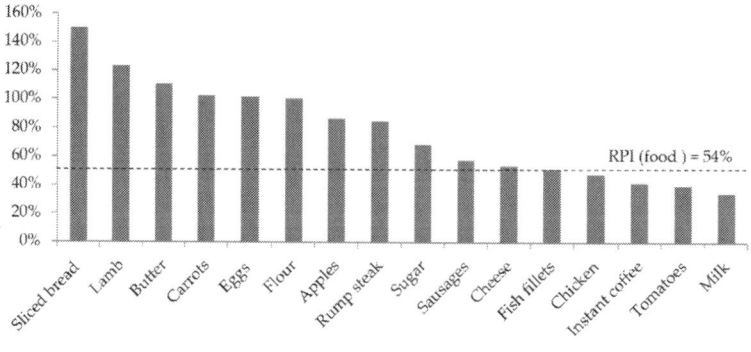

[Bar chart showing food price increases from 2000-2013, with sliced bread highest at ~150% and milk lowest at ~30%. A dashed line indicates RPI (food) = 54%. Items from left to right: Sliced bread, Lamb, Butter, Carrots, Eggs, Flour, Apples, Rump steak, Sugar, Sausages, Cheese, Fish fillets, Chicken, Instant coffee, Tomatoes, Milk.]

Source: ONS

In other countries the index suffers less from this effect as components of the inflation are adjusted less frequently. It is difficult to say what is an optimum review period, but a formal review every three-five years would be a good compromise between consistency and the need to reflect changing purchasing habit.

4b. Quality adjustments

Some items checked in indices have short life cycles and are regularly superseded by improved or different versions. This is particularly the case for technology items, such as computers, cameras and mobile phones. How this is dealt with can cause issues for the index. To some extent, the problem in the UK at least is overcome by ensuring the items being surveyed are revised annually - see above. However, improvements can occur during the year and older spec models may even be discontinued.

In the 1960s the US adopted a process called "hedonic pricing". It involved creating a mathematical model for the prices of items dependent on their features.[17] Therefore, if a product needed to be substituted for a higher spec and more expensive one, a calculation would be done about how much the higher spec one would have cost at the beginning of the year. This aimed to deduce how much of the change in prices were related to the higher spec features and how much, if any, was a real price increase. They then used it extensively for most white goods (e.g. kitchen appliances), technology items and clothing/footwear. Many other countries have followed suit in the last decade and the UK for example uses it for phones, computers and cameras.

INFLATION MEASUREMENT ISSUES

This is a fine idea in theory, but the simple models can rarely portray the intricacies of pricing. Furthermore, the approach usually ends up in estimating that the price of such items has declined, when the absolute price paid for, say a new phone, by the man in the street may have actually increased, as the models offered for sale have new features for which they cannot avoid paying.

To give you an idea of the impact of such measures on some of the components that go into inflation indices, let's consider what has happened to the price of some of the items being adjusted this way in the UK. Between 2005 and 2012, CPI went up by 23 per cent across all goods. However, the price of digital cameras had fallen by 83 per cent and that of laptops by 65 per cent. This implied that the average person buying these products was paying massively less than they were in 2005.

Unfortunately, there was no objective measure of the average price paid for a digital camera or laptop to enable us to verify this method. However, as an alternative, you can look at the average price of all products in the *Which?* magazine review tables from 2005 and compare it to an average price from a similar review in 2012.

Average Prices in *Which?* 2005 vs 2012 compared with CPI hedonic predictions

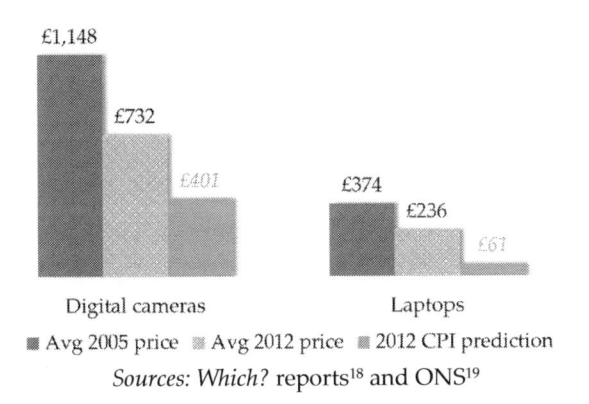

Digital cameras: £1,148 (Avg 2005 price), £732 (Avg 2012 price), £401 (2012 CPI prediction)

Laptops: £374 (Avg 2005 price), £236 (Avg 2012 price), £61 (2012 CPI prediction)

■ Avg 2005 price   ■ Avg 2012 price   ■ 2012 CPI prediction

Sources: Which? reports[18] and ONS[19]

This gives a fairly representative sample of the products being bought in both periods by real people for the purpose of taking pictures and using a computer. It focuses on the prices people are really paying and ignores any of their features and the clever mathematical models.

The results show that indeed the price paid for both a digital camera and a laptop had fallen since 2005. However, the reduction was not anything like that being assumed in the CPI inflation index on the basis of modelling. This analysis is not a precise measure of average prices of these products in 2005 and 2012, but it does show that government modelling was probably causing at least a doubling of the price reduction effect.

Overall this is contributing to a reduction in both of the UK's main inflation indices. The total impact is not that much, probably around 0.1 per cent or even less[20], as the number of items covered by this method is small. Having said that, if the published CPI rate is 1.5 per cent, it would have been 1.6 per cent without this adjustment.

People have argued that in the US, where this technique is much more widely used, it has reduced overall inflation estimates by as much as a third.[21] Clearly, it is a problem trying to determine how best to account for quality changes in products. It would appear though that using mathematical models may not be the most accurate way. However while this practice remains, it continues to help governments make inflation rates look lower than they actually are.

Summary of issues with CPI

Given all the above, CPI in the UK probably underestimates true inflation by 1 to 1.5 per cent.

How much CPI underestimates true inflation

Issue	Reason	Average effect (last 3 years)	Typical range (last 3 years)
Coverage - items	Exclusion of housing costs	0.25%	0.05%-0.45%
Coverage - weighting	Bias towards purchasing of the rich	(variable)	
Calculation	Use of geometric means	0.95%	0.90%-1.00%
Substitution	Annual update of items	0.05%?	
Substitution	Use of quality models	0.05%?	
TOTAL		**1.25%**	**1.00%-1.50%**

Source: ONS for housing and geometric means effects. Author best estimates for substitution effects.

The exact amount is variable and there is no simple consistent adjustment that can be made to determine it. This implies that when CPI is at its target of 2 per cent, inflation in the UK is truly around 3-

INFLATION MEASUREMENT ISSUES

3.5 per cent. The key components of the difference are listed in the table above:

KEY LEARNING POINTS:
- Inflation statistics worldwide are subject to political pressure to ensure they appear as low as possible (but not negative).
- Calculating inflation indices is complicated. Some of the key ways in which they differ are related to: coverage (i.e. the items included and the universe of expenditure), calculation method (and specifically the use of geometric means) and how substitution is dealt with (i.e. revisions to the items and quality adjustments for missing items).
- In the UK, CPI underestimates true inflation by around 1 to 1.5 per cent. For the US, the effect according to recent *Price Stats* data is similar (though *ShadowStats* suggest it may be significantly more).

QUIZ ANSWER:
C

---

[1] "Don't lie to me Argentina", *The Economist Print Edition*, 25 February 2012.
[2] ibid.
[3] The PriceStat index excludes service prices however.
[4] Zumbrun, J., 2014, "Why Weather Could Determine Who Wins a Race To Measure Inflation", *Wall Street Journal Blog*.
[5] House price rises are included in RPI in a convoluted way in a measure called "house depreciation".
[6] Based on ONS price data for September (Q3) 2014. The figure was 0.5% for two person pensioner households excluded from RPI.
[7] Warwick University also has a personal inflation calculator, which allows simulation of both the missing groups. This again suggests that the omission of these two groups is reducing published RPI inflation estimates by around 0.1%. (Their calculator is predicting inflation of 0.5% higher for the 4% very rich and 0.6% higher for 9% pensioners on state benefits. Overall, this equates to a reduction of RPI of just over 0.1%.) For the calculator, see: http://news.bbc.co.uk/1/shared/bsp/hi/pdfs/20_05_13_inflation_calculator.pdf (accessed 1/6/2013).

[8] Walsh, C., 1901, "The Measurement of General Exchange-Value", *The Macmillan Company*.

[9] More recently they have argued it is subject to similar price bouncing biases.

[10] In certain theoretical circumstances, a situation might occur where you get the wrong answer if you use an average of the price relatives (i.e. the Carli mean of the shifts). Take the following example. Say prices are just being checked in two shops A and B. If in month the cost in shop A is £2 and in shop B £3, the average price would be £2.50. In the second month, say the price in shop A increases to £3 and declines in shop B to £2. The average is still £2.50 i.e. inflation should be zero. However if you average the two relative price changes (i.e. +50 per cent and -33 per cent respectively), you do not get zero.

[11] Levell, P., 2012, "A winning formula? Elementary indices in the Retail Prices Index", *Institute of Fiscal Studies*, IFS Working Paper W12/22.

[12] The author had a number of email conversations with the ONS in December 2014 where they confirmed that they do not officially publish this information. They provided an approximate expenditure weighting split but this differed markedly to some figures in another ONS document published in 2012 (ref 13) as part of the RPI consultation. It is difficult to understand why ONS cannot share this factual information. It unfortunately undermines perceptions of the independence and validity of their statistics.

[13] Evans, B., 2012, "International comparison of the formula effect between the CPI and RPI", *ONS*.

[14] Levell, P., 2012, "A winning formula? Elementary indices in the Retail Prices Index", *Institute of Fiscal Studies*, IFS Working Paper W12/22.

[15] Source: *ONS*. Note, the formula effect used to average around 0.6 per cent until the ONS made "improvements" in the way they measured clothing prices in 2010. See: Morgan, D., & Gooding, P., 2011, "CPI and RPI: increased impact of the formula effect in 2010", *ONS*.

[16] ONS only publishes backdata on a few items. There are more items than on this graph, but I aimed to pick a random representation of ones in key categories to illustrate the point.

[17] This takes the form of a regression model, where items have a base

price and fixed amounts are then added for each feature that the product has.

[18] *"Digital Cameras: Which?"* June 2005 (n = 10 cameras), *"Which?"*, December 2012 (n = 28 cameras). *"Laptops: Which?"* April 2005 (n = 13 laptops), *"Which?"*, August 2012 (n = 25 laptops).

[19] Predicted price calculated by taking the *Which?* price and multiplying the CPI index change from 2005 to 2012 in categories: 09.1.2 Photographic, cinematographic and optical equipment and 09.1.3 Data processing equipment.

[20] It is difficult to be precise over the exact effect from the published data and without knowing the unpublished details of the hedonic modelling. However, assuming it is only being applied to certain goods such as PCs, laptops, digital cameras and PAYG mobile phones, its net effect on the published UK prices indices will be to lower them by an amount of around 0.05%. (These items contribute only around 1–2% of CPI/RPI index weights and the hedonic modelling effect in recent years has been to reduce prices by around 10% pa, some of which is a genuine reduction, as was noted by analysis of digital cameras and laptops in the text.)

[21] Freeman, R., 2000, "The Quality Adjustment Method: How Statistical Fakery Wipes Out Inflation", *Executive Intelligence Review*, 27 October 2000.

PART II

INFLATION PAST

Q7. How long have prices been rising in the UK?

A — They have gone up x100 since 1900 and have been trending up for centuries

B — They have only risen markedly since the UK joined the EU in 1973

C — They have mainly just risen since World War II

7

Inflationary Wave Theory

Those reading this at the beginning of the 21st Century may be excused for thinking that price rises are a fact of life, a bit like death and taxes—after all, throughout their lives, inflation has always been there. However an examination of history shows this not to be the case. There have been many periods, some lasting centuries, where prices have remained largely stable and people may have lived their whole lives unaware of the concept. That being said, there appears to be a long-term secular[1] trend towards higher prices over the millennia driven by the increasing world population and competition for resources.

Inflationary Wave Theory

Prices vs Time chart showing:
1. Underlying trend (population growth)
2. Man-made factors create over-trend inflation growth
3. Transition period often turbulent
4. Consolidation phase

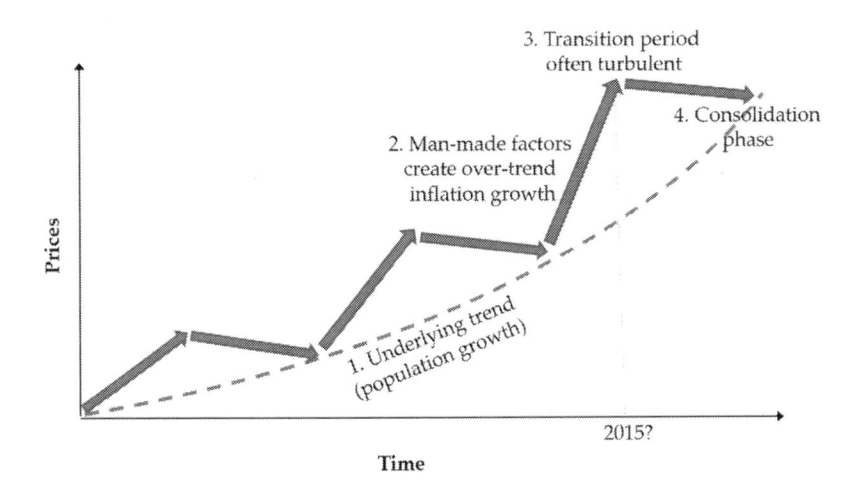

2015?

This chapter introduces a new theory about inflation called *Inflationary Wave Theory*. It is based on a detailed examination of the history of inflation. This shows that there is a marked wave pattern of rising inflation over a century or more, followed by a period of equilibrium with almost stable prices, before the cycle repeats itself. The length of the waves, the intensity of the inflation and its causes all vary, but the broad periodicity remains.

As Mark Twain is reputed to have once remarked, history may not repeat itself but it certainly rhymes. This is very true of inflation. Once you understand this core concept, you have the potential to unlock the learnings of past generations not only to make more sense of the present but also to offer possible scenarios for the future. (See: "Part IV-Deflation yet to come".)

Evidence of inflation in ancient history

There are records of inflation occurring in a number of periods in ancient history. Some have even argued that the concept of inflation predates formal money systems[2].

In Babylonian times the recorded prices of barley rose markedly on a number of occasions, e.g. during the reign of Alexander the Great and the Wars of the Successors that followed from 330–301 BC. This inflation spike has many similarities to those seen more recently in the 20th Century in being related to wars and shortages. However others have hypothesised that the cause might have been related to the amount of silver (and gold) that Alexander brought back from his conquests.[3] This silver would have increased the amount of money in circulation and hence inflated prices.

The ancient Greeks suffered inflation, interestingly at almost the same time as the Babylonians around 350BC. The Romans had periods of inflation too. However we have better records for wheat prices from the Roman Empire. These show it suffered three distinct waves of inflation: one around 300-250BC, another at near the end of the Republic (about 50BC) and then again in the period after at the end of the 2nd Century.

The cause of the third wave is known. It was related to the money supply again. From the reign of Trajan in 117AD, successive Roman emperors started to reduce the amount of silver in a denarius coin from 95 per cent down to less than 1 per cent 100 years later. By melting down the old coins and mixing in copper, emperors could create more coins to pay for their wars and exploits. However, the increase in the number of coins also resulted in significant price rises.

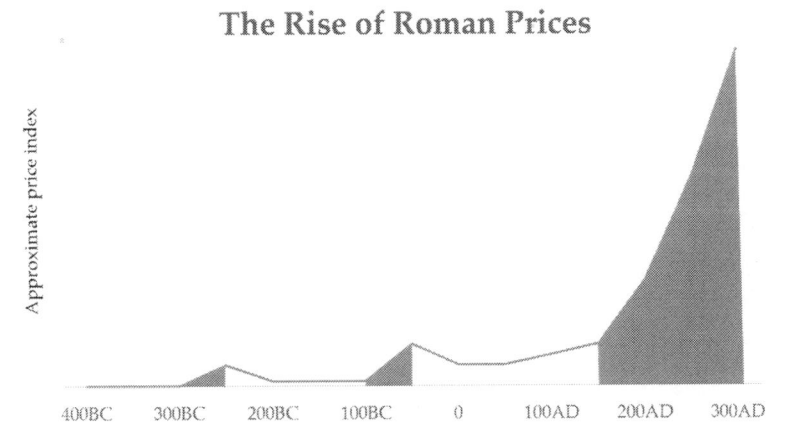

The Rise of Roman Prices

Source: A version of a chart in Fischer (1999), The Great Wave.
Note though that Fischer based his chart of comparatively few data points.

Inflation since medieval times

Official price indices have only been around in the UK for the last century. Calculating inflation during earlier times has taken a lot of painstaking research. The pioneering work was done by Sir Henry Phelps-Brown and Sheila Hopkins who estimated historical inflation from records of household accounts in southern England[4].

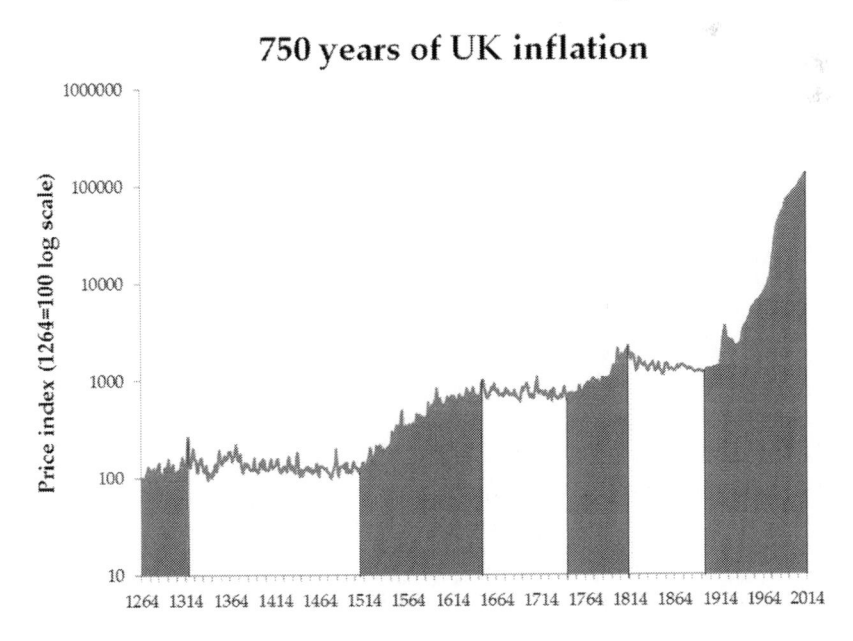

750 years of UK inflation

Source: Phelps-Brown and Hopkins (1956) and ONS.

This chart shows that the UK has experienced waves of price increases (shaded) followed by consolidation periods of relative price stability. The length of each half of the cycle has varied quite markedly between 85 and 190 years. Significantly this pattern of inflation is not unique to the UK but appears to be mirrored with very similar timings across Europe and other countries where records exist[5].

The inflationary waves in the UK since the medieval period have been approximately as follows:

UK inflationary waves

Inflationary part of the wave	Consolidation part of the wave
1180-1320 (140 years)	1320-1510 (190 years)
1510-1650 (130 years)	1650-1730 (80 years)
1730-1815 (85 years)	1815-1900 (85 years)
1900-20?? (115+ years so far)	

Another key factor is that every inflationary cycle has resulted in exponentially larger increases in prices than the previous one. Over the four waves above, the average annual prices increased by 0.5%, 1%, 2% and 4%+ respectively. This may be related to man's increasing ability to exploit inflation over time – see below.

Understanding the inflationary wave

The pattern of inflationary waves followed by consolidation waves is very commonly exhibited in financial markets. You can see similar patterns if you look at major stock indices over the last century. What drives them is an underlying trend; in the case of inflation probably competition for resources. However when humans become involved in trends, self-fulfilling prophecies create feedback loops that exaggerate the change. At this point there needs to be a period of consolidation when the underlying driver catches up with the exaggerated rise in prices.

Note: like the price patterns exhibited by stock prices, the changes never follow simple lines but are much more complex when looked at over shorter time scales like decades. The long-term pattern exists but is overlaid by large short-term effects which can obscure the bigger picture if you look at them over too short a time span. For example in the latest wave of inflation starting in 1900, we have seen spikes of inflation in many countries (particularly around the great wars and again in the 1970s) and we've also even seen periods of declining prices (e.g. the 1930s). However the big picture shows a long secular rise in prices that may be yet to reach its final peak. In the UK prices have risen by a factor of 100 during this period.

The start of a new wave

One of the most detailed historical analyses of inflationary waves around the world was conducted by David Hacker Fischer in 1999[6]. Fischer's hypothesis is that after a period of price stability something triggers the start of a new inflationary wave. He believes the evidence supports the theory proposed by Reverend (Thomas) Robert Malthus in 1798[7] that it is related to imbalances between demographic and economic growth. (See: "3-Other theories about inflation".)

Fischer goes on to argue that the periods of stability lead to more people perceiving life positively and, as a consequence having more children. This gradually puts pressure on resources and it is the effect of this population growth that starts a slow but steady rise in prices.

Fischer's key insight based on his detailed analysis of history is that it is not increases in the money supply that trigger the start of a new trend. Instead changes in the money supply normally *follow* the start of a new trend and then amplify it. You can see this in the start of the latest wave. Prior to World War I, prices went up by 13 per cent in the UK (1899-1913) whilst an index of the money supply[8] rose by just 3 per cent in the same period. World War I then ensued and the money supply more than doubled, only then to be followed by a similar rise in retail prices.

An inflationary mindset takes over

The critical point in the new cycle soon happens when prices break out of their previous range of natural fluctuations. People start to realise that they have entered a new era of apparently permanent increases in prices. A new phase of inflation then takes over and an inflationary mindset sets in. People start adopting different behaviours that reinforce the new inflation trend. These range from workers demanding inflation-related pay rises, through to governments expanding the money supply to ensure there is enough money in the economy.

More specifically the financially astute and wealthy are usually first to spot and exploit the change and start other behaviours which further feed the inflation wave. One of the most important is borrowing money, whether by companies for investment purposes or by individuals to buy assets that will keep their value during the forthcoming inflation. The choice asset is often land and housing. Others in the population then see land and house prices rising and seek to join the bonanza and demand even more credit furnished by private banks. All of these actions expand the money supply since money is created when debt is created. (See: "2-Inflation and the money supply theory.") Those increases in the money supply eventually end up affecting the prices of goods and services too, providing further feedback to the inflation loop e.g. in the form of wage demands.

Governments also exploit the inflationary situation. As they are usually net debtors, they understand that inflation will erode their repayment obligations and it is in their interests to foster inflation. For example the current UK government regulates many prices from train fares, to energy, to education costs and facilitates their rise. This has the effect that welfare and pensions payments keep rising too.

Governments sometimes also decide to print money to fund their current expenditure, rather than borrow it. This might be to finance wars, to expand their economy (short-term) or to act as a substitute for collecting taxes. Such increases in the money supply have the potential to spiral out of control into hyperinflation if not managed carefully. (See: "8-World War I and learning about hyperinflation.")

Exploiters of the inflationary wave

Impact of the inflation

The impact of the initial stages of the new inflationary wave can be positive for the economy. The increased borrowing can result in increased business investment. The increasing prices provide an incentive for people to spend money rather than save it. Some also make gains from asset price inflation (e.g. housing and shares) and then spend this in the goods and services economy.

This stage is initially accompanied by increases in wages as the expanded economy demands more labour. But the inflation pep pill only has short-term benefits. Soon the real gains for the economy decline. At the same time, the population continues to grow. This results in declining labour costs. Concurrently the wealthy continue to profit from asset price inflation and the erosion of the cost of their borrowings. These two factors fuse together and lead to growing inequality. (See: "16-The impact of current inflation.")

Cresting of the inflationary wave

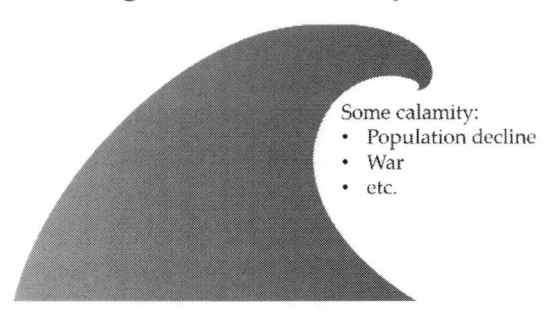

Like waves in the sea, there usually comes a point when inflationary waves build to a final peak and finally collapse, usually cataclysmically. Something stops the whole cycle. Historically this has normally been war and/or population decline. At the end of first great inflation wave around 1320, one tenth of Europe's population had died in the previous decade as harvests failed and prices soared[9]. This was followed by the Black Death a few decades later that wiped out a further 25-40 per cent of many European populations.

Cresting of the inflationary wave

Some calamity:
- Population decline
- War
- etc.

A similar decline was seen at the end of the next wave. Europe was savaged by the Thirty Years War that led up to the end of the second great wave around 1650. The population declined by 40 per cent in Germany alone.

Interestingly, the third great wave was not halted by population decline. Instead it was the after-effect of worldwide revolutions and wars, the most significant being the Napoleonic Wars (1796-1815). These caused prices to reach unprecedented levels whilst real wages plummeted. The impact was such that by 1812 it was estimated that more than a half of English families were dependent on poor relief.[10]

Price stability stage

Normally after inflationary wave peaks, there follows a period of relative price stability. Relative is a key word. The period still exhibits price oscillations but the key factor is that prices typically remain within a range and do not exceed the previous high. In addition, as time goes by, the amplitude of the oscillations typically reduces. This is a reflection of a stable price mindset taking over. A whole generation grows up never witnessing long-term price rises in their life-time. Indeed during these periods, there is typically a gradual decline in overall prices. This is due to certain goods becoming cheaper as productivity or technological advances reduce the cost of production.

The period also sees declining returns on assets such as land and houses. Rents also decline. At the same time, the purchasing power of wages rise from the benefits of the gradual decline in prices over time. In waves following population decline, labour is in short supply too, which again enhances wages as employers compete to recruit from a smaller working population. The net effect is a significant decline in inequality.

History shows that such periods have often coincided with cultural changes in society, e.g. the Renaissance in the 14th/15th Century, the Enlightenment in the 17th/18th Century and the Victorian Empire of the 19th Century. These have helped inspire more positivity and confidence in society, which has sown the seeds for the next wave of population growth and for the inflationary cycle to repeat itself.

KEY LEARNING POINTS:
- There is a long-term secular trend towards higher prices over the millennia. This appears to be driven by the increasing world population and competition for resources.
- Inflation follows a marked wave pattern of rising inflation over a

century or more, followed by a period of equilibrium of relatively stable prices.
- Once a new wave has been triggered, man-made factors such as increases in the money supply drive prices higher. These rises are exponentially increasing over time as man becomes more adept at exploiting the situation.

QUIZ ANSWER:
A. _____

[1] The word secular comes from the Latin saeculum, meaning a generation or a century.

[2] Parsson, J., 1974, " Dying of Money: Lessons of the Great German and American Inflations", *Wellspring Press*.

[3] Van der Spek, R., 2003, "Sense and Nonsense in the Statistical Approach of Babylonian Prices", *Bibliotheca Orientalis*, 60, Leiden.

[4] Phelps-Brown, E. and Hopkins, S., 1956, "Seven Centuries of the Prices of Consumables Compared With Builders Wage Rates", *Economica*, New Series, Vol 23, No 92, Nov 1956, 296-314.

[5] Hackett Fischer, D., 1997, "The Great Wave: Price Revolutions and the Rhythm of History", *Oxford University Press*.

[6] ibid.

[7] Malthus T., 1798, "An Essay on the Principle of Population", *Oxford World's Classics*.

[8] The index of the money supply was calculated from M3 and the GDP increase deducted from it to determine the true excess money supply growth.

[9] Hackett Fischer, D., 1997, "The Great Wave: Price Revolutions and the Rhythm of History", *Oxford University Press*.

[10] ibid.

Q8. Who and what causes hyperinflation?

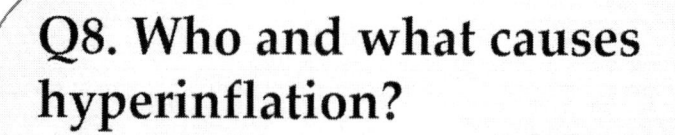

A People cause it by paying too much for goods

B Companies cause it by charging too much

C Governments cause it by deciding to print money

8

World War I and learning about hyperinflation

This chapter looks at hyperinflation and particularly what happened in post World War I Germany in the Weimar Republic in the early 1920s. It shows that when governments decide to fund their economies by printing money, it frequently results in a hyperinflationary spiral of increasing prices. The effect of hyperinflation is to transfer the cash-based wealth and assets of citizens to the government (and other debtors).

Definition of hyperinflation

Before we examine the hyperinflation that occurred after World War I, it is useful to understand what is meant by the term. It is usually defined as prices rising over 50 per cent in a single month.[1] This may not sound a lot, but because of the compounding effects it equates to an annual inflation rate of 12,875 per cent. If you think that is high, inflation reached nearly 100 per cent a day in Zimbabwe in November 2008 and over 200 per cent a day in Hungary after World War II. In those countries, the price of a meal might have literally gone up by 50 per cent from the time it was ordered to when it was paid for.

Hyperinflationary periods

You might think such occurrences are rare in history, but this is not the case and they are not limited to the period since World War I. The

Cato Institute reports 56 such hyperinflations in the last century.[2] Although the two main groups of them followed the World Wars in Europe and the split-up of the former Soviet Union, they have occurred at other times and all around the globe, from Brazil to China.

The increasing frequency of hyperinflation

Inflationary wave	Number of hyperinflations	Average annual price rise in the UK
1180-1320	0	0.5%
1510-1650	0	1%
1730-1815	1	2%
1900-1914 (and still ongoing)	56	4%

Source: Cato Institute

Interestingly, hyperinflationary periods were almost unheard until this latest inflationary wave starting in the 20th Century. Prior to that, the only one was in France during the revolution in the late 18th Century.[3] Part of the reason for their recent rise in frequency is the emergence of *fiat* (or paper) currencies that are neither linked to gold nor pegged to other stronger currencies. This has made it easier for a government to increase the money supply.

Causes of hyperinflation

One key thing that must be understood though is that hyperinflations are always a result of government policies.

Causes of hyperinflation

Reason	Instigator	Situation	Example
Debts	Government	When government debts become so large that it is not possible to pay the interest on them and/or there is no political will or ability to do so.	Weimar Republic in 1922-3
Low tax revenues	Government	When government expenditure suddenly far outstrips the possibility to pay it with tax revenue.	French Revolution in 1795-6
Fiscal power	Government	When a government cares little about the credibility of its finances due to its strong electoral position.	Zimbabwe in 2007-8

In all these cases, governments create money to cover their obligations. If it is created in sufficient quantity, high levels of inflation result in keeping with the Quantum Theory of Money. (See: "2-Inflation and the money supply theory.") According to famous economist Ludwig von Mises,[4] hyperinflation is typified by a "crack-up boom" when people become aware of the fact that inflation is a deliberate government policy and may go on endlessly. Suddenly, people want to swap their money for real goods no matter whether they need them or not, nor how much in currency they have to pay for them. The ensuing lack of confidence of citizens in the currency then causes a spiral of ever increasing prices and money creation.

A key learning point here is that it is not just a massive increase in the quantity of money that triggers hyperinflation. It normally happens when that increase is accompanied by an increase in the velocity of money brought about by the lack of trust in the sovereign currency. Remember the quantity theory of money states that: MV=PQ, where M=the money supply, V=velocity of money, P=prices and Q=size of the economy.

Systems to prevent hyperinflation

In enlightened periods of history, people realised the potential for abuse of the money supply and set out to create systems to prevent it. Historically this meant linking their currencies to something tangible (e.g. gold or silver) or at least pegging it to stronger currencies.

Such a system existed in the UK for many centuries and was made more formal by the creation of the Bank of England in 1694. The coinage from that date was literally worth its weight in precious metal. This persisted, excepting a brief period during the Napoleonic Wars, until World War I.

In more recent times, some countries have created laws to ensure the money supply is not abused. For example Article 123 of the Maastricht Treaty forbids an EU state from printing money to buy its own debt. (Note, this law has been circumvented recently with states such as the UK getting around the letter of the law by instructing their central banks to buy government debt not directly but indirectly via financial companies).

World War I and its effects on inflation

A key time when most governments abuse the money supply is during wars. They are expensive and usually cost much more than can be raised by tax revenue alone. Governments therefore normally fund them by creating the money to do so directly or indirectly via private banks.

The UK government and that of most of the other major combatants therefore suspended the gold linkage of their currencies when World War I started and also permitted banks to create massive amounts of new money. For example, during the war, the number of German Reichsmarks in circulation increased ten times[5]. Without this, some have speculated that the war in Europe would probably have been over within a year.

Inflation increased greatly in all European countries during the war, partly as a result of the increased money supply and partly due to shortages caused by the war. Despite the massive increases in the money supply though, prices only slightly more than doubled in Germany and the UK. However in the years immediately following the war, prices continued to rise in all major economies as the increased money supply finally worked its way into everyday life. In the UK, prices rose by a quarter in 1919/1920 but in Germany they rose over five times in 1919 alone.

Some economies (like the UK) decided to remedy this situation and reinstated the link to gold, implementing policies to try to shrink the money supply and return the economy to the previous pre-war equilibrium. In the UK, the resulting recession was painful and resulted in outright deflation for most of the 1920s and early 1930s until the link with gold was finally abandoned in 1931[6].

The Weimar hyperinflation

In contrast many of the defeated countries decided to follow a different policy. For example the post-war socialist German government continued to use debt finance and print money to finance its promised improvements to benefits, wages and education. They also encouraged lending by keeping interest rates low. The stock market and companies thrived, as the costs of rebuilding business post-war were wiped out by inflation. Similarly the government's war debts shrank as inflation eroded their value.

Berlin became the tourist capital of Europe in the early 1920s with its cabaret lifestyle. Massive mansions were built by the new rich. Corporate entrepreneurs flourished and there was nearly full employment. Inflation even moderated to a fairly low level in 1920 and 1921, despite the declining value of the Reichsmark (caused in part by the massive war reparations being paid).

Source: "Bundesarchiv B 145 Bild-P062899, Berlin, Tanzkabarett im Europahaus". Licensed under Creative Commons Attribution-Share Alike 3.0-de via Wikimedia Commons - by the German Federal Archive (Deutsches Bundesarchiv).

A tipping point was finally reached in May 1921 when prices started to rise again. By July 1921 prices had risen 700 per cent and confidence in the currency vanished. No one wanted to hold paper Reichsmarks anymore and people sought to exchange them for real goods. Up until November 1923, prices increased exponentially and inflation reached 29,500 per cent with prices doubling every few days.

A 50 million mark note printed in Germany in 1923
Source: "50 millionen mark 1 September 1923" by Reichbanksdirektorium, Germany - private source.
Licensed under Public domain via Wikimedia Commons

The cycle was finally halted on 15 November 1923 when the Rentenmark was introduced at an exchange rate of one trillion old

Reichsmarks. The architect behind it, Dr Schacht (later to become Hitler's financial wizard), promised that there would only be so many Rentenmarks created and the government promised to balance its budget. Schacht stopped all credit from the central bank shortly afterwards and the inflation finally abated in early 1924.

Businesses built on the ever-increasing inflation and cheap credit collapsed, government slashed spending and increased taxes, workers were dismissed, wages cut and working hours raised. Unemployment soared. Holders of Reichsmark denominated assets were wiped out.

In contrast the clear winner from the whole episode was the largest debtor i.e. the German government. According to an analysis by Ronald Marcks [7]: *"Inflation relieved it of its entire crushing debt which represented the cost of the war, reconstruction, reparations and its deficit-financed boom"*. In addition, as a by-product of the inflation, speculators who borrowed heavily and bought real assets and shares also profited.

Culpability of the Weimar government

The Weimar government had inherited a state in which the money supply had been grossly increased by the previous German government during the war. However it is difficult to believe that those in charge were not well aware of the likely results of their actions. They not only continued to print more money (to cover their socialist welfare programme) but also encouraged private banks to expand credit money creation.

John Maynard Keynes had already described this type of scenario in his 1919 best seller entitled *The Economic Consequences of the Peace*. Some of those in government would have undoubtedly read the book as it was a good summation of world economy following the Versailles Conference at which the post-war agreements with Germany were made. In this book, Keynes made the argument that further expanding the money supply after the war would be "reckless" and "malpractice" by any government.

He noted in early 1919 just after the formation of the Weimar Republic (and prior to the hyperinflation) that:

"The various belligerent Governments, unable, or too timid or too short-sighted to secure from loans or taxes the resources they required, have printed notes for the balance... In Germany the total expenditure in 1919-20 is estimated at 25 milliards of marks, of which not above 10 milliards are

WORLD WAR I AND LEARNING ABOUT HYPERINFLATION

covered by existing taxation. This is without allowing anything for the payment of the indemnity."

Keynes also noted the power of inflation to deal with debts and the exact process that governments could use to benefit from it. Keynes actually quotes the writings of Karl Marx[8] in this respect, who argued that inflation was a useful tool of the state, i.e.

"By a continuing process of inflation, governments can confiscate, secretly and unobserved, an important part of the wealth of their citizens. ...There is no subtler, no surer means of overturning the existing basis of society than to debauch the currency. The process engages all the hidden forces of economic law on the side of destruction, and does it in a manner which not one man in a million is able to diagnose."

The inflationary process appears therefore to have been consciously pursued by the Weimar government as a method to pay for the war, the reparations and their socialist agenda. Moreover they almost certainly must have been aware of its consequences for the wealth of their subjects, but were probably not strong enough politically to adopt any other solution.

Example of the impact of post WWI hyperinflation

"We poor harassed housewives had a disagreeable Christmas surprise. The kronen and heller, which have lately given us so much trouble, have been changed into schillings and groschen. For 15,000 kronen, we get – one schilling! Thousands of Austrians have been reduced during the last days to beggary. All who were not clever enough to hoard the forbidden stable currencies and gold have, without exceptions, suffered losses.

To give an example: An old married couple, with whom I have been friendly for years, had a holding of government stock amounting to two million pre-war kronen [£83,000 at that time], which brought them in interest 80,000 pre-war kronen a year [£3,300]. They were justly regarded as rich people. Today their stock brings them in eight new schillings a year [25p].

The state has in one stroke relieved itself of all its debts to the population. Panic has seized the stock exchange. Shares too are being converted into new schillings. My millions have dwindled to about a thousand new schillings [£32]. We too belong today to the new poor. The middle class has been reduced to a proletariat. I can escape from starvation only if I find new sources of income."

Anna Eisenmenger, 1924

The Austrian government also used inflation as a policy in the post-war period. The above is an extract from the diary of Anna Eisenmenger[9] who was writing in Vienna in January 1924 just after the country's post-war inflation had been brought under control.

Real example of the effects of hyperinflation

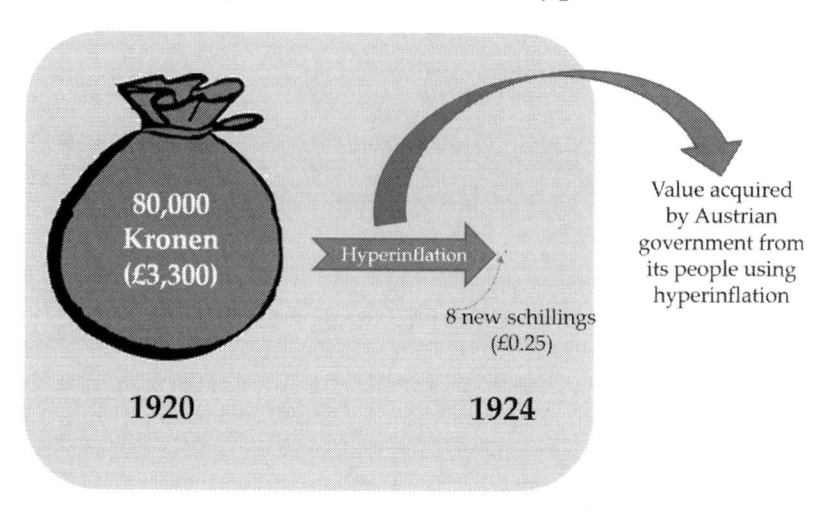

80,000 Kronen (£3,300) — Hyperinflation → 8 new schillings (£0.25)

Value acquired by Austrian government from its people using hyperinflation

1920 — 1924

Hyperinflation - the end game

Hyperinflations normally last for a short period of time—around a year (although inflation may have been building over a much longer period). They carry on exponentially growing until suddenly a tipping point is reached. Most end when a credible new currency is finally adopted as the medium of exchange. This could be a new internal currency (e.g. Rentenmarks in the Weimar Republic in 1923) or an alternative currency that is adopted (e.g. US dollars in Zimbabwe).

The net primary effect of hyperinflation is to transfer the value of *all* cash-based wealth or assets (including bonds) to the state as the currency becomes worthless. All inflation has this transfer of wealth effect, even at the low levels we have today. Hyperinflation is just an extreme illustration of it. (See: "16-The impact of current inflation.")

Will QE cause hyperinflation?

Many are concerned that the programme of Quantitative Easing (QE) recently conducted in the UK, US and Japan might cause hyperinflation.

For example, the Bank of England created £375 billion between 2009 and 2012 to buy its own government's debt. To keep to the letter of the law which forbad an EU nation from financing its own government in such a way[10], it did so via the intermediary of other financial companies such as commercial banks. The net result was the same though i.e. it expanded the money supply. However the level of quantitative easing was negligible in comparison to the amount of money created in other countries that have experienced hyperinflation such as the Weimar Republic - see above. QE in the UK was less than 20 per cent of the UK money supply (of just over £2 trillion then). Moreover, in practice it did not even increase the net money supply at the time.[11] It merely acted as a replacement for the money destroyed by private loans being paid or written off.

More generally, the UK has been adept historically at controlling the level of inflation and it is unusual for the type of low-level inflation seen in the UK since World War II to suddenly spiral into hyperinflation. Indeed, there have been only three recorded instances of UK annual inflation getting to crisis levels (i.e. above about 25 per cent a year) – in 1800, 1917 and 1974. In all these cases, intervention soon returned inflation to much lower levels.

Part of the reason for the relative historic stability of UK prices has been the pound being linked to either gold or, more latterly, the dollar. However, it could be argued that since sterling is now a floating fiat currency without such a peg, historical precedents do not necessarily apply. But UK governments have learnt that with time and patience, the same objectives of debt relief can be obtained at lower levels of inflation and this causes much less disruption to the economy and the social fabric of society.

Remember, it takes a lot of money creation by a government to produce hyperinflation. It is normally the resort of a government that is powerless to raise revenue by any other route.

KEY LEARNING POINTS:
- Hyperinflation is defined as when prices rise over 50 per cent in one month.
- Hyperinflation is always caused by a conscious government policy. It occurs when they decide to print excessive money to finance their economies and/or debts.
- The effect of hyperinflation is to transfer the cash-based wealth and assets of citizens to the government (and other debtors).

QUIZ ANSWER:
C.

---

[1] Cagan, P., 1956, "The Monetary Dynamics of Hyperinflation", in Friedman, M. (Ed), "Studies in the Quantity Theory of Money", *University of Chicago Press*.

[2] Hanke, S. and Krus, N., 2012, "World Hyperinflations", *Cato Institute*, Working Paper No 8.

[3] In addition, the US came close to hyperinflation during the money printing of the Revolutionary and Civil Wars.

[4] Mises, L., 2007, "Human Action: A Treatise on Economics", *Liberty Fund Inc.*

[5] Fergusson, A., 1975, "When Money Dies", *William Kimber & Co, London.*

[6] Note, the UK never did manage to bring prices back to pre-war levels despite their austerity campaign. Prices more than doubled from 1914-1920. By the low point in the 1930s, they had still risen over a half since 1914. The inflation genie, was out of the bottle.

[7] Parsson, J., 1974, "Dying of Money: Lessons of the Great German and American Inflations", *Wellspring Press*

[8] Keynes, J., 1919, "The Economic Consequences of the Peace", *Macmillan, London.*

[9] Eisenmenger, A., 1932, "Blockade: The Diary of an Austrian Middle-class Woman 1914–1924", *R. Long & R. R. Smith*.

[10] Monetization of an EU government's debt is forbidden under Article 123 of The Maastricht Treaty. Interestingly the clause was specifically inserted in the treaty as a result of German requests.

[11] M4 money supply.

Q9. Who and what caused deflation in the 1930s?

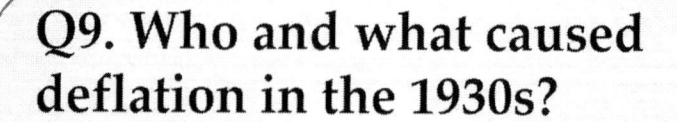

A The government which ordered lower prices to help the poor

B Contraction of the money supply due to a banking crisis

C Crop failures due to droughts on the US prairies

9

The 1930s depression and the deflation bogeyman

Deflation refers to a condition where prices decline over a period in time. The prevailing view amongst economists is that deflation can be the cause of many problems in an economy.

This opinion primarily arose in the aftermath of the Great Depression in the 1930s. It is therefore instructive to review what happened during that time. As you will see, the likely cause of the economic woes was not consumer price deflation per se, but primarily a banking crisis brought about by an asset price bubble. The resulting shrinkage of the money supply eventually led to falling consumer prices.

Antecedents of the 1930s Depression

The epicentre of the Great Depression was the US. Although the ripple effect of the economic collapse of that nation affected the globe, it is important to understand what was happening in that country in the preceding decade to appreciate the true causes of the calamity.

Also known as the "Roaring Twenties", the 1920s were a period of massive expansion of wealth in the US where it more than doubled between 1920 and 1929. Estimated GDP grew over 13 per cent in 1923 alone. The period was associated with increases in consumer spending and mass consumption of products for the first time e.g. fridges and automobiles. For some, it was also an era with constant parties, jazz and a flapper lifestyle.

Source: "Saturday Evening Post cover 2-4-1922" by Ellen Bernard Thompson Pyle in the 1922 Saturday Evening Post - http://www.saturdayeveningpost.com/2009/07/25/art-literature/artists-illustrators/ellen-pyle.html. Licensed under Public domain via Wikimedia Commons

Much of this was a result of changes in the banking industry[1]. The newly formed Federal Reserve oversaw a rapid rise in lending for property and the phenomenon of national banks transforming themselves from institutions that simply held money into organisations selling a wide variety of investments. Banks leveraged their databases of account information to target sales of bonds and (later) shares to the public.

Clients' investments were encouraged by the concept of margin. It was only necessary to put up 10 per cent of the purchase price of shares, the rest being supplied as a loan by the bank. All this caused a public frenzy of stock market activity, driving asset prices higher and higher until the bubble finally burst in late 1929. At that point, the Federal Reserve tried to rein in the bubble by raising interest rates.

The early 1930s in the US

Although stock prices recovered in early 1930, they declined again and by mid-1932 had dropped nearly 90 per cent. Many ordinary people lost fortunes in the stock market over this period. As noted above, many had bought shares on margin and went bankrupt. The resulting tidal wave of defaults brought down many banks. In the runs on those banks even more money was lost by ordinary people.

At the same time, the remaining banks tried to rescue their balance sheets by calling in loans (especially to business) which further shrank the economy. Business confidence collapsed, as did spending. Overall money supply contracted by over a quarter between 1930 and 1933, as money was destroyed in all these ways.

The whole situation was made even worse by a natural catastrophe. Between 1930 and 1936, droughts hit the main prairie lands of the US and turned them into a dust bowl. Not only did this create massive unemployment and poverty amongst migrant workers but farmers had to abandon their farms, unable to pay back the debt on them. This led to further bank failures and made the banking crisis even worse.

Source: "8b33132r" by Dorothea Lange - United States Library of Congress's Prints and Photographs division under the digital ID fsa.8b33132. Licensed under Public domain via Wikimedia Commons.

US unemployment soared to 25 per cent by 1933 and consumer spending was drastically hit. Not only was a large portion of the population living on subsistence having been made unemployed, but those still in work often experienced pay reductions. Those with any remaining cash after the bank failures tried to keep what wealth they could and reduced their expenditure.

The velocity of money therefore also reduced. The resulting decreased demand not surprisingly led to lower prices, as producers and retailers sought to compete for what sales they could. Deflation set in. Consumer prices declined a quarter by 1933, with commodity farm prices declining even more.

However note the causality here. As discussed before, it was not deflation that created the economic problems of the 1930s. It was an outcome of the banking crisis and reductions in asset prices that had caused the overall money supply to shrink.

The Fed's response

At the height of the crisis, the Federal Reserve initially took a non-interventionist position. Many at the Fed believed that the correction seen in asset prices and the resulting foreclosures of unprofitable businesses were nature's way of correcting imbalances and that after a period of pain the economy would recover.

The crisis was a bigger one than had been witnessed before in previous business cycles and its impact was greater. There was therefore heavy political pressure to do something. However the Fed was restricted at that time in its ability to create money by the requirement that 40 per cent of its assets should be backed by gold. So apart from reducing interest rates to help borrowers, it did little to try and alleviate the misery. Instead it was up to presidential initiatives by Hoover and Roosevelt to aid the recovery. A full recovery only came after the advent of World War II.

The debt-deflation theory

Since then there has been much analysis by economists of the Great Depression, why it happened and whether more could have been done to alleviate its affects. A key economist of the time was Irving Fisher. He proposed the debt-deflation theory[2]. In this he argued that there was a chain of events that created the crisis. It started with debt liquidation and distress selling. This contracted the money supply as bank loans were paid off, which led to a fall in the level of asset prices. This resulted in a still greater fall in the net worth of businesses, precipitating bankruptcies and a decline in profits. This created a reduction in output, in trade and in employment. At the same time there was an overall loss of confidence causing people and businesses to hoard money.

This key issue with this theory, which became very influential, is that it links the word deflation in economists' psyche with economic trouble. That is despite the fact that the deflation refers primarily to a reduction in asset prices and not consumer prices. It has subsequently become associated with a situation where the prices of ordinary goods and services decline, even though there was little reference to consumer price deflation in the original theory.

The debt-deflation theory

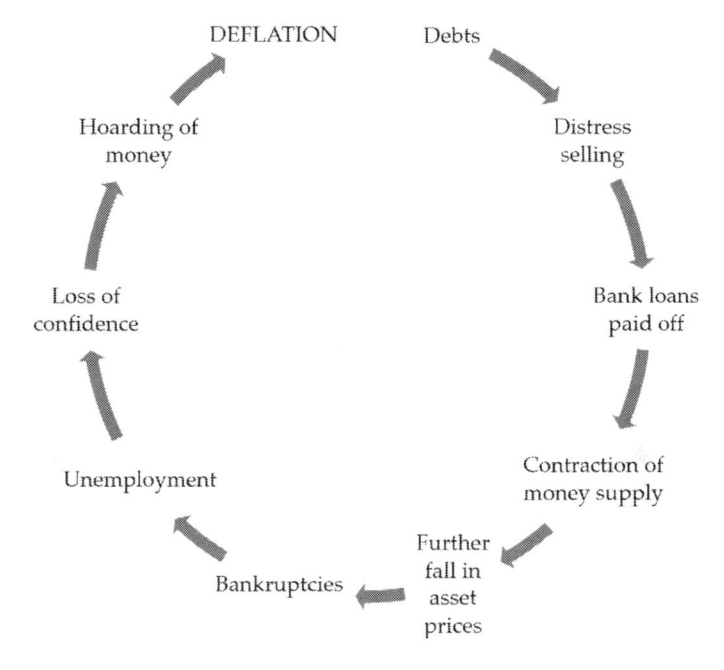

```
DEFLATION → Debts
    ↑         ↓
Hoarding of   Distress
  money       selling
    ↑          ↓
 Loss of    Bank loans
confidence   paid off
    ↑          ↓
Unemployment  Contraction of
    ↑        money supply
Bankruptcies ← Further fall
               in asset prices
```

Ben Bernanke and deflation

Fisher was particularly influential on the thinking of an economist called Ben Bernanke in the 1980s. He not only published his own theories on the causes of the Great Depression but went on to become chairman of the Federal Reserve from 2006-2014 and oversaw the handling of a re-run of the 1930s banking crisis in the post 2007 era.

Bernanke believed that the Federal Reserve was largely responsible not only for creating the Great Depression by trying to curtail the asset boom, but also for ensuring that it lasted so long and was so painful by not helping to alleviate the symptoms. These views very much followed those proposed by the economists Milton Friedman and Anna Jacobson Schwartz in 1963[3].

A key part of Bernanke's theory was that deflation reduced the value of the collateral of assets used against bank loans (for mortgages or by business). This increased banks' risk on those loans and caused them to foreclose on them. He postulated that deflation was so bad because it 'dammed' the flow of credit in the economy.

Source: "Ben Bernanke official portrait" by United States Federal Reserve Licensed under Public domain via Wikimedia Commons

The effects of deflation are complicated. Bernanke is probably right that it affects credit flows in the economy. It certainly has an impact on debtors. However, for the vast majority of the population, steady or slightly declining prices are not an issue and can indeed have benefits. These benefits are often ignored in the economic debate, which primarily uses the 1930s as its framework for analysis.

KEY LEARNING POINTS:
- Irwin Fisher's analysis of the 1930s and his debt-deflation theory inextricably linked deflation to negative economic thinking.
- More recently Ben Bernanke postulated that the problems of the 1930s were due restrictions of credit.
- However it is important to understand that the likely cause of the economic woes in the 1930s was not consumer price deflation per se, but a banking crisis brought about by asset price bubbles created during the 1920s.

QUIZ ANSWER:
B.

[1] White, E., 1984, "Banking Innovation in the 1920s: The Growth of National Banks' Financial Services", *Business and Economic History*, 12.
[2] Fisher, I., 1933, "The Debt-Deflation Theory of Great Depressions". *Econometrica* 1 (4): 337–357.
[3] Friedman, M. and Jacobson Schwartz, A., 1963, "A Monetary History of the United States, 1867-1960", *Princeton University Press*.

Q10. How did governments pay off WW2 debts?

A By increasing taxes and cutting back on the state

B By making the losing countries pay for them with reparations

C They didn't bother – they let inflation deal with them

10

World War II, debts and the low inflation world

World War II created massive debt around the world. After World War I, nations had tried either to reduce their money supply and pay off their debts (e.g. the UK) or reduce the value of them to almost nothing by hyperinflation (e.g. Germany).

After World War II, Keynesian thinking abounded and nations used it to justify a different tactic: reducing the value of their debts by creating a continuous low level of inflation. This achieved the same objective as hyperinflation of reducing the real value of government debts and making the interest on them easier to pay. However it did so in a more subtle way over a much longer period. Moreover it did not break the fabric of society and few even realised how the debts were being dealt with and who was effectively paying them.

World public debts

World War II was the most expensive war in history and left the world with more public debt than had ever been created before. It is estimated to have cost over $4 trillion[1] in current money. The average debt left across all nations reached 123 per cent of GDP in 1947. In some places, like the UK, it was double that level. Yet as the chart below clearly illustrates, the world managed to reduce debt levels down to near historical lows within the space of thirty years. At the same time it witnessed a period of strong economic growth.

Unlike the aftermath of World War I, only one western nation resolved its debt problem by resorting to hyperinflation (Hungary). In addition, many countries instituted expensive reforms and social welfare programmes post-war adding to their fiscal costs. So how, at the same time, did the world afford to pay off all this debt so quickly? The answer is simple. It didn't.

World public debt to GDP levels

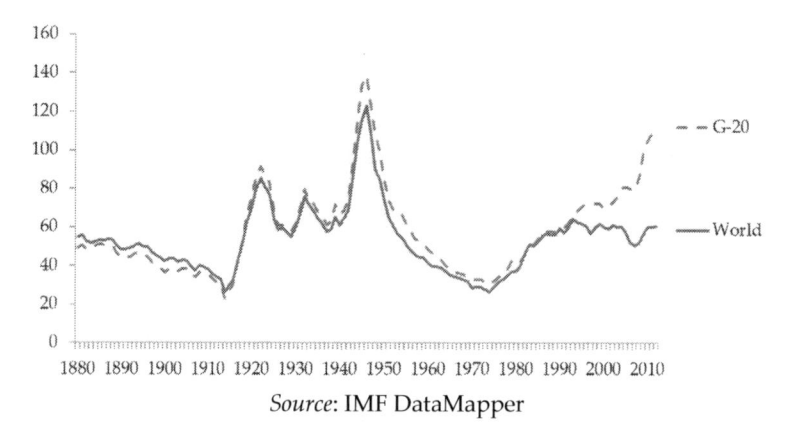

Source: IMF DataMapper

Instead it employed a clever strategy of creating a low, but persistent, level of inflation across the globe. As the world's GDP grew in absolute terms, in large part due to the inflation, the war debt appeared lower as a proportion of national income. At the same time, increases in tax revenues made the interest payments less onerous for governments.

This chapter looks at how this strategy came about and illustrates it with a case study of the UK. Not only did the UK come out of the war as one of the biggest debtors with the most to gain but it was also where the man who most influenced the strategy lived.

Britain and its 'Financial Dunkirk'

After the war in 1945, Britain's finances had a problem. Britain had been on the winning side, but in the process government debt had soared to 237 per cent of GDP. In addition the Americans, who had given billions to the UK under the Lend-Lease programme, demanded to be paid back. To make matters worse, the UK had just elected a new government whose manifesto included expensive nationalisations and to spend even more cash on welfare reforms e.g. by creating the NHS. The famous economist John Maynard Keynes, then working for the Treasury, said Britain faced a *'Financial Dunkirk'*.

Dealing with the post-war debts

Roll on just 25 years and Britain's real debt to GDP ratio had reduced to around 50 per cent. This was a remarkable achievement for a country that was often described in the 1960s and 1970s as the sick man of Europe and whose productivity gains lagged behind other major economies.

However if you look at the government debt statistics, you'll find that over that period, the UK did not pay off any of that debt[2]. Instead it actually increased its debt, from £26bn in 1945 to £33bn in 1970. Historically, this is not unusual. UK governments have regarded their borrowings very much like a credit card without limit, making the monthly repayments and ignoring the escalating capital amount owed, as the following graph of UK public debt clearly shows.

The UK government never pays off its debts

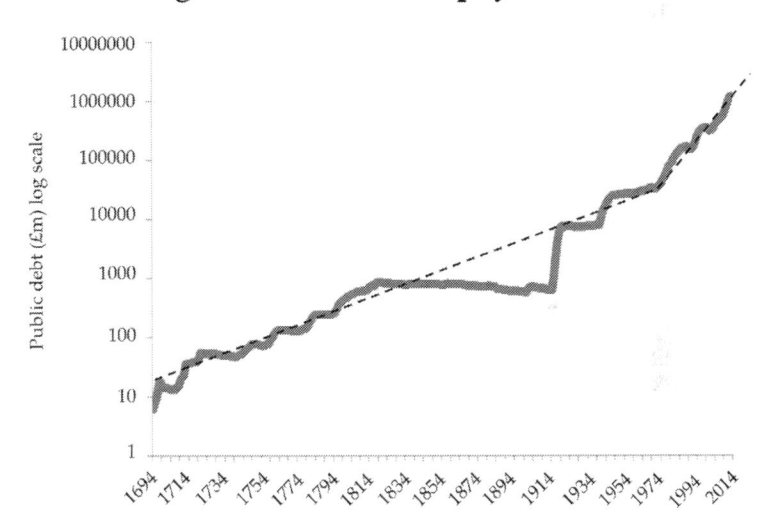

So what did the UK do to deal with its debts post-war?

There are three main ways governments can deal with their debts (assuming they do not plan to pay off the capital). Firstly they can make the payments easier to afford. For example, following the Napoleonic Wars, productivity increased massively in Victorian times, as did the population, and so UK debts became a much smaller proportion of the tax take.

The second option is to default. The UK likes to pride itself that it has not formally defaulted on government debt – although it has adopted lower interest rates on its World War I loan contracts, which some might class as a default[3].

The third option is just to inflate the nominal value of the debts away and reduce their real value. Given the lack of real productivity growth, and freed from the constraints of its own gold peg, the third route was the one that the UK and many other countries followed after 1945.

How inflation became embedded after the war

Previously after major wars, deflation was the norm in the UK, bringing prices back down. In contrast, government policy changed radically with regard to inflation after World War II, setting a path of ever increasing inflation.

The impact of major wars on UK prices

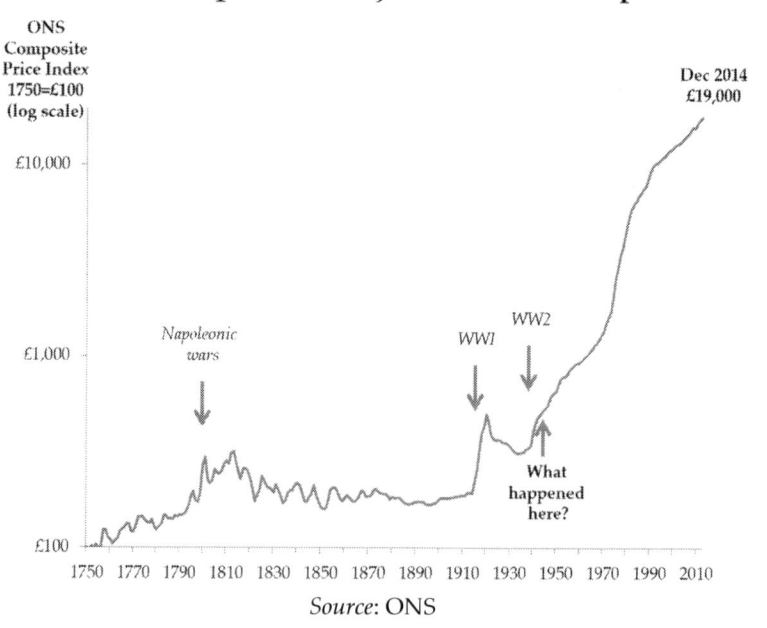

Source: ONS

Examining the history of this period shows there were three key contributing factors to the post-war inflation. All three share a common link: John Maynard Keynes (although the culpability of Keynes is open to debate - see discussion below).

1. **Keynesian economic thinking** appears to be responsible for the change in attitudes towards inflation. Keynes had seen first-hand the economic mismanagement of the post World War I era[4] and

lobbied for things to be different after the next war. Furthermore, many aspects of Keynes's famous 1936 book *The General Theory of Employment, Interest and Money* came to be adopted by post-war governments in the UK and elsewhere. In particular, politicians somewhat simplistically interpreted his writings as saying that if you wanted full employment, you had to have a certain level of positive inflation.

2. **Hugh Dalton**, Attlee's post-war Chancellor, may also bear some of the blame for instilling an inflation policy into UK governments and the Treasury. Dalton, a student of Keynes, really understood economics and public finance. He wrote one of the first textbooks on the subject in 1923, which even mentions the power of using inflation as a method of taxation. He was therefore well placed to help the UK deal with its debt.

Dalton's solution was to nationalise the Bank of England to give him, and his successors, the power to force the Bank to buy government the debt if required. He made cash and bondholders pay for the war by ensuring he kept interest rates low whilst fostering inflation – a policy that today we call financial repression.

3. The **Bretton Woods** monetary system was effectively the brainchild of Keynes and the most important mechanism for inflation to be transmitted around the globe. It was founded on the belief from Keynesian thinking that exchange rates could be controlled to ensure full employment and economic stability. However the final version agreed in 1944 differed from Keynes's original proposal of an independent world bank and a currency free from gold and politics.

Instead the US insisted their system be adopted, pegging currencies to the dollar and ultimately the price of gold. Therefore whatever the US decided about money supply and inflation had a direct impact on the UK and other countries because all the currencies were linked together[5]. In addition to directly increasing the money supply post-war and especially during the 1960s, the US specifically tasked the Federal Reserve in 1952 to maintain "low inflation". This low level of inflation was then exported to other countries such as the UK.

Another key facet of Bretton Woods was the creation of the IMF (International Monetary Fund). This significantly reduced the likelihood of countries having to reduce their money supplies to deal with deficits and thereby creating mass unemployment. Instead they could just devalue against the dollar peg. This also acted as a further positive contributor to inflation by removing the counterbalancing periods of monetary contraction that used to occur. In addition, such devaluations increased prices directly, as imports became more expensive.

Keynes (right) and the US representative Harry Dexter White (left) at the Bretton Woods Conference in 1944
Source: Reproduced with permission of the IMF

Put together these three created a system in the UK where inflation was not only tolerated but apparently encouraged.

Was inflation Keynes's real plan?

Even though Keynes clearly had a significant influence over the people and policies that were adopted post-war, it would appear that creating a world of continual inflation was not his plan and was not the solution he was advocating for paying off the debts accumulated in the wartime period.

Indeed in 1939 and 1940, Keynes spent a lot of time and effort lobbying newspapers, politicians and trade unions for a planned way to pay for the war[6]. He proposed that a system of compulsory savings be set up to help fund it and reduce demand during it. At the suggestion of the economist Friedrich Hayek he also proposed that some form of capital levy be imposed on the rich to help pay for it. Keynes was not concerned that this might harm the idle rich. Indeed, as a socialist he had written a few years before in his *General Theory* of his belief in the 'euthanasia of the rentier' class.

Keynes knew that the expansion of the money supply and the wartime tightening of the labour market would cause inflation, but he was trying to propose a system that would reduce its effects. For example, he advocated controlling the prices of key elements of the constituents of the cost of living index so as to curtail wage inflation demands. Although some elements of his thinking did happen (price controls and a limited form of compulsory savings), his broad proposals were rejected, particularly by the Labour Party and trade unions.

This was because neither overtly reducing the wages of working people and/or imposing annual capital levies on the rich were seen to be politically tenable strategies with the electorate. Instead politicians had to come up with a more subtle approach to dealing with the debts that the public would accept.

The effects of post-war generated inflation
('*Euthanasia of the rentier*')

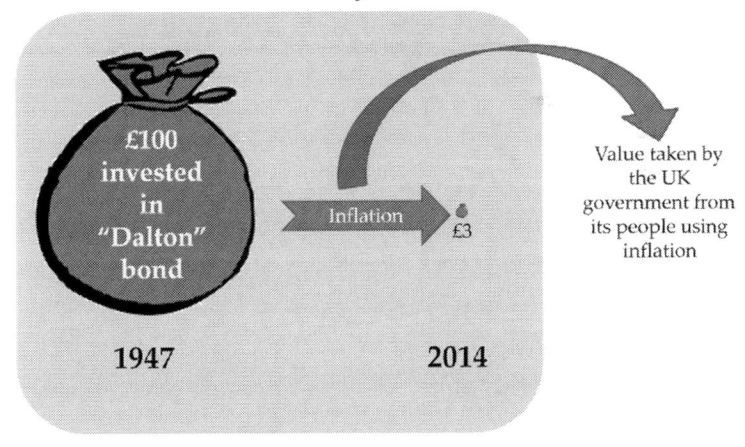

£100 invested in "Dalton" bond — Inflation → £3

Value taken by the UK government from its people using inflation

1947　　　　2014

Therefore, after the war, most economies including the UK permitted a persistent low level of inflation to take hold. The effect of this was to stealthily tax the cash holdings of everyone. During the post-war period, Dalton and successive chancellors forced down interest rates below the level of true inflation and in the process effectively imposed a capital levy on the wealthy rentier class. In addition, price controls were brought in such as "resale price maintenance" which effectively created a lower price for nearly a half of all goods, below which prices could not fall. This also helped push prices higher.

The net effect was almost the same as that noted about hyperinflation, as the diagram above illustrates. However the transfer of wealth to the government was more subtle and far more effective as it did not destroy the fabric of society and few noticed what was going on.

The system was very effective in a number of countries in reducing real debt to GDP ratios. According to detailed analysis by Ray Dalio of Bridgewater Associates[7], it is estimated that about 80 per cent of the reduction in UK post-war debt by 1970 was achieved by inflation alone.

The effect of inflation on the UK's war debts (real value of £26bn debt at each time)

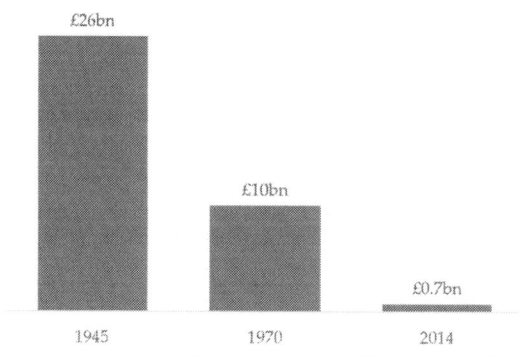

- 1945: £26bn
- 1970: £10bn
- 2014: £0.7bn

Sources: Debt Management Office and ONS.

Unfortunately, having successfully controlled the debt problem in the couple of decades after the war, governments followed a pattern of expanding the economy with money printing and the result was rampant inflation in the 1970s and 1980s.

KEY LEARNING POINTS:
- Debts escalate in wars and World War II was the world's most expensive to date.
- Few war debts have ever been paid back. Instead most governments have adopted a policy of reducing their value by creating a continuous low level of inflation. They have justified this on the basis of Keynesian thinking that it would ensure full employment.

- This achieved almost the same objective as hyperinflation after World War I, but in a more subtle way and over a much longer period. Few realised how the debts were being dealt with i.e. the public was effectively paying them by an inflation tax on their cash-based assets.

QUIZ ANSWER:
C.

---

[1] Therichest, 2013, "The Top 10 Most Expensive Wars", Blog post.
[2] Some of those debts were redeemed but new debt was then immediately created to refinance them.
[3] These potential increases were permitted within the original War Loan contract, but few buying them probably realised the full consequences of the terms and some therefore regarded it as a default.
[4] Keynes, J., 1920, "The Economic Consequences of the Peace", *New York: Harcourt, Brace, & Howe.*
[5] Indeed during that period, UK and US inflation had a correlation of over 70 per cent.
[6] Toye, R., 1999, "Keynes, The Labour Movement and 'How to Pay for the War'", *Twentieth Century British History* 10 (3).
[7] Dalio, R., 2012, "An In-Depth Look at Deleveragings", *Bridgewater Associates, LP.*

Q11. What was the primary cause of the 1970s inflation?

A Increases in the money supply during the 1960s and 1970s

B Increased trade union power which created a wage-price spiral

C The 1973 Arab–Israeli War which resulted in higher oil prices

11

The 1970s inflation crisis and fiat currencies

World inflation rose sharply during the 1970s. In the UK for example, it reached 26.9 per cent in August 1975—the highest level seen since 1800. It then took more than a decade for it to be forced back to 3 per cent (the level previously seen in 1967). This chapter looks at the reasons that caused inflation to take off around the globe at that point and the solutions that were adopted to bring it back under control.

The rise and fall of UK inflation

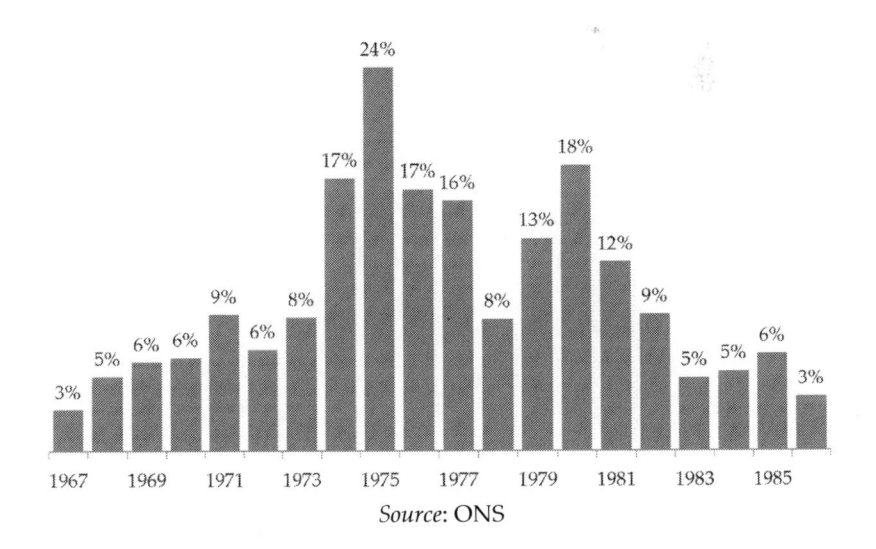

Source: ONS

The rise of true fiat currencies

The Bretton Woods currency system that emerged after World War II effectively led to the US dollar becoming the world's reserve currency. It permitted the US government to run massive budget deficits, which it used to finance things like the Vietnam War. In addition, the US had been following an expansionist policy since 1962 when Kennedy was elected to bring down unemployment. This greatly increased business and private lending. The increases in the money supply thus created in the US were exported all around the world as foreigners increasingly financed (i.e. owned) more and more US debt.

Normally when currencies are freely traded, their value is strongly correlated to the amount of money circulating[1]. Therefore if a country strictly controls its money supply (e.g. Switzerland), the value of the currency rises. In particular it rises against those of countries that have increased their money supply above their needs i.e. faster than the speed of economic growth. Despite the benefits of Bretton Woods, it imposed a strait jacket on its members' exchange rates that did not permit this mechanism to function normally, especially for the reserve currency.

This fundamental flaw eventually broke the system as confidence in the value of the US dollar dwindled and many demanded to exchange dollars into gold at the official Bretton Woods price. Finally President Nixon was forced to terminate the conversion to gold on 15 August 1971, and the Bretton Woods Agreement effectively ended at that point as currencies began a period of floating freely against each other.

The other key implication of the end of the agreement was that major world currencies were no longer linked to gold and became true fiat (paper) currencies. The limit on the expansion of the money supply created by the gold peg was therefore lifted and inflation was one of the consequences.

Causes of the 1970s inflation

There are three likely causes for the 1970s inflation, which are all interlinked: expansion of the money supply, commodity price rises and a resulting wage/price spiral.

THE 1970S INFLATION CRISIS AND FIAT CURRENCIES

Key causes on the 1970s inflation

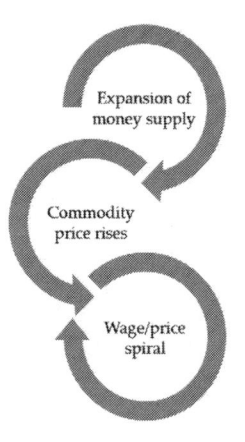

It was not just in the US that the money supply had been increasing in the run-up to the breakdown of Bretton Woods. In the early 1970s, UK Prime Minister Edward Heath was also stimulating the economy in an attempt to reduce unemployment, which had risen to 1 million for the first time since the war. Released from the ties of the Bretton Woods currency agreement, the UK could create whatever money it wanted (within reason) and so it did.

Tax relief on mortgages was introduced in 1969 to help encourage home ownership. Heath then deregulated the mortgage market, allowing not just building societies to lend but also banks. The net result was that house prices doubled in just over two years prior to 1974. They had doubled again by the late 1970s. At the same time, consumer credit was also mushrooming as credit cards started to be used for the first time in the UK.

In addition to increases in the money supply, inflation rose in the 1970s due to the direct effect of rising commodity prices. (Note, some have argued that those price rises were simply a result of the increases in the money supply since the 1960s[2].) The oil price rises in 1973 and 1979 caused inflation to spike higher in 1975 and then again in 1980. Inflation was further exacerbated by food crop failures, which saw increasing prices in other commodities. This triggered governments around the world (including the UK) to adopt policies allowing the money supply to increase further.

Finally inflation also increased in the 1970s due to a 'wage-price spiral'. This was a particular issue in the UK at that time due to weak governments and the power of some trade unions. For example, the

111

1970s witnessed miners' pay strikes that brought the country to its knees with widespread power cuts and resulted in the infamous *Three-Day Week*. The breakdown of industrial relations in the 1970s was also accompanied by a rise in a new phenomenon called stagflation, i.e. a period of both rising inflation and unemployment without real economic growth.

How the 1970s inflation was brought under control

Writing in 1974 with inflation at over 10 per cent in the US, Ronald Marcks proposed that there were basically three scenarios that could play out in resolving the debts and inflation of the 1970s[3]. He suggested that these were as listed below.

Marcks's suggested solutions to the 1970s inflation

1. Regaining control over monetary policy by raising interest rates and reducing the money supply.

2. That the world came to live with the higher inflation and maintained increases in the money supply and inflation at a new higher stable equilibrium of around 5-6 per cent.

3. That money supply carried on increasing until the geometric rises in prices reached a point of hyperinflation. Soon after the system would collapse and a new monetary order would be created.

In the end, it was a version of scenarios one and two enacted by the US that finally brought inflation under control. Paul Volcker was appointed Chairman of the Federal Reserve in 1979. He promptly tried to enact part of scenario one i.e. the higher interest rate part, but he did not reduce the money supply. He raised short-term interest rates to over 20 per cent in early 1980 prompting a deep recession. The impact of this spread around the world as interest payments rose sharply on dollar debts and this resulted in the Third World Debt Crisis.

However the policy was very successful for the US, and inflation fell from 12.5 per cent in 1980 to 3.8 per cent in 1982. At the same time, President Reagan cut tax rates and reduced business regulation to increase the production of goods and services. He deregulated the price of oil, which broke the OPEC oil cartel. He also fired strikers, which helped get the wage-price spiral under control. These, together with the rising value of the dollar which cut the cost of imports, all contributed to a swift end to the 1970s inflation in the US.

However the political cycle is short in the US and by 1983 the next election was in sight and a version of scenario two was enacted. Volcker cut interest rates and flooded the economy with money. He kept the money supply growth at around 10 per cent per annum[4] until 1986, despite the lower inflation rate. This stimulated a great expansion of business and asset prices, which lasted throughout Reagan's presidency. At the same time price inflation remained low— mainly in the 3-5 per cent range.

On the other side of the Atlantic, Prime Minister Margaret Thatcher aimed to emulate the US policies. The Bank of England raised interest rates to over 15 per cent in 1980, the highest level in its three hundred year history. Thatcher copied some of Reagan's other policies on deregulation and also managed to break the wage-price spiral in some key industries. However, the overall policy was slightly less successful in the UK. It took until 1986 before inflation fell below 4 per cent. This was partly the result of the declining value of sterling increasing import prices. The pound had declined from $2.4 to £1 in late 1980 to just above parity to the dollar in 1985.

The other difference in the UK was the amount of monetary expansion the Thatcher government permitted and the length of time it lasted. The UK money supply was increased by an average of over 15 per cent per annum through the whole of the 1980s. This fuelled massive rises in asset prices such as shares and property.

Despite this, consumer price rises remained below 5 per cent per annum (except for a brief period at the end of the 1980s). What the UK effectively did was to store up a large amount of potential latent inflation, which still remains locked up within asset prices to this day. It remains to be seen how and when this will unwind. (See: "18-The transition period and near-term inflation.")

KEY LEARNING POINTS:
- The great inflation of the 1970s followed the breakdown of the Bretton Woods currency agreement in 1971, which ushered in true fiat (paper) currencies with no link to gold or other pegs.
- Following this, money supply around the world increased sharply and this helped trigger commodity price rises and ultimately resulted in wage-price spirals.

INFLATION MATTERS

- The situation was eventually brought under control by Paul Volcker of the US Federal Reserve, who raised interest rates in 1980 and created a worldwide recession.

QUIZ ANSWER:
A.

---

[1] It is also affected by government policy, interest rates and perceived political stability of the regime.

[2] Parsson, J., 1974, " Dying of Money: Lessons of the Great German and American Inflations", *Wellspring Press*.

[3] ibid.

[4] M3 monetary growth - source St Louis Federal Reserve.

PART III

INFLATION PRESENT

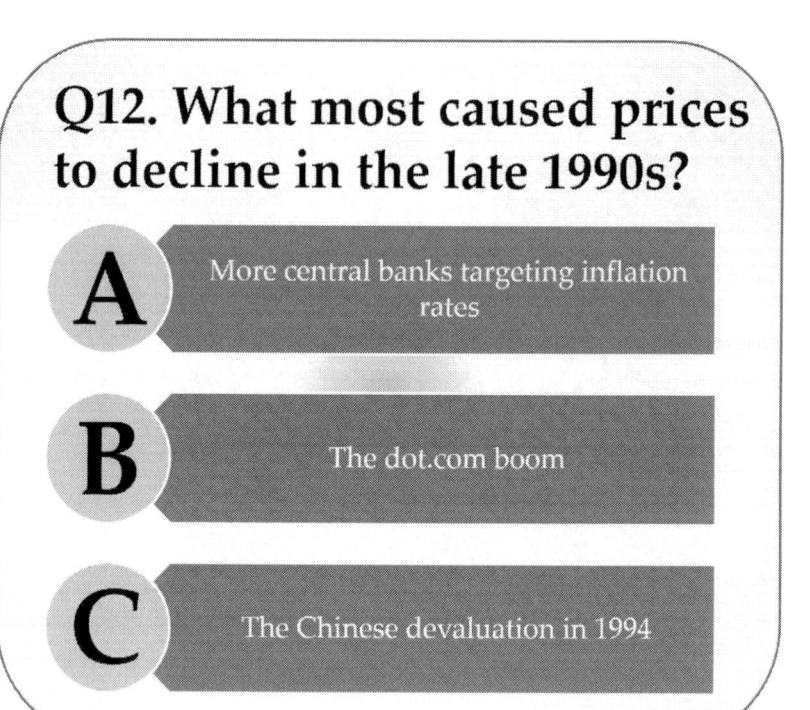

Q12. What most caused prices to decline in the late 1990s?

A More central banks targeting inflation rates

B The dot.com boom

C The Chinese devaluation in 1994

12

The Great Moderation and the Great Recession

This chapter looks at what has been happening to inflation over the last few decades and the factors that are influencing it right now. It shows that during the 1980s the world entered a period that has been called the *Great Moderation*, where inflation rates declined from double digit levels to almost zero by the turn of the millennium. A key contributor to this was a decision by China to devalue its currency and flood the world with cheap goods.

Inflation picked up a little in the early noughties, brought about in part by expansionist monetary policies, especially in the US. However the *Great Recession* and the resulting debt overhang have brought that trend to an abrupt halt, and prices in 2014 were heading back to near-zero levels in many major economies.

The sudden decline of inflation worldwide

From the early 1980s, inflation in most countries around the world declined. Inflation in the G7 countries (+ China) dropped from an average of 12 per cent in 1980 to nearly zero by the end of the 20th Century. In the UK for example, inflation was 18 per cent in 1980 and declined to just 3 per cent by 2000 (and just 0.8 per cent as measured by CPI).

The reduction was a truly worldwide phenomenon. In only two of the G20 countries did inflation exceed 10 per cent in the year 2000 - Turkey: 55 per cent and Russia: 21 per cent.

The decline of world inflation from 1980-2000
(G7 + China average)

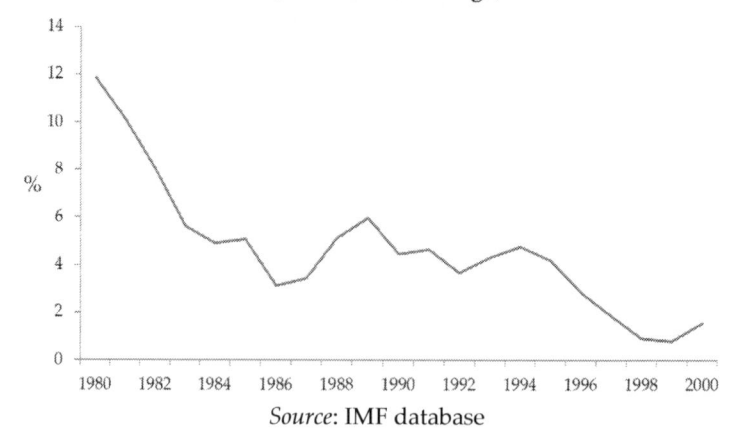

Source: IMF database

However even in these countries, inflation had come down massively in the previous decade. For example, Russia experienced a peak of 874 per cent inflation in 1993 following the dissolution of the Soviet Union. Furthermore the near hyperinflation seen in certain South American countries in the early 1990s were a distant memory by the turn of the century:

The decline of inflation in South America

Country	1990	2000
Argentina	2314%	-1%
Brazil	2948%	7%

Source: IMF database

The most frequently espoused explanation for the decline of inflation was that it was due to the skill of central bankers who had learnt how to control western economies. Indeed as noted previously, the plan of Paul Volcker of the US Federal Reserve contributed significantly to the reduction of the inflation rate in that country and had knock-on effects across the rest of the world. (See: "11-The 1970s inflation crisis and fiat currencies.")

The Great Moderation (1985-2007)

Another explanation for the decline was that it was related to the so-called Great Moderation[1]. This was a term coined to describe the period of economic history from the mid-1980s through to the start of the Great Recession in 2007 during which volatility declined and the extremes of the business cycle seemed much reduced. Although there were recessions (e.g. in 1991 and the dot.com crash), they tended to be less extreme than previously, and many countries saw long periods of sustained economic growth, particularly towards the end of the century. Indeed in 1999, the then Chancellor of the Exchequer of the UK, Gordon Brown, infamously claimed that the 'boom and bust' business cycle was no more.

It was also a period of great technological change with the advent of the internet. In addition, new processes allowed shortened supply chains and just-in-time inventory methods. At the same time, cheap labour from Asia and the era of offshoring not only helped increase company profits but ensured companies were leaner and better able to cope with economic shocks.

This era was one where consumers witnessed reductions in prices in many categories of goods as cheap imports flooded in from the Far East and particularly China. Discounts shops (such as Poundland and Primark in the UK) abounded and helped consumers substantially reduce what they paid for many household goods and clothes. At the same time, the rise of online shopping increased competition in high-street stores, ensuring that the average price paid for many goods was held in check.

A key factor contributing to keeping inflation down in many countries in the West was exchange rates. China devalued its currency by a third in 1994 and then pegged it to the US dollar at the new low rate. This ensured that the prices of its exports would significantly undercut those of goods produced in many western countries. As the market share of these products increased in the West, inflation was simultaneously suppressed.

The return of inflation in the noughties

Despite the decline of prices in the run up to the turn of the millennium, prices then started to rise again. In part this was related to government policy in many countries targeting inflation of around 2 per cent. However the early noughties also saw a number of key countries (especially the US) adopt very "accommodative" monetary policies.

After the dot.com crash of 2001, the then Federal Reserve chairman, Alan Greenspan, cut interest rates from 7 to 1.75 per cent. This created an era of cheap money which caused an explosion of debt across the financial and consumer worlds. US money supply

(M3) was allowed to grow over 6 per cent a year from 2000-2007 and it grew in the UK at an even higher rate (over 8 per cent).

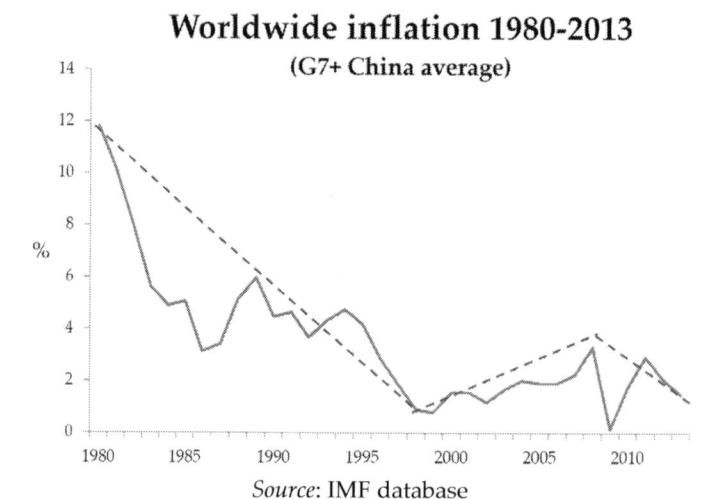

Worldwide inflation 1980-2013
(G7+ China average)

Source: IMF database

Although most of this went into increased asset prices (houses, shares, commodities etc.), some did leak across into consumer prices too. This was in part because the increased credit caused a boom in a wide variety of commodity prices, which have a direct impact on inflation indices. For example in the UK, price inflation steadily rose prior to the Great Recession and was above 4 per cent by 2007. Note, had a flood of cheap Chinese imports not been balanced against this, prices would have risen even more during this period.

Another implication of the credit boom was to create a *global savings glut*. The money created allowing countries like the US to continue spending beyond their means also generated cash balances elsewhere in the system. This led to massive savings accumulating in producer nations like China. These savers bought US government bonds and this helped keep down interest rates during this period, further prolonging the boom.

The Great Recession (2008 onwards)

The financial crisis of 2008 brought an end to the expansion of the money supply but not before creating another asset bubble, this time in commodities. The rising prices of oil and foodstuffs in that year caused a final peak in inflation rates, particularly in less-developed countries where they counted more in the cost of living indices.

The shock waves from the demise of Lehman Brothers and other banks caused a sudden contraction of the economies in most nations, as business and consumer confidence collapsed. The decline in demand brought with it a strong deflationary influence on world prices. 2009 brought deflation to some of the world's largest economies including the US, Japan, China and the UK (RPI measure only).

The recession also had an impact on the psyche of the world and further enhanced the global savings glut. This time however it was companies and individuals that were saving. The uncertainty surrounding the recession caused many to hoard money and delay spending on investment.

The response from governments was varied but all tried to increase demand by whatever methods they could. This ranged from money printing in the form of Quantitative Easing in the US and the UK, to state sponsored borrowing and infrastructure projects in China, to subsidies for buying new cars in many developed nations (the so-called "cash for clunkers" schemes). At the same time base interest rates were reduced to levels never seen before in many countries such as the UK.

The initial effect of this was some form of recovery. But for most leading economies it took half a decade to recover their former GDP levels. Moreover the crisis took its toll on long-term economic growth rates.

Looking into the future, some economists now think that growth rates will be impaired for many decades to come as a result of the debts that have been accumulated. Indeed recent analysis[2] shows that the world's debts are continuing to rise, even in 2014. In order to help these debts be serviced and to reduce the chances of a disorderly default, governments are expected to keep interest rates low for a very long time to come. It is therefore very likely that inflation will remain subdued. This will be a particular problem for Eurozone countries that lack the structures and systems to alleviate the debt issues, such as money printing and devaluation.

The impact of the Great Recession on inflation is therefore still being felt and likely to remain for a long time to come. The effects of this and the likely prognosis for inflation are discussed in detail in later chapters. (See: "Part IV-Inflation yet to come.")

INFLATION MATTERS

KEY LEARNING POINTS:
- The Great Moderation describes the period starting in the mid-1980s that saw growing economic stability and global inflation rates decline markedly to near-zero levels by the turn of the millennium. A key contributor to the latter stage of this was a decision by the Chinese to devalue its currency and flood the world with cheap goods in 1994.
- Inflation picked up in the early noughties, brought about in part by expansionist monetary policies, especially in the US.
- The Great Recession of 2008 and the resulting debt overhang have brought the above trend to an abrupt halt, and inflation in 2014 was heading to near-zero levels again in many major economies.

QUIZ ANSWER:
C.

---

[1] Stock, J. and Watson, M., 2002, "Has the business cycle changed and why?", *NBER Macroeconomics Annual*.

[2] Lane, P., Reichlin, L., Reinhart, V.,and Wyplosz, C., 2014, "Deleveraging? What Deleveraging? The 16th Geneva Report on the World Economy", *International Center For Monetary and Banking Studies*.

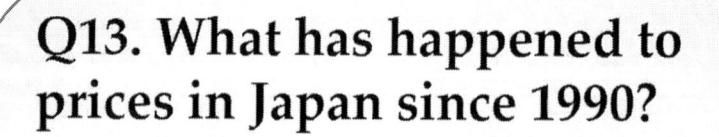

Q13. What has happened to prices in Japan since 1990?

A — Prices have gone up by about 10 per cent

B — Prices have declined by about 5 per cent

C — Prices have declined by about 20 per cent

13

Japan and deflation

Unlike the rest of the world, Japan has been a special case for the last couple of decades and has experienced more or less stable prices. This chapter looks at the story in more detail and examines what implications it might have for prices elsewhere in the world. The chapter shows that the tale of woe frequently told about Japan's deflation is missing a few key details.

Its economy has not grown significantly. However this ignores the fact Japan has a declining workforce and an ageing population, both of which depress consumption and GDP. In addition, Japan has not actually experienced much deflation. The chapter highlights alternative explanations for the lower prices seen in Japan and in particular the impact of the historical strength of the Yen.

The 1980s financial bubble

Post World War II, the US poured money into countries like Japan to ensure they became economically sound and depended on world trade in order to resist the onslaught of communism. Japan became the world's centre for producing tech goods and during the 1980s was regarded as one of the most successful countries in the world.

During the 1980s, money supply was allowed to grow sharply in Japan (around 8-11 per cent in most years). In addition, the Bank of Japan slashed interest rates to 2.5 per cent in 1987 in order to try to stem the appreciation of the Yen. Not only did it fail to do that, it helped stoke the already growing bubble in asset prices as speculators took advantage of the low interest rates to borrow and invest in property and shares. From 1984, the Nikkei almost quadrupled in value in the space of five years.

INFLATION MATTERS

The Japanese asset bubble

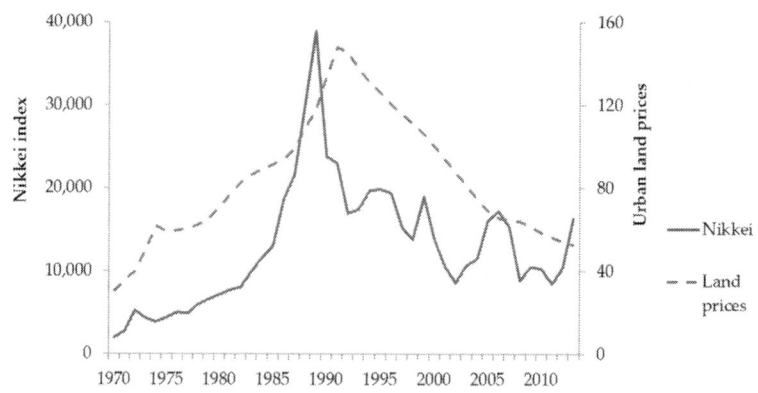

Sources: Nikkei and Japan Real Estate Institute (nationwide urban land prices).

Finally at the end of December 1989, the Bank of Japan raised interest rates to 4.25 per cent. Within days the Nikkei peaked at its record high of 38,957. Within a year it had nearly halved. Over the coming years it continued to decline and it reached lows of just above 7,000 in both 2003 and again later in that decade. House prices also peaked in the early 1990s and have since been in decline for nearly two and a half decades.

The aftermath of the bubble

There has been much discussion about the response of the Japanese government to the bubble bursting. Initially it allowed many financial companies to ignore their losses and indeed to carry on lending. However, eventually, bank collapses ensued and the government nationalised those banks. Companies followed a policy of paying back their debts, as did consumers.

The net effect of all this was a marked contraction of the economy. GDP growth stagnated within a few years. The revival of 1995 was hit by the effects of the Asian financial crisis of 1997 that finally forced Japan into recession in 1998. However for much of the mid-noughties Japan grew by around 2 per cent a year until the Great Recession hit.

Nearly all historical reporting now focuses on "the lost decades" and blames deflation as one of the main causes. For example, as I write, deflation is back on the front cover of *The Economist* magazine. Their lead article highlights the "struggling" Japanese economy and how it fell into "deflation with unpleasant... consequences for both itself and the world economy." (Source: *The Economist*, "*The world's biggest problem: Deflation in the euro zone is all too close and dangerous*", 25 October 2014).

A key part of the argument is that when deflation took hold in Japan people stopped buying goods and awaited cheaper prices and that this caused the economy to falter. (As we saw before, this is not necessarily true - see: "4-Deflation and why it is regarded as a problem.") The BBC website's article[1] about "*Japan's economic battle with deflation*" is similar to most others. It claims: "*deflation gripped the economy - and its effect filtered through all sectors of society affecting all parts of life... As corporations went through the vicious deflationary cycle of falling prices, declining sales and, subsequently, plunging profits; they were forced to make lay-offs and pay cuts.*"

The evidence however does not back this up and suggests the story is more complex.

What deflation?

A key part of the above argument centres around the deflation that Japan has suffered during the lost decades. The following chart shows the Japanese prices index since the bubble burst in late 1989. Far from showing deflation, it shows that prices actually carried on rising for five years until 1994, during which time they rose by 10 per cent. In the last 20 years there have been dips but no overall deflation, with prices now almost higher in Japan than they have been before.

Japanese Price Index

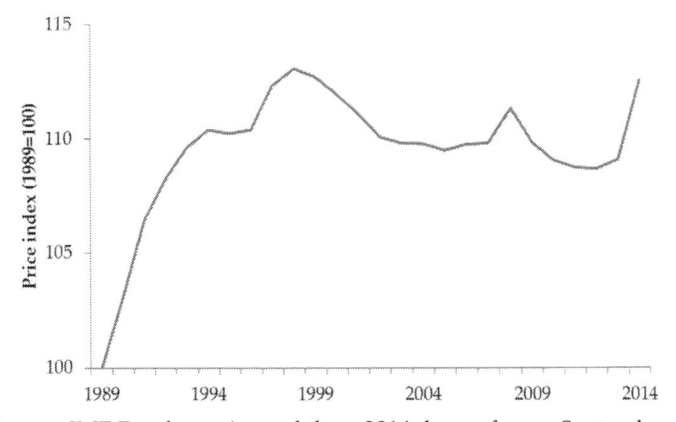

Source: IMF Database. Annual data. 2014 data refers to September.

Perhaps a better description of Japanese prices during the latter part of the lost decades is that they were largely stable. In years when they went down, the declines were all less than 1 per cent a year, with the exception of 2009 when they declined by 1.4 percent. (But remember, in 2009 worldwide prices declined due to the recession - e.g. UK RPI was down 0.5 per cent.)

It seems unlikely that such small price changes would have caused the Japanese consumer to delay purchasing products. Instead what did significantly affect Japanese retail sales were increases in sales taxes such as the hikes in 1997 and 2014.

The myth of the lost decade

The other part of the argument often cited about Japan's deflation is that it caused wages to decline. Undoubtedly the country went through tough economic times due to the recession resulting from the asset bubble. This caused structural changes in the jobs market; for instance more Japanese were employed on short-term contracts. This resulted in slightly lower actual average wages during the first part of the noughties. At the same time however, this was the time when prices edged lower temporarily. Therefore the net effect on wages after inflation was again negligible—see chart below. A better description of average Japanese wages was that in terms of purchasing power, they were largely stable after the crisis.

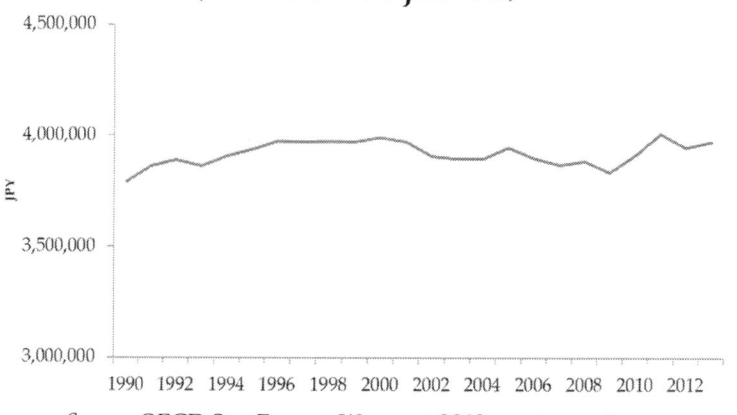

Average Japanese wages (inflation adjusted)

Source: OECD Stat Export. Wages at 2013 constant prices.

However, the main criticism of the Japanese economy has been that its economy has declined because of the deflation. A recent economics article in *The Guardian* said[2]: "Japan, a country gripped by deflation, which over the past two decades has struggled with stagnant growth..." Again the answer is more complex than this superficial comment implies.

In absolute terms the GDP in Japan in 2013 was almost the same as in 1991, very much supporting the notion of lost decades of economic growth. However this ignores a key characteristic of the Japanese economy: its ageing and declining workforce. GDP is the sum of things produced in an economy. If there are less people working, GDP will be lower. Over the last 15 years the Japanese labour force has declined over 3 per cent. In contrast, the workforces of most other developed countries have continued to increase. Over the same period, the US workforce grew by 13 per cent and that of the UK by 14 per cent.

When you fully take the declining workforce into account and instead examine GDP per worker, you end up with a very different story about Japan. As the chart below shows, this measure shows a GDP increase of 20 per cent in Japan, a figure that outstrips most major European countries such as Germany, France, Italy and Spain. Only in the UK and the US did apparent[3] output increase more. Moreover, in absolute terms at *Purchasing Power Parity*, the level of output of Japanese workers seems very similar to that of other developed countries, the US being an exception.

GDP per worker by country

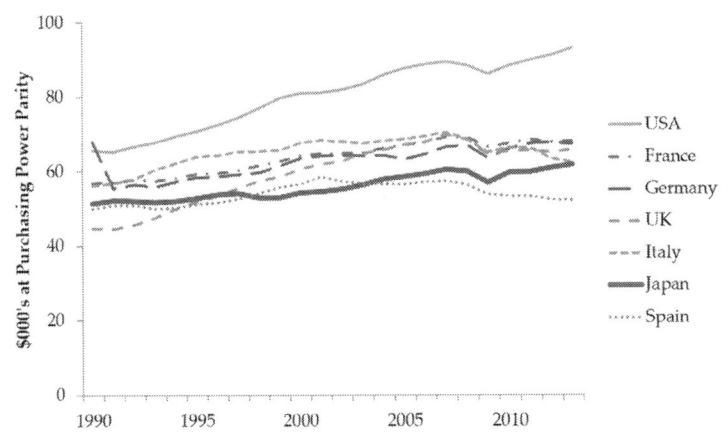

Source: OCED Stat extracts. Data shows GDP at constant prices, constant PPPs divided by total civilian labour force.

INFLATION MATTERS

The impact of the demographics

Another factor rarely considered when interpreting events in Japan is the true impact of demographics on purchasing. It has an impact on production and GDP as noted above, but it also has a major impact on consumption. The decline in consumption in Japan has been significantly influenced by demographics.

Births peaked in Japan after the war and to a lesser extent during the 1960s Baby Boomer period. By 1990 however the birth rate had declined to a half that of the 1970 level. In 2014, only 1.4 babies were being born for every woman. The falling birth rate is causing the population to decline and has already reduced the number of workers in the population as the post-war boomers move into older age. The average age of a Japanese citizen was 46 in 2012. This was higher than any other country in the world and had increased from just 38 when the bubble burst in 1990.

Japanese population - average age

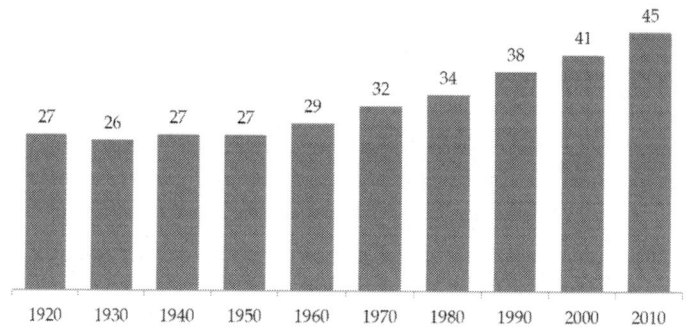

Year	Average Age
1920	27
1930	26
1940	27
1950	27
1960	29
1970	32
1980	34
1990	38
2000	41
2010	45

Sources: Nikkei Research Institute of Industry and Markets and CIA World Factbook.

The average age matters, because consumption in the economy is strongly correlated with age. Research in many countries has shown that around 46 is the peak age for consumption for an individual, being the age when the demands of supporting children are at their greatest. Consumption changes as people get older and eventually becomes focused on basic commodities and healthcare. However the net effect is that total spending steadily declines with age. (See chart in: "7-Inflationary Wave Theory.") .

The increasing average age of Japanese citizens since the crisis will also have had an impact and must have in part contributed to decline in consumption levels. Given this, it is actually somewhat surprising that GDP has not declined more during the period.

So the story of Japan is not as simple as portrayed in the media. Not only has the Japanese economy performed predictably for one with a declining workforce and ageing population, but it has not actually experienced much deflation, merely a period of more stable prices. Admittedly government debt has increased significantly in Japan but it is debatable whether its economy has really suffered lost decades as often depicted.

Why prices have stabilised in Japan

One is still left with the question of why price rises remained so low in Japan and inflation did not return despite all the best efforts of the Japanese government to increase it by printing money over the last decade. Indeed it could be argued that there should be substantial latent inflation built into the system following the attempts to expand the money supply.

The answer probably lies in something unique about the Japanese currency and perceptions of the government's economic control. Despite the evident woes with the economy, the Japanese Yen has continued to be perceived as a safe-haven currency - that is one that people park their assets in during times of turmoil. Unlike most other developed countries, it has run a balance of payments surplus for decades, and hence owns many assets abroad. This has caused the Yen to continue to appreciate against virtually all other currencies since the Bretton Woods currency agreement broke down in the early 1970s.

Yen trade weighted exchange rate

Source: Bank of England

INFLATION MATTERS

This has had a major impact on inflation rates in Japan, as over time the cost of key imports has declined. This effect appears so great that it is likely that this has contributed more than anything else to the lower level of price rises in Japan versus other economies.

The chart below shows the inflation rate in Japan and compares it to the average for other G7 developed countries (+ China). The results are striking, particularly for the period *before* the asset crisis struck. Japan had an inflation rate about 4 per cent less than the rest of the developed world before its crisis struck. It even experienced deflation two years before it in 1987.

Japanese inflation has always been lower

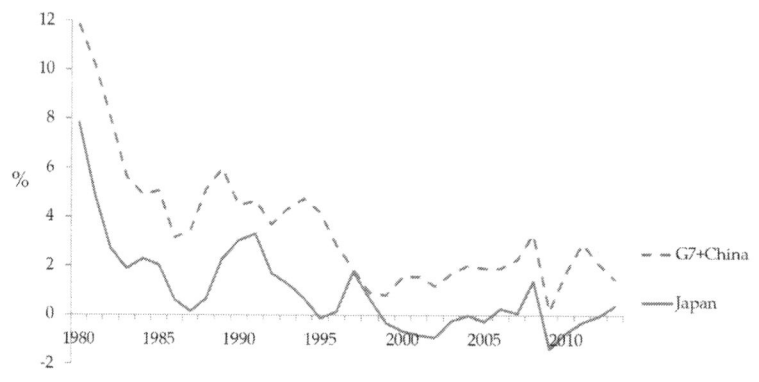

Source: IMF World Economic Outlook Database, April 2014

An alternative explanation for the reasons for Japanese deflation (or more correctly, stable prices) is that this differential continued as the Yen has carried on appreciating. Worldwide prices declined markedly in the 1990s, partly as a result of central bankers' actions and partly due to deflation being created by China's cheap exports. Therefore, assuming the differential of 4 per cent less inflation in Japan after the crisis, it was forced towards near-zero inflation rates as world inflation rates came down.

A key implication of this is that prices probably declined in Japan not because of the effects of the crisis, but more because of the continued appreciation of the Yen and the flood of very cheap imports from China. The logical response of the consumer to such cheap prices (and the resulting proliferation of 100-yen shops) was probably not as portrayed in the media i.e. a decline in consumption. They just bought more cheaper goods, the sum total of which may have been the same as it was before, so that GDP didn't change.

KEY LEARNING POINTS:
- Japan has not actually experienced significant deflation and prices in 2014 are higher than at any time before.
- Japan had an inflation rate approximately 4 per cent lower than the rest of the world before the so-called lost decades. This difference has persisted and has been erroneously attributed to the aftermath of the banking crisis. Lower inflation has actually been caused by the gradual strengthening value of the Yen over the last 30-40 years.
- Japan's economy has not grown significantly, but this does not factor in its declining workforce and ageing population. On a GDP per worker basis, Japan's growth has actually exceeded that of most major European economies. Furthermore, GDP calculations do not factor in the effect of a rapidly ageing population that is simply consuming less.

QUIZ ANSWER:
A.

---

[1] Takeshita, S., 2009, "Japan's economic battle with deflation", *BBC News*, 23 March 2009.

[2] Collinson, P., 2014, "Oh what a lovely stock market crisis", *Guardian Money Blog*, 18 October 2014.

[3] Some have argued that the UK and US growth figures only appear higher due to the manipulation of their GDP deflator statistics. (See: "6-Inflation measurement issues.")

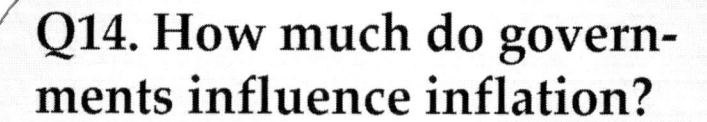

Q14. How much do governments influence inflation?

A — A lot. Inflation is largely a governmental choice

B — Not much. It depends so much on external factors

C — Not at all. Inflation is a random act of economics

14

Governments and inflation

The legacy of the economic policies from the post-war period is that we now have governments throughout the globe that rely on inflation as both a form of taxation and a way of dealing with their fiscal imbalances. (See: "10-World War II, debts and the low inflation world.") This chapter looks at the adoption of inflation as a fiscal tool, the many ways in which present governments gain from inflation and how much that "inflation tax" is worth. It then examines the governmental policies that have been adopted to ensure inflation is perpetuated.

Inflation is a governmental choice

If you doubt the influence of governments in creating inflation, consider Switzerland. Price stability has been a government policy since 1973. Moreover, since 2000 it has required that its national bank (SNB) ensures that inflation stays within the range 0-2 per cent. It has averaged just 0.7 per cent since then.

Consider also the UK, which has tasked the Bank of England to create 2 per cent inflation (and has achieved 2.3 per cent measured by CPI). Indeed in every G20 country except Japan, inflation since the millennium has averaged around two per cent or above. Countries with higher inflation targets have had even higher levels. For example, both Russia and Turkey have 5 per cent targets and have averaged respectively around 10 per cent and 20 per cent inflation over 2000-2013.

Evidence that governments influence inflation rates

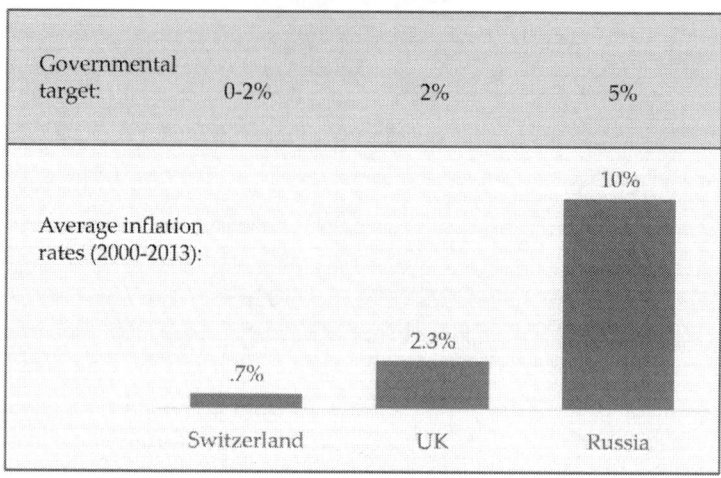

Governmental target:	0-2%	2%	5%
Average inflation rates (2000-2013):	.7% (Switzerland)	2.3% (UK)	10% (Russia)

Source: IMF Database

Inflation usually results from governmental actions. It is not a random act of economics.

The origins of government interference in inflation

Governments often over-promise to the electorate in order to gain power. They usually end up spending more than they can raise in direct taxation to fund these promises. There is therefore an incentive to utilise more subtle methods of indirect taxation that permit their increased spending (and associated deficits) to be funded while avoiding the anticipated revolt from more direct and visible forms of taxation. The answer to this problem for many governments has been "inflation tax"[1].

The concept may have been adopted unwittingly in historical times such as during the French Revolution, but its usage only became prominent following the establishment of economics as an academic discipline around the turn of the 20th Century. Much work was done on the economics of public finances and politicians became well acquainted with the power of inflation as an alternative method of taxation. As Keynes wrote in a key work in 1922[2]:

GOVERNMENTS AND INFLATION

> "A Government can pay its way ... by printing paper money. That is to say, it can by this means secure the command of real resources — resources just as real as those obtained by taxation. The method is reprobated, but its efficiency cannot be disputed. A Government can live by this means when it can live by no other. This is the form of taxing the people which it is most difficult to evade and which even the weakest Government can enforce when it can enforce nothing else.
>
> On whom has the tax fallen? Clearly on the holders of the original notes ... The burden of the tax is well spread, cannot be evaded, costs nothing to collect, and falls, in a rough sort of way, in proportion to the wealth of the victim. No wonder its superficial advantages have attracted Ministers of Finance."

John Maynard Keynes, 1922

It is also a form of taxation that very few really understand. In one of the UK's first economics books on Public Finances in 1922[3], Hugh Dalton wrote:

> "The comparative acquiescence of a public opinion in taxation by inflation is a measure of public ignorance of economic principles and of the inability of wage earners, and still more the recipients of fixed money incomes, to safeguard their economic interests. Thus persons, who would certainly vote against a government which added one shilling in the pound to their income tax, have been found to tolerate a government which, by doubling the price level through inflation, has in effect, imposed upon them an additional income tax of ten shillings in the pound."

Hugh Dalton, 1922

During that time, many European governments with debts that were impossible to pay with ordinary taxation resorted to printing vast amounts of money and using inflation tax to pay them off. (See: "8-World War I and learning about hyperinflation.") A similar inflationary episode followed World War II in many countries. However this time a more subtle policy of lower but persistent inflation was adopted by most developed countries. This more closely followed the economic textbooks in being effected without the awareness of most of the population. (See: "10-World War II, debts and the low inflation world.")

Inflation tax is worth about £30bn a year to the UK government

We are still living in that era now. The key benefit of inflation is that it reduces the real value of government debt. It does this because tax revenues increase approximately in proportion to inflation. Government's fixed debt payments therefore become a smaller part of the tax take and more affordable.

The benefits to the UK government of inflation tax depend on the inflation rate and is currently around £29bn in 2014. Inflation at this time is lower than it has been and so the value of inflation tax is less than a few years ago despite the rising value of government debt. Cumulatively over the last five years, inflation tax has theoretically been worth an estimated £182bn to the UK government.

The value of inflation tax

Year	UK fixed interest debt	UK inflation (RPI)	Inflation tax
2010	£848bn	4.6%	£39bn
2011	£949bn	5.2%	£49bn
2012	£1012bn	3.2%	£32bn
2013	£1081bn	3.0%	£32bn
2014 (est)	£1173bn	2.5%	£29bn
Total			£182bn

Sources: Debt Management Office and ONS.
To calculate inflation tax, you multiply the total government debt excluding index-linked bonds (but including NS&I) by the inflation rate.

I say "theoretically" as this calculation omits one key thing. The Bank of England now owns £375bn of government debt acquired through the Quantitative Easing programme, and it pays the interest it receives back to the Treasury. Therefore the net inflation tax benefit to the government is not as high as these numbers might imply, but nevertheless it is still over £20bn per year currently. Furthermore, we have to assume that at some point fairly soon the Bank will return that debt to the private sector.

Moreover, government debt is projected to keep growing in the UK —increasing by £170bn in the next two years alone according to the Office of Budget Responsibility, and the actual numbers could well turn out much higher. Therefore, if inflation persists at the same level, inflation tax receipts will increase further.

Other benefits of inflation to governments

In addition to debt relief, governments experience a number of other benefits from inflation.

The benefits of inflation to governments

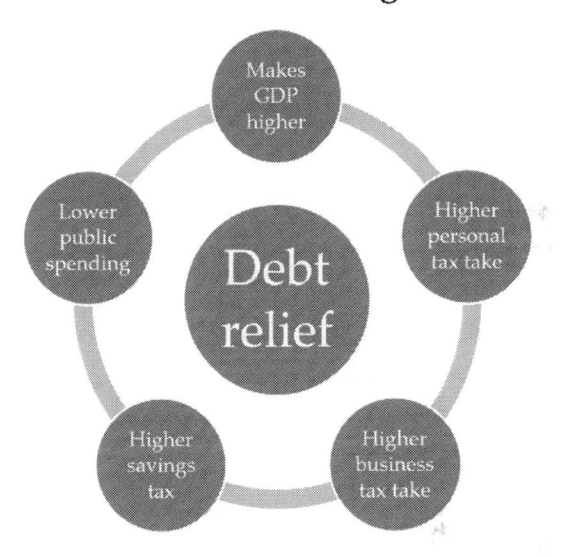

Diagram: Central circle "Debt relief" surrounded by: Makes GDP higher, Higher personal tax take, Higher business tax take, Higher savings tax, Lower public spending.

Note that in the current abnormal time of below-inflation interest rates and salary rises, some of these effects are temporarily negated. The normal benefits are:

1. Increased personal tax revenue: Personal tax revenues and national insurance contributions increase as wages increase. They do so because governments rarely index higher tax thresholds in line with inflation[4] – a concept called "fiscal drag".[5] This means inflation pushes more people into higher rate tax brackets and the government benefits from increased tax revenues accordingly. According to government statistics, the number of higher rate taxpayers in the UK more than doubled from 1.7 million to 4.1 million over the last 20 years.[6]

However, balanced against this trend is the fact that UK employers have been awarding pay rises significantly below inflation over the last few years. Coming to an exact calculation of the extra tax benefit of this in the current economic climate is therefore more difficult than it is when wages keep up with inflation.

2. Increased revenue from business taxation: As a general rule, provided inflation is fairly low and does not change too quickly, business profits increase in line with inflation in the economy. This is very useful for governments as it means corporation tax revenue also increases. The effect is enhanced further because the government tends not to increase tax threshold levels for corporations.

For example, since 2006 the threshold for the lower level of corporation tax in the UK has remained at £300,000 and the higher one at £1.5 million. Therefore, any rise in profits which companies have made since then will have directly translated to increased tax revenue. Even assuming just 3 per cent (RPI) inflation going forward, the UK government gains extra corporation tax revenue of over £1 billion cumulatively each year.

3. Extra revenue from saving account interest taxation: In "normal times", interest rates on savings accounts are higher than the base level of inflation. For example, in the decade prior to 2010, the top savings rate in the UK averaged 5.6 per cent,[7] while the mean annual inflation rate was just 2.7 per cent. So, assuming basic rate tax was paid on all savings during that period at that rate, tax revenue would have been 5.6 per cent x 20 per cent tax – i.e. 1.12 per cent of all UK savings. Had there been near-zero inflation during that time, and assuming a similar premium for savings accounts (i.e. 5.6% - 2.7% = 2.9%), tax might have been just 2.9 per cent x 20 per cent tax – i.e. 0.58%. Therefore, inflation effectively doubled the government's revenue from savings account interest over that decade.

We currently live in a world of *financial repression*, where governments are artificially manipulating savings interest rates to be lower than the rate of inflation. In this climate, this extra revenue effect actually goes into reverse and governments make less tax revenue this way – an unfortunate by-product of the low interest rate policy. However, this is more than balanced by lower debt repayments because of the near-zero rates.

4. Relatively lower public expenditure: A reduction in public expenditure is achieved by creating an official inflation measure that underestimates true inflation. In the UK the CPI index probably underestimates it by around 1-1.5 per cent. (See: "6-Inflation measurement issues.") The government then uses the official (lower) measure to pay increases in pensions and benefits whilst seeing revenues from taxation rise in line with the true inflation rate.

GOVERNMENTS AND INFLATION

5. Making GDP appear higher: Governments are judged in part on how successful they are in growing the economy, i.e. GDP growth. Before this is calculated, the raw GDP figure is adjusted for inflation.[8] This adjustment is summarised by the *GDP deflator*.

The deflator should approximate to the true inflation rate in the country. However the key consumer prices element of GDP in the UK was switched recently to being adjusted not by RPI but by CPI, which produces lower estimates of inflation. Accordingly, UK GDP is now being overestimated by about 1 per cent per year.

If that were not bad enough, the process by which prices for government services in the UK are adjusted for inflation is effectively a black box, not open to scrutiny. It also normally involves hedonic adjustments and is not based on real price changes. The net effect is that there is now a very wide disparity between the GDP deflator and true inflation rates in the UK. A comparison of the deflator versus the slightly more accurate RPI inflation rate in the UK in the last three years shows an average difference of 2.1 per cent[9]. This has massively enhanced apparent GDP growth in the UK. Similar enhancements can be seen in most countries around the world.

Governments and the money supply

The primary way in which governments have been influencing inflation is by sanctioning an ever-increasing money supply above the level required for the growing economy. Over the medium-term these excess increases in money supply feed through to price inflation.

UK money supply growth since the war

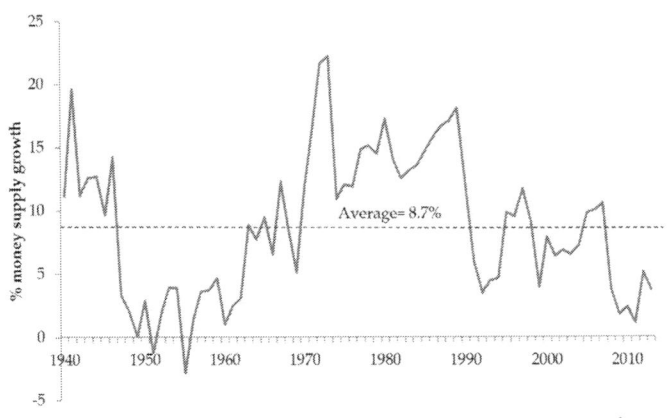

Source: Bank of England. (M3 up to 1963, M4 1964 onwards.)

The money supply growth that UK governments have allowed since World War II is a good example. It has grown by 8.7 per cent a year (see chart above) whereas during that time the economy has grown by just 2.3 per cent a year.

Moreover since the mid-1960s, governments, starting with the Wilson administration, have allowed the money supply to grow above that long-term trend and significantly ahead of economic growth. This has created price inflation, particularly so during the 1970s and 1980s when money supply growth was at its peak.

How governments create inflation via the money supply

Governments influence the money supply in two ways:

1. Directly by bond creation or money printing
2. Indirectly via permitting private banks to expand credit.

Governments can directly increase the money supply by the creation of new government bonds to finance their budget deficits. For example, no UK government for nearly 300 years has had a plan to pay back the capital of these debts. This is acting to increase the money supply.

In addition, more recently various governments around the world (e.g. the USA, UK and Japan) have been directly expanding the money supply by getting their central banks to print money in a process called Quantitative Easing (QE). The size of these operations in some countries has been huge. In 2013, the Japanese government embarked on a plan to double the money supply within two years.

Still, the primary way in which the money supply is expanded by governments nowadays is by permitting private banks to create more money, i.e. credit. Those banks have an incentive to expand the money supply to make more profits.

Governments have little reason to curtail this expansion, as they gain not only from tax on the banks' profits, but also from inflation tax through the reduced value of the money thus created and also electorally from the feel-good factor when the economy is seen to be expanding.

Inflation-friendly government policies

In addition to increasing the money supply by the methods outlined above, there are a number of other 'inflation-friendly' policies that governments can follow to help further enhance their inflation rates. These include:

1. Having an inflation target. This is the primary method used by many governments to ensure that they have inflation. They task their central banks to follow policies to ensure that inflation occurs in their economy. (See a much more detailed discussion of this: "15-The era of inflation targeting.")

2. Regulated prices. A large part of the inflation rate is under the direct control of governments through regulated prices. In the UK currently these include utilities, train fares, student loans and many other areas. Indeed, Mervyn King, the previous Governor of the Bank of England, often pointed out that this was arguably the largest factor driving UK inflation and accounted for about half its level at that time[10].

3. Government sponsored borrowing. Governments can expand the money supply by encouraging the electorate to borrow more. This could be via student loan schemes but is often done through housing incentives. For example, in the UK there have been a number of recent schemes to assist homebuyers (such as "Help to Buy") that have significantly increased the amount of mortgage loans and consumer credit[11]. This has increased house prices, which have a direct impact on inflation measures such as RPI and indirect effects through increased money supply and enhanced consumer spending, which also boost prices.

4. Devaluations. Currency devaluations are another way in which governments can increase inflation. A lower currency means that imports (particularly commodities like oil) become more expensive and push up the inflation rate. Some have argued[12] that the effect of devaluation on inflation is not that great in the UK as the imported element of goods manufactured here is quite small. Despite this, it is still a simple policy for a government to follow to foster some extra inflation and has been, for example, part of the strategy followed by Japan in 2013/2014.

5. Wage agreements. Governments are in direct control of public sector wages and have an indirect influence over other wage rises in the private sector. Wages are a key component of the prices of goods and services and so rises in wages can quickly flow into increases in retail prices. Although many governments curtailed public sector wage rises during the downturn, there will come a time when this changes and governments may well help trigger a wage-price spiral which increases inflation.

6. Increased government spending. Despite the current era of austerity, governments can also increase the money supply by investing in large infrastructure projects, which may not appear in the national accounts. For example, the UK government has recently sanctioned the construction of many new nuclear power stations (with funding provided by the private sector). Another large UK project recently agreed is the proposed high-speed railway between London and the north of England. All such large-scale projects add to inflationary pressure by competing for resources in an economy.

KEY LEARNING POINTS:
- Inflation usually results from governmental actions. Countries that want low inflation (e.g. Switzerland) have low inflation.
- Inflation tax was worth £29bn to the UK government in 2014. Other key benefits of inflation to governments include increased tax take (due to fiscal drag) and making GDP appear higher (through downward manipulation of the GDP deflator).
- Governments primarily create inflation by sanctioning above-GDP growth increases of the money supply. They also pursue many inflation-friendly policies, including setting high targets for inflation, using regulated prices, high wage agreements, devaluations, government sponsored borrowing, infrastructure spending, and more.

QUIZ ANSWER:
A.

GOVERNMENTS AND INFLATION

[1] Comley, P., 2013, "Inflation tax: The plan to deal with the debts", Self-published.

[2] Keynes, J., 1922, "Inflation as a method of taxation", *Manchester Guardian Commercial*, Series of Supplements 'Reconstruction in Europe', No. 5.

[3] Dalton, H., 1922, "Principles of Public Finance", *London: Routledge*.

[4] For example, in 2003/04 the higher rate tax threshold was £30,500. In 2013/14, it is set to be £32,011 i.e. just a 5% increase, while inflation rose by 38% over that ten year period.

[5] "Economics A-Z terms beginning with F", *The Economist* website (accessed 1/6/2013).

[6] http://www.hmrc.gov.uk/statistics/tax-statistics/table2-1.pdf
(accessed 1/6/2013).

[7] Source: Author's calculations in Comley, P., 2012, "Monkey with a Pin: Why You May Be Missing 6% a Year From Your Investment Returns", Self-published.

[8] The adjustment occurs at the individual level of each aspect going into GDP. The overall effect can then be calculated by looking at the difference between the total GDP figure in pounds and the adjusted one where each aspect has inflation taken out of it. The government does this division and publishes it as the GDP deflator.

[9] The respective figures for RPI/deflator for the last three years were: 2011- 4.6%/3.1%, 2012- 5.2%/2.3%, 2013- 3.0%/1.7%. The data sources were: ONS and the June 2014 National Accounts version updated in September 2014.

[10] "Money and Credit: September 2013", *Bank of England Statistical Release*, 29 October 2013.

[11] Giles, C., 2013, "Four Charts That Explain Bank Lending", *Financial Times*, 29 October 2013.

[12] Mills, J., 2013, "Devaluing the pound will not lead to a race to the bottom", *Daily Telegraph*, 9 August 2013.

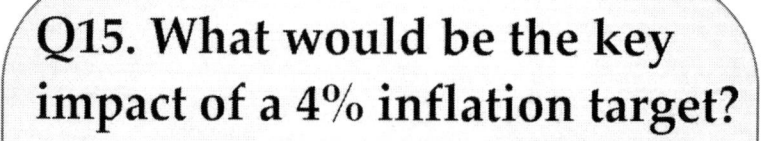

Q15. What would be the key impact of a 4% inflation target?

A None, apart from it would be easier for central bankers to control the economy

B The transfer of wealth from savers to debtors would increase

C Central bankers would hit their inflation targets more often

15

The era of inflation targeting

This chapter looks at one of the key tools that post-war governments created to ensure that inflation persists: inflation targeting. It examines its origins and where it is now used, as well as the mechanisms by which it is claimed to work. It also critically evaluates the recent case put forward to set higher inflation targets in developed nations like the US and the UK.

Definitions and purpose

Inflation targeting is usually defined as[1]:

"A framework for monetary policy characterised by the public announcement of official quantitative targets (or target ranges) for the inflation rate over one or more time horizons, and by explicit acknowledgement that low, stable inflation is monetary policy's primary long-run goal."

Its primary purpose is to provide economic stability to aid economic growth. However it serves another purpose that is rarely explicitly acknowledged: ensuring that inflation keeps on increasing. This is very useful to governments (who gain by inflation tax) and also to other debtors such as businesses and speculators who also see the real value of their debts diminished.

The Swedish experience

The origins of inflation targeting go back to the great Swedish economist Knut Wicksell. In 1898, he published his seminal work *Interest and Prices*[2] in which he suggested that governments should control interest rates as a way to stabilise the economy and prices. Following his death, a version of his policy was enacted by the Swedish government in the 1930s. Having left the gold standard in 1931, there was concern that prices might rise without that constraint on the money supply and there was similar concern that the worldwide depression might bring temporary deflation to Sweden.

Knut Wicksell – the originator of inflation targeting
Source: "Wicksell2". Licensed under Public domain via Wikipedia

The government passed a law in September 1931 tasking the Riksbank to maintain price stability. It did this primarily by a combination of interest rate changes and devaluations of the Krona. The system was very successful. Five years later, the price index was unchanged and had fluctuated only a few per cent during that time. Indeed by the onset of World War II, prices had only risen about 5 per cent[3].

The Fed and Bretton Woods

After World War II, the idea of overt inflation targeting fell out of fashion as most countries had their currencies linked to the US dollar either directly via the Bretton Woods Agreement or indirectly via other pegs. The currency linkage meant that the Swedish system proposed by Wicksell (and by others such as Keynes[4]) would be less effective, as altering exchange rates was perceived to be a key element of controlling inflation.

However that logic did not apply to the US itself. Indeed in the early 1950s, the Federal Reserve in the US was specifically tasked with maintaining a low level of inflation[5]. This was done ostensibly on account of the Keynesian belief that it would help keep employment high. No precise target was set but this policy did ensure that positive inflation persisted in the US and that it then got transmitted around the world for two decades until the collapse of the Bretton Woods agreement.

New Zealand and the birth of modern inflation targeting

The collapse was accompanied by a surge of inflation in the 1970s and 1980s. The need to control prices was high on the political agenda. Italy, Greece and Portugal were amongst the countries that had attempted, and failed, to control inflation by targeting it at specific levels during the early 1980s.

It took until the late 1980s before any country succeeded. New Zealand had suffered persistent inflation rates of over 15 per cent for most of that decade. The then finance minister, Roger Douglas, was a reformer and had already brought in a raft of economic changes under the banner of Rogernomics. In 1988 he decided to tackle inflation. On April Fool's Day that year, on live television and without consulting anyone, he decided to announce a policy to completely stabilise prices and target an inflation rate in New Zealand of "around 0 or 0 to 1 per cent".

Roger Douglas – the instigator of modern inflation targeting
Source: "Roger Douglas 2008" by Alan Liefting. Licensed under Public domain via Wikimedia Commons

In the resulting consultation with his government, the Reserve Bank of New Zealand and other interested parties, this was watered down to a target of under 2 per cent by the early 1990s in the Reserve

Bank of New Zealand Act of 1989. To give Douglas credit (and the Reserve Bank tasked with achieving it) this was indeed achieved and inflation fell to just below 1 per cent in 1992 and remained on target for the following three years.

This experience was inspirational to other governments and set a trend that was quickly followed by many. In 1991, Canada, Chile and Israel all adopted inflation targets and they were joined by Sweden and Finland in 1993.

Currently in 2014 there are nearly seventy countries worldwide with inflation targets. In most developed countries, these targets are to keep inflation at or around 2 per cent. In emerging markets, inflation targets tend to be higher with many setting targets at or above 5 per cent.

2014 inflation targets by country

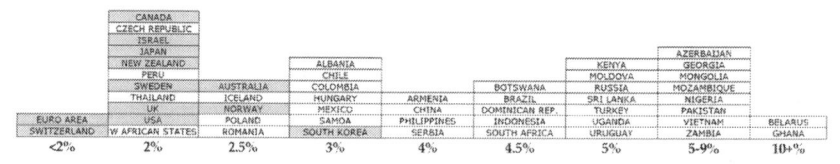

<2%	2%	2.5%	3%	4%	4.5%	5%	5-9%	10+%
	CANADA							
	CZECH REPUBLIC							
	ISRAEL							
	JAPAN							
	NEW ZEALAND		ALBANIA			KENYA	AZERBAIJAN	
	PERU		CHILE			MOLDOVA	GEORGIA	
	SWEDEN	AUSTRALIA	COLOMBIA		BOTSWANA	RUSSIA	MONGOLIA	
	THAILAND	ICELAND	HUNGARY	ARMENIA	BRAZIL	SRI LANKA	MOZAMBIQUE	
	UK	NORWAY	MEXICO	CHINA	DOMINICAN REP.	TURKEY	NIGERIA	
EURO AREA	USA	POLAND	SAMOA	PHILIPPINES	INDONESIA	UGANDA	PAKISTAN	BELARUS
SWITZERLAND	W AFRICAN STATES	ROMANIA	SOUTH KOREA	SERBIA	SOUTH AFRICA	URUGUAY	VIETNAM	GHANA
							ZAMBIA	

Source: centralbanknews.info. Where targets are a range, the midpoint is shown.
Shading indicates a developed market.

How targets differ now

There is a critical difference between the current inflation target world and that envisaged by its forefathers such as Wicksell and Keynes. The original intention was to set a target on the absolute price level. The purpose was to keep prices approximately constant over time to ensure that standards of living were preserved. The system would allow prices to deviate in one direction or the other temporarily, but it would then be the central bank's aim to bring the absolute level back to where it was before.

Although this also appeared to be Douglas's original aim in New Zealand, it was not the policy that was enacted into law and that then became replicated around the globe. Instead the policy was set on the change in inflation rate and not on the absolute price index level. Under this approach, policy decisions set by central banks ignore the cumulative effects of inflation over a period of time.

Furthermore no allowance is made for setting a lower inflation target in the year following one when it was exceeded. For example in the UK, inflation in 2010 was 3.3%. The Bank of England still targeted 2 per cent in 2011, rather than 0.7%, which would have led to an average rate of 2 per cent over the two years.

Another difference is that most countries now target a specific inflation level, e.g. 2 per cent. This was not the format of the original inflation targets created in the early 1990s. For example, in the original letter launching the idea in the UK in October 1992, the Chancellor, Norman Lamont, sought a "rate of inflation in the long-term of 2 per cent or less". In 1997, his successor, Gordon Brown, swiftly increased this in the Bank of England Act 1998 to a target of exactly 2.5 per cent. Not only was the long-term target changed but it set a policy of always ensuring that inflation was maintained at the higher level and the desire for some form of constant prices was abandoned. Brown's subtle change had major implications for inflation rates in the UK and was copied elsewhere.

The ever-increasing UK inflation target

Year	Instigator	Actual target	RPI equivalent target
1992	Norman Lamont (Chancellor)	0-2% RPI	0-2%
1997	Gordon Brown (Chancellor)	2.5% RPI	2.5%
2003	Gordon Brown (Chancellor)	2% CPI	3.0%
2010	Olivier Blanchard (IMF – *proposal only*)	4% CPI	5.0%

More recently others have proposed that the UK inflation target be raised still further. For example, Olivier Blanchard[6] of the IMF suggested it should rise to 4 per cent. Some[7] have suggested that major economies such as the UK should adopt a nominal GDP target instead an interest rate target. What this means is a target is set on the value of economic growth *before* that number is inflation-adjusted. The logic being that when the economy hits a bad time for economic growth, inflation can be higher than normal to compensate for it. Many propose that such a target should be around 5 per cent with around a half of this being inflation. Others[8] however just see it as a way to increase inflation.

Finally, the use of a per cent target is a very clever device to covertly permit higher inflation over a period of time. The 2 per cent target used by many countries seems a very small number and therefore one that most members of the public ignore[9]. Had they instead been focusing on a price index, the true cumulative impact on their standards of living would be more obvious to see. For example the RPIX index initially used for inflation targeting in the UK and set to 100 in 1987[10] stands at 257 in 2014. If a raw index like this had been used for targeting, the public would clearly have seen how much prices had actually risen.

How inflation is controlled by central bankers

The whole purpose of inflation targeting is to control the economy to make it more stable and therefore more economically productive. However, it is worth understanding a little of the theory behind the way that central bankers aim to control inflation to achieve this objective. The main lever they have is controlling interest rates.

The logic of this is as follows. If inflation takes off (above say a 2 per cent target), a central bank increases interest rates, so private banks tend to lend less money, thus reducing the expansion of the money supply. As less money is chasing the same amount of goods being sold, prices should decline. As they do, interest rates can be reduced. Therefore, in general, interest rates are highly correlated with inflation rates.

How inflation targeting is supposed to work

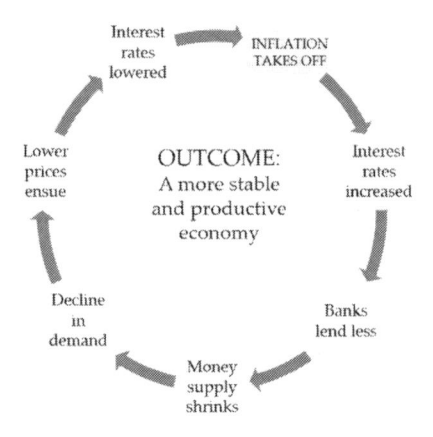

- INFLATION TAKES OFF
- Interest rates increased
- Banks lend less
- Money supply shrinks
- Decline in demand
- Lower prices ensue
- Interest rates lowered

OUTCOME: A more stable and productive economy

The system also works the other way round. So when an economy is in recession, reducing interest rates helps stimulate it. Setting interest rates lower than inflation acts as an incentive for people to spend and borrow, rather than to save. This policy is continued until demand picks up and prices start to rise.

Like interest rates, exchange rates can also be a useful method for controlling inflation. The theory here is that if inflation is too high and a country can revalue its currency higher, the prices of imports will drop, hence helping to bring down inflation. The converse policy of devaluing to help create inflation was adopted by Japan in 2013/14. Note though that most central banks today use only interest rate adjustments to attempt to manipulate inflation; few use exchange rates.

Finally, central banks also control inflation in part by the expectations they set for inflation. If people believe that inflation rates will be at a certain level in the future, they are likely to seek pay increases in line with that prospect. Similarly, companies often plan pricing strategies on the basis of future expectations for inflation. The more credible the central bank, the more successful this strategy tends to be in helping keep inflation in check.

The problems with inflation targeting

The era of inflation targeting has been trumpeted as a great success. Since its inception, many developed economies implementing it have seen sustained lower levels of inflation. Central bankers have been quick to attribute this to the success of their policies and in particular have claimed it justifies their ability to control inflation[11].

However, an alternative explanation is that the period of inflation targeting largely coincided with the Great Moderation, the latter part of which saw China reduce its exchange rates and flood the West with cheap goods. This probably helped keep inflation on target at low levels just as much as central bankers' policies. (See: "12-The Great Moderation and the Great Recession.")

Another issue with inflation targeting as now practised is that it does not aim to control all prices but only a limited subset of them. This can result in accusations that the system is not as effective as claimed. For example, in the US the Federal Reserve only targets core inflation, leaving out food and energy prices. (The apparent logic for their omission is that they are volatile. Cynics might argue that "volatile" is jargon for the part of the index most likely to exhibit price rises.)

Moreover the Fed switched in 2012 from using a core index of CPI to a core index of something called PCE (Personal Consumption Expenditures). PCE is normally about 0.3 per cent lower than CPI and one can but surmise that the switch was made to make it easier to achieve the target. The UK did a similar thing in 2003 when it switched from its existing RPI measure to CPI, which has typically estimated inflation to be 1 per cent lower due mainly to a statistical calculation effect. (See:"6-Inflation measurement issues."). The CPI measure leaves out house prices, and this had implications on the inflation policy of the Bank of England. Some have argued that the Bank failed to stop the housing boom of the noughties because of this.

The argument for higher inflation targets

There has been a debate on whether a higher inflation target (than 2%) might be best for developed economies like the US and the UK. As noted before, Olivier Blanchard of the IMF proposed that it should be raised to 4%[12].

His primary argument for having a higher inflation target was to help central bankers implement their policies. This is linked to what is called in the jargon the *Zero Lower Bound* (or ZLB). Central banks need to be able to lower interest rates by a significant amount to help stimulate the economy if it falls into recession. However if the normal state of affairs was zero inflation and interest rates of around 1%, they would not have the flexibility to reduce them very much, as it is very difficult to set negative interest rates.

The severity of the recent recession has led some to argue that it would be better if we had a higher inflation target to allow central banks more flexibility before the ZLB is reached. A number of articles have been written proposing a higher 4 per cent target be set[13]. These argue that there is little evidence that a little higher inflation would hurt the economy. They contend that where people have tried to quantify the effects of higher inflation, they have not found a large effect.

Another argument in support of a higher target is the belief that consumer inflation measures overestimate the true inflation rate. This is mainly on account of how they factor in quality improvements. Some central banks (e.g. Canada[14]) are still arguing this as a reason for needing a higher inflation target.

The arguments for and against a higher inflation target

Argument for a higher target	Counter argument
1. Higher targets would make it easier to control economy in the current climate (ZLB problem)	Central banks have other tools to control the economy e.g. QE, direct credit easing, helicopter money, etc.
2. Inflation measures under-estimate real inflation	Not true. All evidence suggests that the reverse is in fact the case
3. More inflation would have little net impact on the economy	Ignores the massive impact that inflation has in transferring wealth from savers to debtors. Also ignores risk that it would create an inflationary spiral

Why a 4 per cent inflation target might be a problem

There are number of issues with the arguments for a higher inflation target:

1. What the positive inflationists often fail to point out is that the central bank does have other tools to stimulate the economy in these conditions e.g. quantitative easing and credit easing. Both of these have been used by the Bank of England in recent years. Money could also be directly injected into the economy by tax cuts – a concept the famous economist Milton Friedman once referred to as "helicopter money"[15]. Therefore the lower inflation targets do not preclude central bankers from stimulating the economy.
2. Ben Bernanke (ex Federal Reserve chairman) also argued against it[16]. He was concerned not only that a higher target would be more volatile but that it also risked others suggesting that an even higher target be then set (once the credibility of maintaining low inflation had been breached). As the economist Mishkin wrote[17] "when inflation rises above the 3 per cent level, it tends to keep on rising".
3. The attempted quantifications of the effects of inflation[18] have often focused on the overall effect on the economy and have not looked at the size of the transfer of wealth that takes place between creditors and debtors when inflation is higher, i.e. they have ignored the real costs of inflation on the population.
4. The argument that consumer price indices overestimate inflation,

so a higher target needs to be set, is unlikely to hold true now. As highlighted elsewhere, most price indices underestimate inflation—in the UK by about 1.25%. The quality adjustments in the US are also making inflation there look a lot lower than it really is, as is the adoption of different indices as key benchmarks. Furthermore, the *Economist* magazine found clear evidence for inflation statistics underestimating inflation in virtually all countries using its BigMac Burgernomics calculations[19].

Given the above issues, the case for increasing the target for inflation to 4 per cent in developed economies looks weak and indeed is potentially dangerous for the precedent it might set.

KEY LEARNING POINTS:
- Inflation targeting is a process of trying to maintain a consistent level of inflation to aid economic stability and growth. The main mechanism used to do this is control of interest rates by central banks.
- Inflation targeting took off around the world in the early 1990s. The original targets were often to get it as low as possible (typically below 2 per cent). Since then higher targets have been set in most countries.
- Some are now arguing for a 4 per cent inflation target primarily to make it easier for central bankers to control the economy using interest rates. Not only is that not required (as other techniques exist), it would also massively increase the transfer of wealth from savers to debtors that results from inflation and also risks the world entering another inflationary spiral.

QUIZ ANSWER:
B.

---

[1] Bernanke, B., Laubach, T., Mishkin, F., and Posen, A., 1999, "Inflation targeting. Lessons from the international experience", *Princeton University Press*.

[2] Wicksell, K., 1898, "Interest and prices". For a translation, see: http://mises.org/books/interestprices.pdf (accessed 12/12/2014).

[3] Berg, C., and Jonung, L., 1998, "Pioneering Price Level Targeting: The Swedish Experience 1931-1937", SSE/EFI Working Paper Series in

Economics and Finance No 290.

[4] Keynes, J., 1923, "A tract on monetary reform (Great Minds Series)", *Amherst, MA: Prometheus Books*.

[5] Bernanke, B., 2012,"The Federal Reserve and the financial crisis. Lecture 2: The Federal Reserve after World War II", *Federal Reserve*.

[6] Blanchard, O., 2010, "Rethinking Macroeconomic policy", *IMF*

[7] Summer, S., 2011, "The case for NGDP targeting: Lessons from the great recession", *Adam Smith Institute*

[8] Chu, B. 2013, "Martin Weale: NGDP target is playing with fire", *Chunomics* blog

[9] Comley, P., 2013, "Inflation Tax: The plan to deal with the debts", Self-published.

[10] Inflation targeting was instituted in an Act of 1992.

[11] Bernanke, B., 2013, "A Century of U.S. Central Banking: Goals, Frameworks, Accountability", Speech at *NBER* conference.

[12] Blanchard, O., Dell'Ariccia, G. and Mauro, P., 2010, "Rethinking Macroeconomic Policy", *IMF Staff Position Note* SPN/10/03.

[13] Ball, L., 2013, "The Case for 4% Inflation", *Central Bank Review (Central Bank of the Republic of Turkey)*, May.

[14] Bank of Canada, 2011, "Why has Canada's Inflation Target Been Set at 2 Per Cent?", *Backgrounders*, December 2011.

[15] Friedman, M., 1969, "The Optimum Quantity Of Money". Macmillan

[16] Bernanke, B., 2010, "The Economic Outlook and Monetary Policy", *Jackson Hole Symposium*, 27 August 2010.

[17] Mishkin, F., 2011, "Monetary Policy Strategy: Lessons from the Crisis", *NBER* Working Paper #16755.

[18] Fischer, S. and Modigliani, F., 1978, "Towards an Understanding of the Real Effects and Costs of Inflation", *Weltwirtschaftliches Archiv* 114 (4): 810–32.

[19] "The McFlation index: Lies, flame-grilled lies and statistics", *The Economist* Print Edition, Jan 27th 2011.

Q16. Who gains and who loses with current inflation?

A It depends - there are no consistent winners and losers

B Debtors such as governments and companies gain whilst cash savers lose

C Trick question – everyone is equal as you can hedge against inflation!

16

The impact of current inflation

Inflation, even at today's low levels, is having a major impact. What is important to comprehend is that inflation now is massively more detrimental than it was before the banking crisis. As we will see, it is currently acting like a conveyor belt, transferring wealth from one group in society to another. This chapter looks at the true impact of current inflation and examines who are the real winners and losers. The size of the transfers is truly staggering, probably totalling nearly £100bn a year currently in the UK alone. They are taking place so subtly that few are aware of their magnitude and impact.

The effect of inflation past

Until recently, many regarded the effects of inflation as somewhat random and often fairly benign. For example a paper published in 1998 by the Institute of Economic Affairs[1] concluded that the effect of inflation very much depended upon the ability of people to anticipate it and there being mechanisms available for them to mitigate it:

"Inflation actually levies a tax on those who failed to anticipate it – or who were in no position to protect themselves against it – and redistributes it to those who were smart enough – or lucky enough – to anticipate it and take appropriate action. There is no obvious correlation between those who gain (or lose) from inflation."

It is true that there were systems that did help to mitigate inflation. For example, historically there had existed a small premium over inflation for depositing money in some form of long-term savings account, thereby ensuring most savings apart from cash were protected to a reasonable extent[2]. In addition, mechanisms existed for employees, pensioners and welfare claimants to ensure that their standard of living largely kept up with inflation. Therefore the spending power of the majority of the population appeared at first sight to be largely unaffected by inflation.

However, even this analysis was too simplistic. It missed out the fact that there were some clear winners with inflation, for example debtors who saw their repayments (both capital and interest) decline over time as inflation eroded their real cost. The key counterparty to them was cash-holders who saw the value of their money destroyed.

The process of transfer of wealth between creditors and debtors was quite complex. For one thing, the two parties involved in the debt contracts both actually gained from inflation. In entering into the debt, new money was created and this expanded the money supply. This ultimately ended up creating the inflation.

Not only did debtors then gain from lower real repayment costs, but the counterparty to the debt (the lender) usually received a premium over inflation for lending the money[3]. Moreover as time went by, those debts became less risky to lenders and thereby permitted them to lend more whilst maintaining their capital ratios. It was a clever arrangement for both lender and borrower.

The debt-inflation process

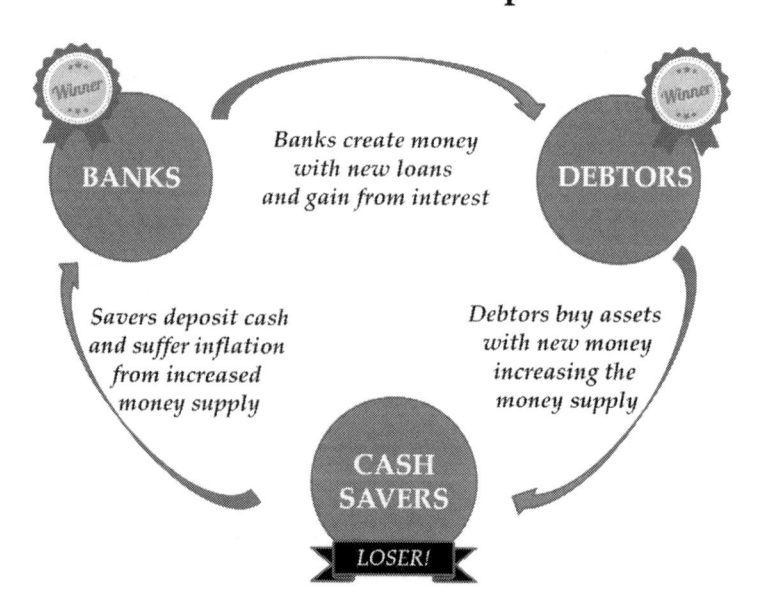

Banks create money with new loans and gain from interest

BANKS (Winner) → **DEBTORS** (Winner)

Savers deposit cash and suffer inflation from increased money supply

Debtors buy assets with new money increasing the money supply

CASH SAVERS — LOSER!

The problem for society was that someone had to pay for the inflation and the gains of these two parties. Moreover it was someone completely different who suffered, someone who was a mere bystander in their speculative games. That someone was the people who either had cash, money in cheque accounts or savings money held at interest rates lower than inflation. The 80/20 rule applies here as it does in many aspects of life. The gains accrued to the 20 per cent richest (plus governments) and the losses were disproportionally borne by the remaining 80 per cent in society and the poor whose assets were primarily cash-based.

The above chart depicts what used to happen with inflation in the past in what I will call more normal times. Its impact now is much more far-reaching and damaging.

Inflation now: the new winners and losers

Everything has changed since the financial crisis of 2007/8. We now live in a very different world. The way that governments have been forced to deal not only with their own debts but also those of their citizens, companies and banks, is to impose financial repression. A key facet of this is keeping interest rates below the rate of inflation. This means that there is no longer the opportunity for savers to mitigate the impact of inflation.

The winners and losers from inflation

Scenario	A. Inflation (Post Great Recession)	B. Inflation (normal times)	C. Near-zero inflation
Treasury	++	+	-
Mortgage holders	++	+	-
Companies	++	+	o
Banks	++	+	o
Employees	-	o	o
Pensioners	-	o	o
Welfare claimants	-	o	o
Cash holders	--	-	o
Savers	--	o	+
Government bond holders	--	o	+

At the same time, many governments have been forced to make austerity cuts and so welfare and pensions are often now failing to keep up with the rising cost of living. Finally, employees' wages have

INFLATION MATTERS

been allowed to lag behind inflation in many countries as the recession has weakened the hand of wage negotiators.

The chart above summarises the net winners and losers from inflation. Scenario A depicts the current situation that exists after the Great Recession. It contrasts it to Scenario B describing the impact of inflation in more normal times that have persisted over most of the last few centuries. By contrast, Scenario C shows what the impact would be in a near-zero inflation world where the so-called risk premium has been restored and there is a small positive return for cash savers.

The inflation conveyor belt

The current scenario of inflation is very harmful for the majority of the population. It is creating a massive transfer of wealth from anyone with cash and savings towards debtors. This includes the majority of the population who hold such money as part of their pension savings.

Inflation is effectively the conveyor belt that is responsible for the transmission. It is necessary as the world has become over-indebted and, barring outright default on some of those debts, inflation is the only simple way to reduce the burden. Moreover, the mechanism is quite subtle such that the bulk of people are unaware of what is happening and how money disappears into the hands of beneficiaries.

The inflation conveyor belt

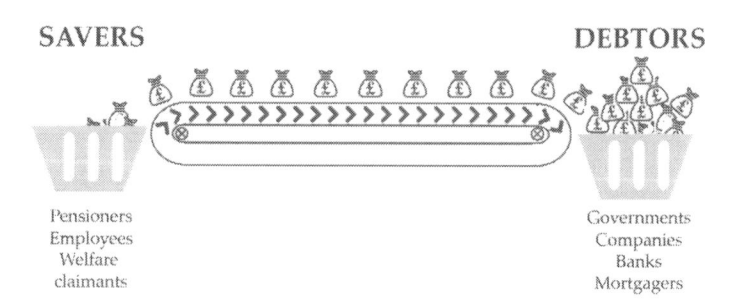

SAVERS   DEBTORS

Pensioners   Governments
Employees   Companies
Welfare   Banks
claimants   Mortgagers

The following sections look in detail at those most affected by the inflation conveyor belt.

THE IMPACT OF CURRENT INFLATION

The £23bn annual loss to savers

The interest rate on cash savings is almost zero now and is destined to remain that way for potentially a decade or even longer to come. This means that everyone who holds cash in their wallets, chequeing accounts or many instant savings accounts, is losing purchasing power of that money at a rate equivalent to that of inflation. Even though official rates of inflation have fallen in many countries, what matters is the true rate of inflation of the cost of living experienced by those cash-holders.

For example in the UK, I estimate that a more accurate cost of living index for the average person is 1-1.5 per cent higher than the official CPI statistics. However even if one uses the more conservative and less misleading RPI measure of inflation, this is still around 2.5 per cent in mid-2014.

Therefore, every year, every person in the UK is effectively donating £2.50p to the debtors for every £100 they keep in their wallets or effectively hold as cash elsewhere. That is a staggering amount, particularly when looked at over a period of time. Even at this low inflation rate, the value of all our cash is going to halve within 28 years.

It is not just cash that is impacted but all forms of savings. My calculations suggest that UK savers and companies are currently losing a total of £23bn a year in this way, nearly half of which comes from the low rates of interest on instant access accounts. In 2014 these rates were generally around 0.4 per cent after tax, significantly below RPI inflation at 2.5%.

The annual loss of UK savers to inflation

Account type	Total saved (£bn)	Avg. after tax interest rate	Inflation (2.5%) - interest rate	Savers loss
Cash	£135bn	0.0%	2.5%	£3.4bn
Instant access savings	£520bn	0.4%	2.1%	£10.9bn
Fixed time savings	£245bn	1.1%	1.4%	£3.4bn
ISAs	£225bn	1.0%	1.5%	£3.4bn
National Savings	£110bn	1.1%	1.4%	£1.5bn
TOTAL	£1235bn			£23bn

Sources: Save our Savers, Bank of England, ONS, NS&I and Building Societies Association.

See endnote[4] more details on the method of calculation and assumptions.

It must be remembered that this is a cumulative loss. UK savers have transferred more than £100bn to debtors in the last four years alone. Furthermore during the period from 2009-2013, the real purchasing power of all UK savings declined by an estimated 13 per cent and will continue to do so as long as financial repression persists.

Savers' loss of purchasing power (2009-2013)

Year	Inflation (RPI Dec)	Avg. after tax savings rate (Dec)	Net loss each year	Cumulative loss
2009	2.4%	0.4%	2.0%	-2.0%
2010	4.8%	1.0%	3.8%	-5.7%
2011	4.8%	1.3%	3.5%	-9.0%
2012	3.1%	0.8%	2.3%	-11.1%
2013	2.7%	0.6%	2.1%	-13.0%

Sources: Building Societies Association and ONS.

What is fascinating is how so few of those savers really comprehend the true impact that financial repression and inflation is having on them. In Cyprus in 2013, the public took to the streets in violent protest when their government tried to impose a levy of just half this loss (i.e. 6.7 per cent on savings). The people forced their government to retract the proposal. In contrast, in the UK the acquiescence of savers is such that a campaigning group called "Save Our Savers" has all but closed down in 2014 for lack of support.

Indirect loss to savers

The current low savings returns are causing many to seek better returns elsewhere – often on the stock market. However, things are not looking much more promising there either. Since 2000, the FTSE has traded sideways and so capital returns have been minimal on shares.

Admittedly dividend income has averaged around 3%. However, as I showed in my book *Monkey with a Pin*,[5] most people investing in the stock market get a return that is about 6 per cent less than they expect, as they've not factored in charges, their low skill in stock picking, bad market timing and something called survivorship bias. Therefore, until the UK stock market breaks out of this trading range and we start to get capital growth again, returns are not going to keep up with inflation. Some leading economists like Martin Wolf are predicting that this may not happen for a long time[6]. (However that may not be the case as we will see later. See: "20-Managing wealth as we head towards near-zero inflation.")

Therefore those opting to invest in shares, might also lose

purchasing power over time. But this time the transfer of wealth would not be via inflation but to the financial services industry through their charges and losses to their professional investors.

The loss to bond holders

The loss by cash savers is mirrored by those buying government bonds. Although this issue appears not to concern the general public, it should do since they primarily hold this debt, albeit via intermediaries.

As the chart below illustrates for the UK, the bulk of public debt (that the Bank of England has not bought), is owned by financial organisations such as pension funds, insurers and banks. They are investing it on behalf of their customers who are typically long-term savers and those with pension schemes. A large part is also held by foreigners, but again the ultimate owners are mainly just savers and pension schemes residing in other countries (just as UK pension schemes invest in other countries' bonds).

Who owns UK government debt?

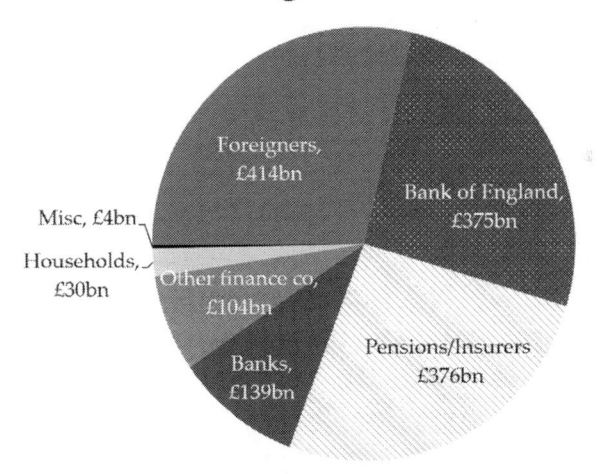

- Foreigners, £414bn
- Bank of England, £375bn
- Misc, £4bn
- Households, £30bn
- Other finance co, £104bn
- Banks, £139bn
- Pensions/Insurers, £376bn

Source: United Kingdom Economic Accounts (Q2 2014)

The problem with such bonds is that governments have helped push down their yields in the aftermath of the financial crisis with exercises such as Quantitative Easing. Therefore the yields have fallen significantly in 2014, the 2-year debt in key countries is producing close to zero return in many leading markets.

INFLATION MATTERS

Example of the inflation loss of government bond holders

	2 year bond yield	Inflation	Holders loss
Japan	0.0%	3.3%	-3.3%
Germany	-0.1%	0.8%	-0.9%
USA	0.3%	1.7%	-1.4%
UK	0.6%	2.4%	-1.8%

Source: Bloomberg. Bond yields are from October 2014 and inflation levels are latest published at that time i.e. August/September 2014. For the UK, inflation is RPI.

The 2-year bond yields are below the rate of inflation in each country in the above table and purchasers of such debt are guaranteed to lose money if inflation remains at its current level. Clearly the loss is different for different bond maturity dates, but even buyers of 5-year bonds are making a loss in all these leading countries.

The £33bn question

This wealth is being transferred to national governments, which are benefiting when they issue new debt through being able to do so at these low rates. The counterparty is typically a saver or someone with a pension scheme. In theory it should be possible to determine the magnitude of the wealth being transferred due to the impact of financial repression on government bonds yields. However in practice it is difficult to determine both the size of the gain and the recipient.

This is because only a limited proportion of new bonds are issued in any given year at the new low rates. New ones only need to be issued to cover the budget deficit and to refinance ones maturing in that year. Therefore the vast majority of UK government bonds continue to pay out the interest rate that was set when they were issued. When base rates declined, the price of those existing bonds increased, making their yield to any new purchaser very low. However, long-term holders of government debt were unaffected and are only being gradually impacted as their portfolios of bonds mature. If that is not complicated enough, different length bonds are issued at different yields. In 2014 new bonds issued by the UK government yield around 2%-3%.

Having said all that, here is my attempt at the calculation. In the last five years (2010-2014), the average after RPI inflation yield of UK debt issued was -1.1%. Contrast this to pre-crisis where the average after inflation yield used to be around +2.2 per cent (from 1998-2006). In the last five fiscal years ending 2010-2014, the UK government issued about £900bn of new debt. Therefore, in 2014, it was benefiting by about £33bn a year in reduced interest payments because of financial repression. That gain is all at the expense of the typical bondholder, which as explained above, is ultimately pension holders and savers, i.e. the general public.

In late 2014, the UK government has decided to redeem some old debt dating back originally to the 17th and 18th Century and to World War I. They are doing so because they can now re-issue it at even lower rates of interest. It remains to be seen if the UK (and other governments) will take advantage of financial repression to re-issue much larger quantities of debt they owe, saving themselves even larger amounts in interest payments. If they do, it will be paid for by savers and pension scheme owners in further diminished returns over the coming decades, making the net annual loss to bondholders much larger than my current estimate of £33bn.

The £20bn-£50bn question

In addition to this, one needs to factor in that pension schemes also frequently invest in corporate bonds (debt issued by companies). The average yield of these has been forced down by financial repression as well and is only about 0.3 per cent higher[7] than the average UK government bond yield. Moreover that premium is unlikely to be enough to cover the higher default risk of such bonds versus sovereign debt, so their true yield is probably even lower. As the size of the UK corporate bond market is similar to that of the UK government debt market, it is likely that UK businesses are benefiting in similar sums to that of government, probably in the range £20bn-£50bn a year.

The ultimate losers with debt and inflation

Returning to the conveyor belt analogy this chapter started with, it is useful to summarise who are the beneficiaries from inflation related to debt in the current situation and who are ultimate losers. The table below summarises this together with estimates of the size of each of the associated debt markets.

What is clear is that the eventual losers with inflation are nearly always individuals, via erosion of the purchasing power of their savings or pension wealth.

The inflation conveyor belt beneficiaries/losers

Beneficiary:	Approx. size of UK debt market	Main intermediary	Ultimate loser
Government	£1.4 trillion	Pension companies/ insurers	Pensions
Companies	£1.5 trillion	Pension companies/ insurers	Pensions
Banks	£3.4 trillion	Banks	Other banks/ Tax payers*
Mortgagers	£1.3 trillion	Building societies/ Banks	Savers
Personal debtors	£0.2 trillion	Banks/Credit cards/ Lenders	Savers

Sources: Bank of England, ICMB[8], The Money Charity
* Although other banks/speculators are the ultimate loser with bank debt, tax payers have also been a loser in the bailouts following the financial crisis as bank debt was taken on to government balance sheets.

The impact on pensioners and welfare claimants

Apart from debt, one of the other key impacts of inflation on those living on state benefits is the almost worldwide abuse by governments of their inflation measures. As we've seen, most employ methods (such as geometric means, substitution and hedonic modelling) that ensure that their official statistics underestimate the true cost of living rises in their countries to a greater or lesser extent. This means that anyone receiving such benefits will see their standards of living gradually decline when there is any form of inflation. In contrast, governments' tax receipts normally rise in proportion to the true inflation rate, as these are derived from consumption taxes on the actual prices paid, corporation taxes on actual company profits and employment taxes that are linked to real wage rises.

This situation has been exacerbated in many countries as governments try various methods to reduce their expenditure. For example, in the UK in April 2011, the government switched the inflation measure they used for calculation of welfare increases from the old RPI index to CPI. This was a clever way of still promising inflation-linked rises while ensuring that they would be smaller than they used to be. At the same time the government also changed public sector pensions so that they too were indexed by CPI. This has been estimated to save around £6bn a year and reduce overall pension pay-outs by 15%.[9].

The impact on employees

The Great Recession has had an impact on employees in many countries as their wages have not kept up with inflation and, in places like Greece, have even been cut. Determining the precise amounts and collating the statistics is notoriously difficult, especially given the multiplicity of definitions of inflation and different governments' attempts at manipulating them. However sources like the OECD do their best and also publish average annual wage estimates. The table below shows one estimate of what has happened to wages after being adjusted by the official inflation stats in each country from 2008 to 2013.

Change in real wages 2008-2013

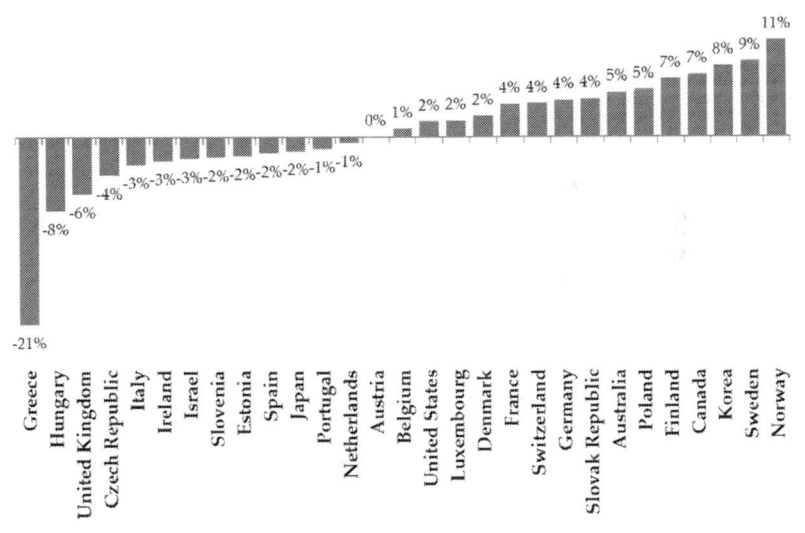

Greece	-21%
Hungary	-8%
United Kingdom	-6%
Czech Republic	-4%
Italy	-3%
Ireland	-3%
Israel	-3%
Slovenia	-2%
Estonia	-2%
Spain	-2%
Japan	-2%
Portugal	-1%
Netherlands	-1%
Austria	0%
Belgium	1%
United States	2%
Luxembourg	2%
Denmark	2%
France	4%
Switzerland	4%
Germany	4%
Slovak Republic	4%
Australia	5%
Poland	5%
Finland	7%
Canada	7%
Korea	8%
Sweden	9%
Norway	11%

Source: OECD series - CPI and annual average wages.

This shows that in nearly a half of OECD countries, real wages have lagged behind the official inflation statistics. Remember the lag behind true price rises in many of these countries will portray an even more concerning picture for living standards.

For example, if you do a similar comparison in the UK using the monthly average weekly wage data (including bonuses) and RPI from the wage peak in February 2008 to August 2014, it shows a much worse situation. Over this time, average weekly wages have risen 5 per cent (from £457 to £479) whilst the RPI index has risen 22%. The average person is earning a staggering 17 per cent less in real terms than they were in early 2008. This equates to over £2,500 a year for the average worker. Furthermore, other commentators[10] have pointed out that the effect may be even more serious than this on the lower paid. This group consumes relatively more commodities (heating, petrol, food, etc.), which have seen above-inflation rises during this time.

KEY LEARNING POINTS:
- The impact of inflation now is radically different from what it used to be. It is acting like a conveyor belt, stealthily transferring wealth in immense quantities from one group in society to another.
- The size of the transfers is highly significant and probably totals nearly £100bn a year currently in the UK alone.
- Inflation's winners are any form of debtor, including governments, companies, mortgage holders and speculators. The losers are anyone with cash holdings, bonds, pension savings and welfare claimants. These represent the vast majority of the population.

QUIZ ANSWER:
B.

---

[1] Dowd, K., 1988, "Private Money: The Path to Monetary Stability", *Institute of Economic Affairs*, Hobart Paper 112.

[2] Although taxation may have resulted in a below inflation yield for many.

[3] Although tax might reduce this such that their final receipts are below inflation.

[4] Savings amounts were derived from calculations made by *Save our Savers* based on November 2013 data from the Bank of England. Average interest rates were derived from data provided by the Building Societies Association for July 2014 and the tax rate assumed was 20%. For NS&I, a half of savings were assumed to be tax free e.g. premium bonds and other accounts. Inflation was based on RPI for

July 2014.

[5] Source: Comley, P., 2012, "Monkey with a Pin: Why You May Be Missing 6% a Year From Your Investment Returns", Self-published.

[6] Wolf, M., 2014, "The shifts and the shocks", *Penguin Books Ltd.*

[7] Data source: *Fixed Income Investor* on 16 October 2014.

[8] Lane, P., Reichlin, L., Reinhart, V.,and Wyplosz, C., 2014, "Deleveraging? What Deleveraging? The 16th Geneva Report on the World Economy", *International Center For Monetary and Banking Studies.*

[9] Evans, R., 2011, "Public pensions: switch from RPI to CPI declared 'lawful' by the High Court", *Daily Telegraph*, 2 December 2011.

[10] Meadway, R., 2014, "The Real Britain Index: a more accurate measure of living standards", *New Economics Foundation blog*, 15 October 2014.

PART IV

DEFLATION YET TO COME

Q17. How could population affect 21st Century inflation?

A Population is predicted to decline in most countries and so prices might stabilise or decline with it

B World population is still growing and so it cannot affect future inflation

C Inflation is only influenced by the money supply and nothing else matters

17

The big picture: a century of more stable prices

This chapter draws together the strands from the rest of the book and aims to provide a vision of the likely path of inflation in the century to come. Note, it is not a precise prediction of inflation tomorrow, next year or even next decade but an indication of the likely future path of prices given the tendency of history to repeat itself when presented with similar stimuli. From this it would seem quite possible that the world will return to a state where prices are moderately stable over the long run and that this might persist for up to a century.

Can inflation be predicted?

I am savvy enough to realise that accurately predicting the future is a mug's game and almost impossible. Even the best experts in the world cannot do it. For example, Philip Tetlock published a seminal book[1] about a decade ago in which he looked at tens of thousands of predictions made by hundreds of so-called experts from academics to politicians to journalists. His findings were very clear. The best experts make predictions that are no better than chance and indeed could be beaten by dart-throwing monkeys[2]. Furthermore, the accuracy of an expert's predictions seems to have an inverse relationship to their self-confidence and renown.

Economists are not exempt from this general finding. In fact they are probably worse than the average futurologist because of their over-reliance on econometric modelling. These models are often simplistic, reliant on limited data from certain countries over very specific time-frames and are usually dependent on many assumptions that challenge their validity and predictability.

In a speech at the LSE in 2014[3], David Miles from the Bank of England demonstrated just how wrong most of their expert economist advisors usually are. In 2007, virtually none of them predicted the possibility of a massive rise in commodity prices, the economic slump or the huge decline of sterling. Normally the experts' predictions with regard to the path of future inflation were worse than chance. He quoted many examples of predictions of inflation and how their economists usually got them wrong. He showed an example (below) of the distribution of the Bank of England's experts' predictions of inflation in Q1 2009 (made in Q1 2007). 94 per cent of them were wrong.

Bank of England's experts' predictions for 2009 inflation (in 2007)

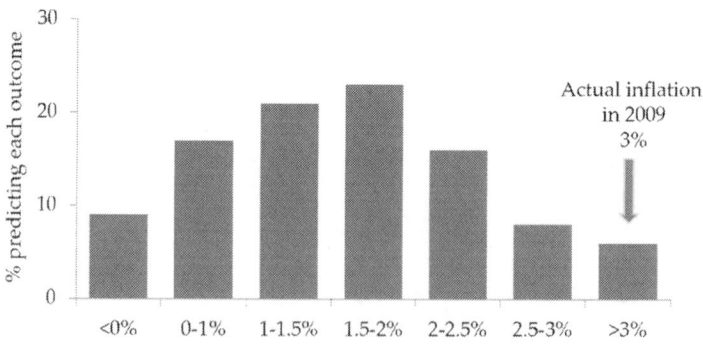

Source: Bank of England Speech by David Miles (2014).

Oleg Kitov at Oxford University summarised the poor record of predictions given by inflation economic models succinctly as:[4]

"There is no unique and comprehensive model in mainstream economics and econometrics, which is able to explain observations and predict inflation."[5]

Eating humble pie

Given all this, you might be wondering how this chapter could even start to attempt to offer a prediction for the future path of inflation across the world. Although I am not a psychic nor in possession of some magic power to see into the future, I do have a good knowledge of the history and factors that have influenced inflation in broad terms in the past.

There is a science fiction term coined by Issac Asimov called *psychohistory*. In his famous *Foundation* trilogy, the author imagines a universe where supercomputers have collated the response of large groups of people across the whole universe to major events. From it, they have derived a model that creates probabilities of different scenario outcomes to future events. Asimov uses the analogy of a gas: an observer has great difficulty in predicting the motion of a single molecule in a gas, but can predict the mass action of the gas to a high level of accuracy.

Although a fictional concept, it went on to influence many people such as the famous economist Paul Krugman and help create the Generational Dynamics Theory. Moreover the broad principle of history repeating itself in some form is well accepted within our culture. But the world is full of people who think they can see connections in random elements of the past and use this as the basis for their claimed insight.

This might turn out to be the case for Inflationary Wave Theory. However the theory does have face validity. Therefore in this chapter it is worth examining what might be its implications, should it be broadly correct.

Recap of the theory

The inflation data from the best part of the last millennium follows a wave pattern of cycles comprising around a century or so of rising prices followed by a slightly shorter period of stability and gently falling prices. The overriding trend is upwards and increasingly so.

What drives the underlying trend is imbalances between the population's need for resources and the satisfaction of those demands. What creates the wave-like pattern is an inflationary mindset that prevails once people realise that a new wave of price rises is happening. Speculators and governments then exploit the opportunity for their own gain and create a self-reinforcing trend of higher prices until finally a tipping point is reached. Some external factor (eg falling demand due to declining population) causes prices to stop rising. A stable price mindset returns and productivity improvements allow prices to decline until they reach the underlying trendline again around a century later. The process then repeats.

Inflationary wave theory

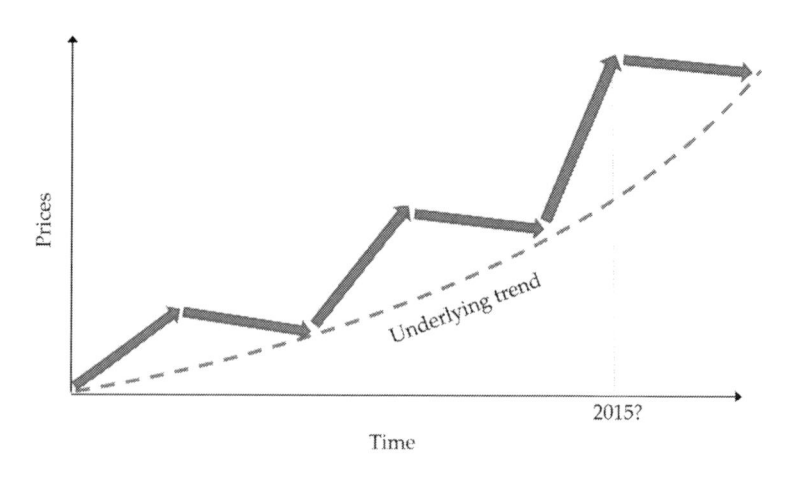

(Chart showing Prices vs Time, with stepped arrows rising above a dashed "Underlying trend" line, ending around 2015?)

How the 21st Century fits into the theory

Following a period of around 85 years of relatively stable or declining prices, they started rising again around the turn of the 20th Century. (Some have argued the low point was 1896 when commodity prices bottomed).[6] Since then we have experienced a period of inflation. The cumulative impact of this has been enormous. Prices in the UK for example have risen by a factor of around 100: £1 in 1900 would now buy £100 worth of goods.

The world is now populated only by people who have lived with this inflation throughout their lives. It is therefore not surprising that most think it is just a fact of life and that this trend will continue forever. However, as we have seen, historically that is unlikely to be the case. Just like many other financial trends, there comes a point when a trend changes or it has a consolidation period where it might even go in the opposite direction for a while.

The timing of the end of the inflationary wave

The up-cycle in the previous three inflationary waves in the UK have lasted between 85 and 140 years. We are about 115 years into the latest one. So there has to be some chance that within the next 25 years we may have a major secular shift. The latest great wave of price rises would come to a halt and a new phase begin. Indeed it is possible that this new wave of stable and declining prices may have already started in some places e.g. Japan.

There is some evidence that the length of the waves is shortening over time whilst their degree of volatility is increasing. Given that the up-cycle in the previous inflationary wave lasted only around 85 years, it could be argued that we are long overdue a peak.

It is most likely that we have not reached the crest of the current inflationary wave yet. As we'll see in the next chapter, there are some specific conditions that need to be fulfilled before we can move into the consolidation phase. Not all of these are in place yet. (See: "18- The transition period and near-term inflation".)

Having said that, today's big inflationary wave is clearly beginning to come to an end. The evidence for this can be seen in the declining world prices around us. It also fits with other trends.

Peak population

It will be remembered that what appears most likely to be the underlying driver of inflation over the long-term is the Malthusian concept of population growth and competition for resources.

The possible impact of population decline on inflation

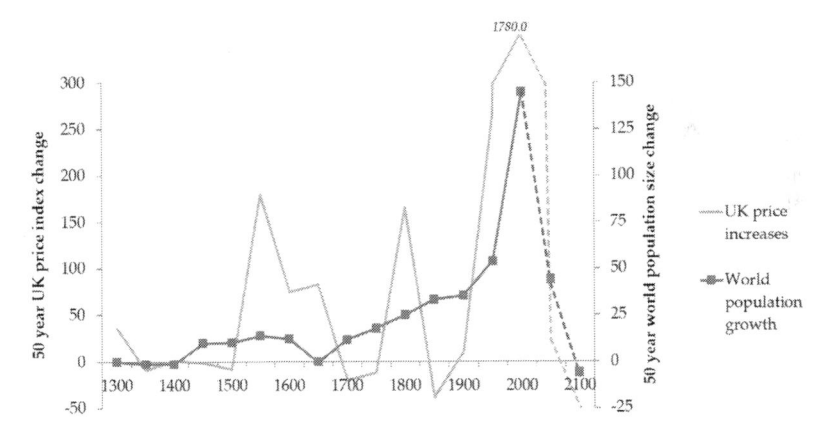

Source of population statistics: 1300-1950: McEvedy, Colin and Richard Jones, 1978, "Atlas of World Population History" and 2000-2100: Sanyal, S., 2013, "The Wide Angle Predictions of a Rogue Demographer".
Source of prices: 1300-1900: Phelps-Brown and Hopkins and 1950-2000: ONS and 2050-2100: author projections.

Although the world population is still growing overall, this increase is being driven primarily by Africa and a few countries in South East Asia, all of whom use few resources. In most other countries which consume more, the level of births is below replacement levels. Even though improvements in life expectancy are still driving populations higher short-term, that trend is about to go into reverse. Populations are already declining in Japan, Russia and Germany. According to recent forecasts by Deutsche Bank[7], the total world population will peak around 2050 and then start declining.

For some developed countries with high immigration like the UK, the picture is slightly less clear. Immigrants typically are younger and often have more children than the indigenous population. This may initially act against the trend but the weight of deflationary force elsewhere will spread even to countries with higher immigration.

At the same time the world's population is ageing. Older people consume fewer goods and services. Therefore there will start to be downward pressure on prices from reduced demand caused by the double whammy of declining population size and reduced consumption by those who remain.

We are starting to see these factors have an impact. In Japan, the stagnation of prices (and GDP) over the last two decades probably has as much to do with demographics as it does to the aftermath of the financial crisis[8]. Its working population is predicted to decline by a half over the 21st Century—see graph below[9]. Even China is predicted to see a similar decline in working population. These demographic changes are going to have a massive impact on consumption and demand for goods.

The decline of the Japanese population

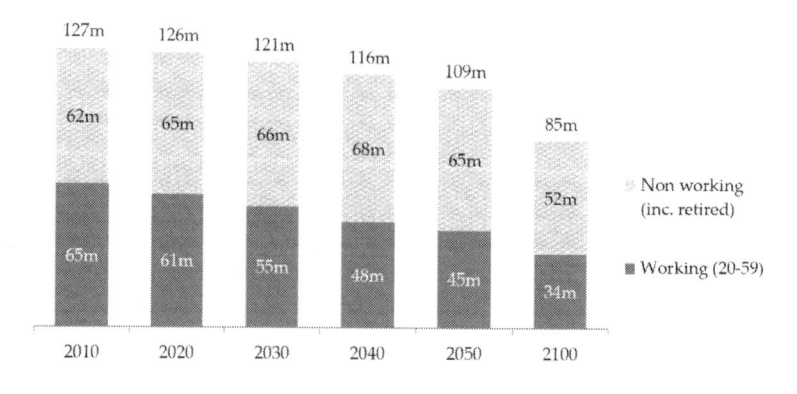

Year	Total	Working (20-59)	Non working (inc. retired)
2010	127m	65m	62m
2020	126m	61m	65m
2030	121m	55m	66m
2040	116m	48m	68m
2050	109m	45m	65m
2100	86m	34m	52m

Source: Deutsche Bank[10]

These demographic trends are important and are probably going to be the force behind the new secular trend. They are starting to have an impact on the world.

Near-zero inflation occurred around 2000

The 1990s witnessed a steady decline in prices. Worldwide inflation actually came very close to zero almost 100 years after the start of the latest inflation wave. The main trigger was the downward pressure on prices created by China's devaluation and export boom. It was also helped by declines in commodity prices towards the end of the decade.

However, in themselves these were insufficient forces to keep prices low enough and for long enough to start the new down-cycle as other key conditions had not been met. (See: "18-The transition period and near-term inflation.") Indeed, within a few years of the start of the new millennium, the US started adopting very "accommodative" policies after the dot.com bust and 9/11. In these the Federal Reserve reduced interest rates and helped create a credit/debt boom. This process increased the world's money supply and asset prices soared. Consumer prices also started rising again.

2008 could have been the peak

Although those actions may have forestalled the end of the wave, they have probably also sown the seeds of its final collapse. They have done so by stoking the world debt boom to such proportions that it created the Great Recession when many of those debts became unsustainable. The ensuing destruction of wealth plunged the world into a deep recession and also threatened to reduce the money supply massively as bad debts were written off. Had this process been allowed to take its natural course, the world would probably have experienced a very sharp reduction in prices, the like of which has not been seen since the cresting of the last wave during the Napoleonic Wars.

The US Federal Reserve again stepped in following 2008 to try to avert basic economic forces restoring the natural equilibrium. The Fed, together with central banks of other nations like the UK and Japan, have printed massive amounts of money to pump into the financial system to compensate for the destruction of the money supply. However the basic problem of the debt overhang has not gone away. The main holders of the debts, banks, did not and have not fully admitted their liabilities. Most banks worldwide are hiding

INFLATION MATTERS

massive loan losses on their balance sheets and have yet to own up to the true level of the destruction of capital[11]. To make matters worse, worldwide debts are even higher in 2014 than they were in 2008[12].

Although there are some signs of a weak recovery in some countries (notably the US and the UK), the bulk of the world, in both the developed and emerging markets, seems stuck in perpetual stagnation caused by the overhang of these massive debts. In 2014, the head of the IMF, Christine Lagarde, stated that the world had entered a new phase she described as the "New Mediocre".

Another reason the peak in inflation did not happen after the Great Recession was commodity price rises. Key commodities like energy and foods hit all-time highs in 2008 and again in 2011. This made its way through to consumer prices, as illustrated by the chart below, which compares changes in the global commodities index with worldwide inflation (in the G7 and China).

The impact of commodity prices on world inflation

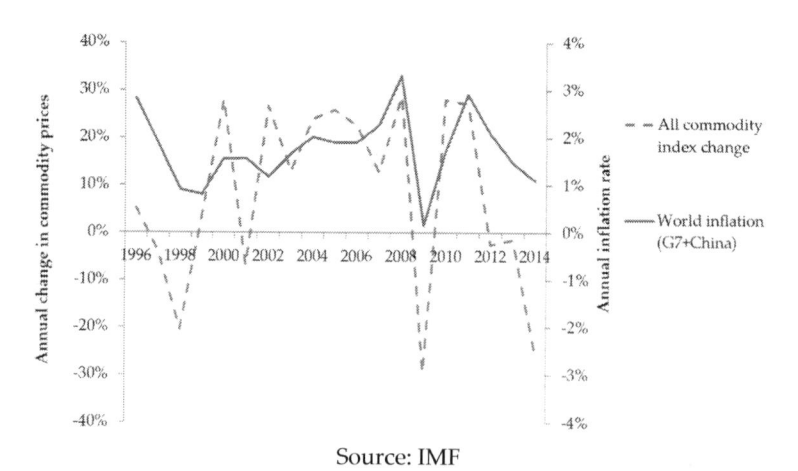

Source: IMF

Is the world heading towards deflation?

Despite the best efforts of central bankers to target inflation rates of 2 per cent or more in most countries, inflation rates declined in 2014 and the world was experiencing what is called disinflation i.e. declining inflation. Indeed rates were heading towards zero or even deflation in many European countries. In Europe in October 2014, Italy, Spain, Greece and Sweden all had deflation and other countries appeared to be heading that way. Europe was not alone; Israel had deflation too.

These falls in inflation were primarily being driven by the contraction of the economy (and money supply) in Europe, especially in the peripheral countries. The fall in world commodity prices also speeded up the decline. As of December 2014, the oil price had declined about 50 per cent in the space of a few months and iron ore by a third over the previous year. Cereal crops like wheat and maize were down by a fifth in 2014 and the overall commodity index by around a quarter.

Therefore you might be excused for thinking that peak inflation is maybe already here. I suspect that these declines will be temporary and worldwide inflation rates will increase again when commodity prices recover in the future. Furthermore, I believe that we have yet to reach the key turning point in inflation for reasons I'll discuss in the next chapter. (See: "18-The transition period and near-term inflation".)

The zero inflation mindset is beginning to appear

Even though the world has probably not quite reached peak inflation yet, a new lower inflation mindset is starting to set in. Long-term expectations amongst traders have declined for all leading economies[13].

Consumer inflation expectations are declining in France

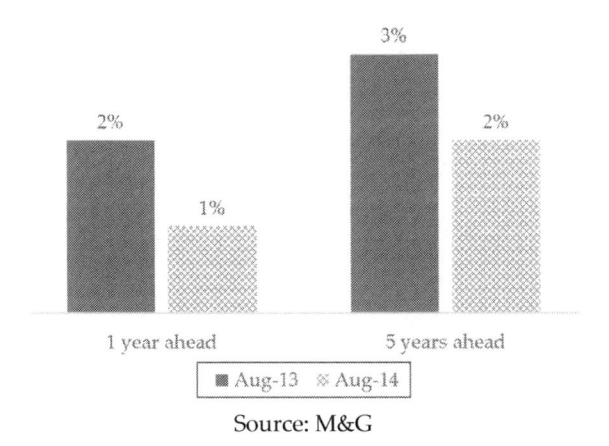

1 year ahead: Aug-13 2%, Aug-14 1%
5 years ahead: Aug-13 3%, Aug-14 2%

Source: M&G

Consumer inflation expectations have also moderated in every single one of the nine countries covered in a recent survey by M&G[14]. For example, in August 2013 French consumers expected inflation to be 2 per cent a year ahead. A year later in August 2014 they expected just 1 per cent. Their outlook for inflation five years ahead similarly declined from 3 per cent to 2 per cent.

These expectations are critical as it is man-made inflation that creates the price rises seen in the inflation wave. Therefore if enough people in society (particularly in the financial and political world) come to believe that inflation is going to be low and trending towards zero, it is likely to become a self-fulfilling prophecy to some extent. People and businesses may stop creating contracts that ensure inflation is built into the system. Workers may stop seeking cost of living pay rises.

How long would the near-zero inflation world last?

The transition to the near-zero inflation world may well not be a smooth one but once it does arrive, it could well last into the 22nd Century. The last two consolidation waves have lasted around 80 years or so in the UK. They seem to have a shorter periodicity than the inflation waves.

Given this, it is quite possible that many of those born today may never experience long-term inflation in their lifetime. They might be part of a more fortunate generation who enter the workforce and their adult lives at a time when many of the financial issues of the world today have been resolved in some way.

KEY LEARNING POINTS:
- The previous three inflationary waves in the UK have lasted between 85 and 140 years. We are about 115 years into the latest wave. Therefore there is some chance that within the next 25 years we may have a secular shift towards more stable prices.
- Population and demographics are again likely to be the underlying driver. Many countries already have live birth levels below replacement levels and this is beginning to impact on working population sizes. Once the baby boomer generation die, total population size will decline. Total demand for goods will decline, exerting a massive downward pressure on inflation throughout the 21st Century.
- The world already has low inflation levels and a corresponding mindset is beginning to set in. Even so, the world has yet to reach the point of peak prices.

QUIZ ANSWER:
A.

[1] Telock, P., 2005, "Expert Political Judgment: How Good Is It? How Can We Know?", *Princeton University Press.*
[2] A concept I expanded in my previous book: Comley, P., 2012, "Monkey with a Pin: Why You May Be Missing 6% a Year From Your Investment Returns", Self-published.
[3] Miles, D., 2014, "Mensch tracht, und Gott lacht: Giving guidance on future monetary policy", Speech at *LSE* on 30 September 2014, text published by *Bank of England.*
[4] Asimov, I., 1951, "Foundation", "Foundation and Empire" and "Second Foundation", *Gnome Press.*
[5] I.O. Kitov, I. and Dolinskaya, S., 2007, "Inflation as a function of labor force change rate: cointegration test for the USA", Working Paper, MPRA Paper from *University Library of Munich, Germany.*
[6] Hackett Fischer, D., 1997, "The Great Wave: Price Revolutions and the Rhythm of History", *Oxford University Press.*
[7] Sanyal, S., 2013, "The Wide Angle Predictions of a Rogue Demographer", *Deutsche Bank.*
[8] Somerset Webb, M., 2014, "Japan diary: There are worse fates for the West than to end up like Japan", *Moneyweek Blog,* 13 September 2014.
[9] Sanyal, S., 2013, "The Wide Angle Predictions of a Rogue Demographer", *Deutsche Bank.*
[10] ibid.
[11] Wolf, M., 2014, "The shifts and the shocks", *Penguin Books Ltd.*
[12] Lane, P., Reichlin, L., Reinhart, V.,and Wyplosz, C., 2014, "Deleveraging? What Deleveraging? The 16th Geneva Report on the World Economy", *International Center For Monetary and Banking Studies.*
[13] Source: Barclays five year forward inflation swap rates.
[14] M&G, 2014, "M&G YouGov Inflation expectations survey", *M&G Investments,* Q3 2014.

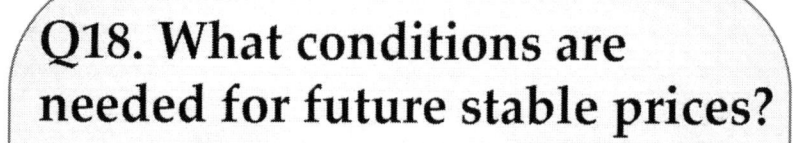

Q18. What conditions are needed for future stable prices?

A The government just needs to impose strict controls on all prices

B We just restrict the money supply

C We need to stop the money supply increasing, resolve latent inflation and restructure debts

18

The transition period and near-term inflation

The outlook for near-term inflation is probably best described as *lowflation*. There are many deflationary forces supressing world prices largely as a result of the financial crisis and the aftermath it has left for governments. It might appear that it is really only central bankers that are preventing us currently transitioning into a zero inflation world in the consolidation part of the inflationary wave.

However history suggests that the transition towards the near-zero-inflation world may not be smooth. There are three conditions that in all likelihood need to be fulfilled for the transition to take place. These are: a stable money supply, no latent inflation in the system, and debt restructuring to a sustainable level. None of these conditions are currently met.

Any number of scenarios could result in this happening though. For illustration this chapter uses two examples: (1) a future bond market crisis and (2) the *Chicago Plan*[1] i.e. a planned debt jubilee and reform of the banking system. It also examines whether Japan has already met the conditions and the likelihood of high inflation returning to the world prior to either of the above scenarios.

The outlook for near-term inflation

The world has not yet moved into the wave of price stability and this may well not happen for quite a while. The pattern of near-term inflation in developed economies and the wider world prior to that point is difficult to predict with any certainty. It is made more difficult by the fact that there could be marked divergence across different economies. This is in part because any transition period is never a simple one and prices would not change completely in sync everywhere at the same time.

There are a number of big themes that are going to affect prices in the near-term, but their impact will pull prices in different directions at the same time.

Factors affecting near-term inflation

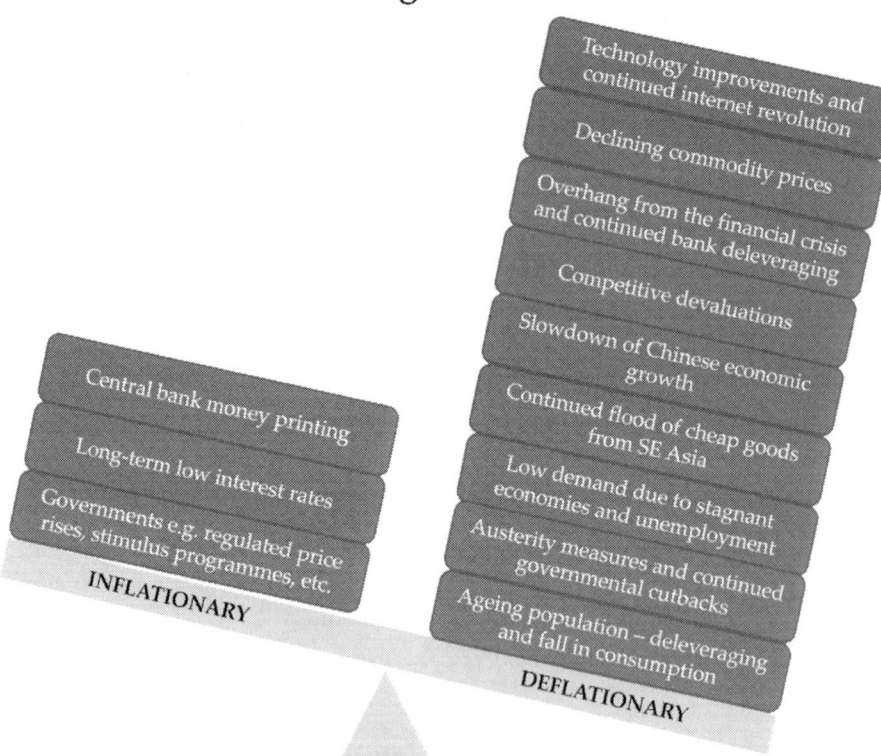

INFLATIONARY
- Central bank money printing
- Long-term low interest rates
- Governments e.g. regulated price rises, stimulus programmes, etc.

DEFLATIONARY
- Technology improvements and continued internet revolution
- Declining commodity prices
- Overhang from the financial crisis and continued bank deleveraging
- Competitive devaluations
- Slowdown of Chinese economic growth
- Continued flood of cheap goods from SE Asia
- Low demand due to stagnant economies and unemployment
- Austerity measures and continued governmental cutbacks
- Ageing population – deleveraging and fall in consumption

There are many powerful forces that are acting negatively on near-term inflation. The most important is the overhang from the financial crisis and the continued deleveraging taking place amongst banks. This crisis has also led to stagnant economies and high unemployment in many countries and this has contributed further to the deflationary pressure. A typical response of governments has been to devalue their currencies when they can (e.g. Japan) to reduce the effective price of their exports. Each wave of these devaluations puts pressure on other countries to lower theirs too and these competitive devaluations are exporting deflation.

Deleveraging has also taken place in China (although the precise amount is debatable due to the state control over finances). This has caused house prices to decline and production to slow. This in turn has helped reduce global commodity prices, which has sparked another strong deflationary wave across the globe in 2014. Furthermore, wages in China have been rising, so other SE Asian countries with cheaper costs of production have been competing to export even cheaper products to the West.

Added to this have been the effects of technological advancement. The true impact of the internet is only now beginning to be felt in many sectors – the latest being taxi companies with the launch of companies such as Uber. As it continues to revolutionise the way business is done in different areas, this will create a further downward pressure on prices for many decades to come.

Government debt levels continue to rise in most economies and the need to try to reduce them has caused many governments to cut back on spending. This has added yet another deflationary force.

Many countries (especially European ones) have ageing populations. The lower per capita consumption of this group acts negatively on prices. In addition as the baby boomers now retire they are starting to pay off their loans and downsize – all of which helps shrink the money supply.

The central banks' fight against the deflationary forces

"Janet Yellen official portrait" by United States Federal Reserve - Obtained from Federal Reserve OPA. Licensed under Public Domain via Wikimedia Commons.

The only thing that has stopped the world moving towards near-zero price rises has been central bankers and governments. There seems to have been an informal game of pass-the-parcel going on between central banks ensuring that one country after another is always trying to stave off world deflation by printing more money. The impact of this to date has largely been on asset prices and increasing the money supply to compensate for that destroyed as debts were written off after the crisis. However, moves by the Bank of Japan in late 2014 might be taking QE to a different level in its attempts to foster price inflation. It remains to be seen if the European Central Bank will finally succumb to similar large scale money printing too at some point.

The other key impact central bankers have had on inflation is their policy of maintaining very low interest rates. This has an expansionary impact on the economy by encouraging further lending. The debt so created expands the money supply again and creates a backdrop of inflationary pressure via the latent inflation it stores up. Central banks can also follow other expansionary polices to reverse the declines in money supply and fight against the deflationary forces, one example being the Funding for Lending Scheme in the UK.

Governments are also directly pushing against deflation. They ensure regulated price rises continue and they can also create stimulus schemes (such as High Speed rail in the UK) which can all help keep inflation positive. Moreover, it should not be forgotten that virtually all central banks are under the direct or indirect control of governments, which can have a strong influence on their policies. The motivation here is simple: it is beneficial to most governments to have positive inflation as it helps reduce their real debt liabilities.

Therefore, for the time being, governments and their central bankers seem to have managed to keep inflation positive. They have, after all, the power to control monetary policy. It remains to be seen for how long they will be able to maintain this - there are scenarios discussed below which could change things. In the meantime, the most likely near-term outlook for inflation in developed countries is lowflation[2].

The end of the cycle

Given the above, it is possible that the world might just gently move into the consolidation phase of stable prices. However looking back into history, the transition between the inflationary part of the wave and the consolidation phase has usually not been a smooth one. Instead it has often been a turbulent time for prices.

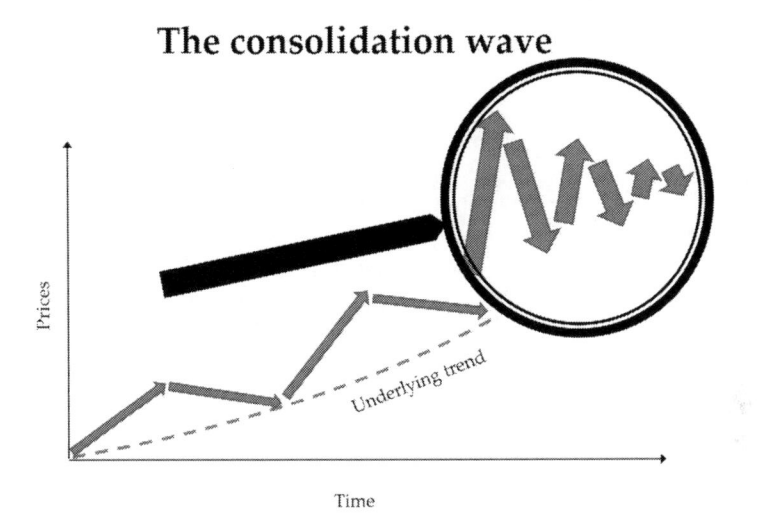

The consolidation wave

The start of the new phase is often some sort of pivot point in time as the trend changes. It appears to have always been some sort of major event. It has been accompanied by declines in prices of up to a half over a period of 4-8 years. This is followed by a period of price recovery to below the previous peak and then gradually reducing oscillations over time towards a new equilibrium.

Wave peaks and their decline

Wave peak (UK)	Years of decline	Price decline	Possible trigger for decline
1316	4	-51%	Famine and floods
1650	5	-37%	Revolution
1813	9	-45%	War

Despite the evidence of the previous wave peaks, the sharp decline in prices seen at the pivot point may not be a requirement for the change in trend. However it is a likely outcome of some of the circumstances that might cause it – see below.

Conditions required for the change of trend

In his analysis of the great inflations of the world, Ronald Marcks[3] proposed that there were three requirements that had to be fulfilled to stop inflation in a country.

Conditions required to stop inflation

1. A process must be put in place to stop the money supply from rising more than that required by the economy.

2. Latent inflation must be extinguished either by allowing prices to rise to the level implied by the previous increases of the money supply, or the money supply must be reduced accordingly.

3. Debts must be restructured to a sustainable level i.e. money wealth must be allowed to be devalued as debts are written off or rerated.

It could be argued that Marcks was writing in a different time (1974) and in different circumstances – namely in a period of sharply rising worldwide inflation. It is possible therefore that not all these conditions might need to apply now for us to shift from lowflation to stable prices. Moreover there might even be some other special conditions that are required at the transition point which no one yet knows about.

However having said that, all his conditions make sense. If any of them were not complied with, there would be the potential for the inflation trend to quickly re-emerge and for us to remain in that part of the wave. Therefore in the absence of alternative special conditions, it makes sense to use Marcks's conditions as a working hypothesis for the transition point. It is difficult to predict what exact situation might bring these three conditions into alignment and when. But history suggests that it will come at some point in the coming few decades.

The following sections look at where the world currently is in relation to Marcks's three conditions. It then reviews the current status of Japan and finally provides two examples of scenarios that might fulfil them, namely a bond market crisis and the *Chicago Plan*. To be absolutely clear, I am not predicting either of these will necessarily happen. They are just two possible circumstances that might result in the conditions being met. They also act as a good illustration of the pattern that inflation might follow in the early part of the consolidation phase and the corresponding implications.

Condition 1: Stable money supply

Already, there seems in place something that is beginning to restrain money supply growth. Money is primarily created by private banks. However many banks became so over-leveraged in the run-up to the Great Recession, that they have subsequently shrunk their balance sheets. This was due in part to the need to write off bad loans and in part to legislation and regulation that has forced them to hold higher ratios of collateral. Either way, the effect is that net money supply (after a deduction for GDP growth) is declining in many developed markets, including Europe.

The effect is not worldwide though. US banks restructured their debts much quicker and are continuing to increase the money supply there. Money supply was also increasing in some developing markets in 2014. And Japan embarked on a massive quantitative easing programme in 2013, which is adding to the money supply there.

Therefore currently this condition is only partly met in some countries.

Condition 2: No latent inflation

Latent inflation is a situation where inflation is yet to happen but the mechanism to generate it has already been created. Over the long-term, increases in the net money supply (i.e. over and above that required by the growing economy) lead to price inflation. Moreover the long-term relationship is almost one to one, so if the net money supply is doubled then so are prices eventually. However the effect is more complex than this and involves the interaction of two separate money supply systems: asset prices and consumer prices.

In addition, Marcks's model assumes that the velocity of money is constant. It could be argued that in the world's ageing economies, velocity would decline as people spend less as they get older. This indeed is probably part of the mechanism by which demographics have an impact on inflation rates in the inflationary wave theory.

The calculation is thus not as simple as it might seem. Furthermore, changes in the net money supply do not immediately impact on prices. They are affected by many factors and a situation can occur where the money supply can outstrip inflation for many years or vice versa. (See: "2-Inflation and the money supply theory.")

To determine latent inflation, you need records that span the whole of the latest inflationary wave, meaning records going back to the beginning of the 20th Century. Unfortunately, obtaining accurate

INFLATION MATTERS

and consistent broad money supply figures, GDP and price data over this long period is very difficult. Such datasets only exist for a few countries, and even fewer when you remove those that have had resets due to hyperinflationary periods.

The UK is one of the few that have such quality data readily available. The chart below compares the UK price index since 1900 with that of an index of net broad money supply having deducted increases required for economic growth (GDP growth). It clearly illustrates the strong long-term relationship between the variables and how in the last two to three decades money supply increases have been far outstripping those required for real economic growth and have also outpaced consumer price rises.

The massive latent inflation in the UK

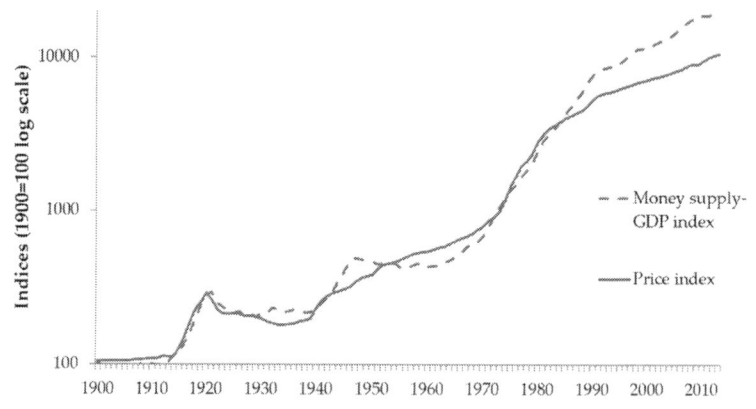

Sources: Price index - ONS longitudinal series. Money supply - The Bank of England's preferred measure (M3/M4/M4x). GDP - measuringworth.com

This implies that a very large amount of latent inflation has been built up. This can be resolved in one of two ways, or by a combination of both. The first is that prices could increase. To restore the equilibrium, prices would need to double approximately in the UK. Alternatively, net money supply needs to shrink by a half, although in practice an even larger reduction might be required in some scenarios[4].

Note it is possible that the UK is in some way unique and unrepresentative of the latent inflation that exists throughout the world. The UK has always had a strong financial services sector and this could have resulted in more excess money being created than elsewhere. However given the worldwide nature of the recent debt boom, it is likely that latent inflation has built up in most other nations too. Either way, determining its size is difficult without full, consistent datasets. Certainly the quantitative easing exercises in the US and Japan will have increased the potential of latent inflation in both those countries.

Overall, this analysis shows that the second condition for transition into a period of more stable prices has not been met yet—there is still latent inflation in the system.

Condition 3: Restructuring of debt

In 2012, total world debt was estimated[5] to be around $223,000,000,000,000 ($223 trillion) and is probably currently much higher. In developed countries debt averaged nearly four times each country's annual income (GDP) [6]. Many countries have debts much higher than that; in Ireland it is over ten times GDP.

These debt levels are still rising at a staggering rate. Some estimate[7] them to have risen by a quarter in the last five years alone, partly as a result of governments taking on even more debt. This means that the average debt for every man, woman, and child in developed nations is around $170,000.[8]

In the UK, debts are even greater by the time you add up all the corporate, banking, consumer and governmental debts. They total some £7.8 trillion[9]. That equates to about £300,000 debt for every one of the 26.4 million UK households. The average household income, after tax and including all benefits, is just over £30,000[10]. A leverage ratio of ten times annual income is already far beyond any normal threshold of sustainable debt.

UK debt levels are unsustainable

£300,000 average debt/household

£30,000 average household income

Sources: Bank of England, ICMB, The Money Charity, and ONS.

Yet there is little sign of willingness on the part of governments around the world to restructure these debts. Indeed many are trying to deal with the problem by adding to them. The only exception is the US, where banks have been encouraged to write off some bad debt and a sizeable proportion of real estate debt has been defaulted upon. The ratio of financial debt to GDP has therefore declined significantly and is at its lowest level since the millennium. Even so, balanced against this, other US debts have risen, particularly government debts.

Therefore world deleveraging and debt restructuring has not really started yet. Condition 3 is not currently met.

Has Japan already entered the consolidation phase?

We have already examined the situation of Japan in detail. (See: "13-Japan and deflation."). That analysis showed that the current state of near-zero inflation in Japan had been brought about by a combination of three factors:

1. The aftermath of a financial crisis reducing spending
2. A reduction in demand due to ageing of the population
3. A generally lower inflation rate on account of the long-term strengthening of the currency.

It is interesting to consider that if Japan has started the consolidation wave, it has done so without experiencing first a massive fall in prices. It has also probably not fully met the other criteria that Marcks suggests might be required to permanently stop inflation.

In terms of the money supply, this was stabilised after inflation peaked in 1998. Over the following decade or so, net money supply growth (after deducting GDP) was effectively zero. However, since 2013 it has started to grow significantly beyond the 1999 level. This rise largely coincides with the Bank of Japan's decision to embark upon a massive quantitative easing programme to double the money supply within two years. The long-term implications of this for Japanese inflation are yet to be seen. However, largely as a result of the subsequent depreciation of the Yen and tax rises, inflation in late 2014 had already risen to 4%.

Marcks's second condition - the absence of latent inflation - is difficult to accurately calculate due to a lack of consistent historic records. However, given the high rises in the money supply during the 1980s and to a lesser extent the 1990s, it is likely that latent inflation still exists. This should have been rectified by a write-off of bad debts in the 1990s, but many of those debts may still remain hidden on company and financial institution balance sheets. It is possible that the condition is therefore satisfied as such excess money is effectively neutralised. Alternatively, the impact of latent inflation may also have been reduced by the velocity of money declining thanks to Japan's ageing population.

Marcks's last condition required that debts be restructured. This has not really happened in Japan. Instead, the government has taken on the liabilities of many banks and other debts probably still reside on the books of so-called zombie companies. Again it is arguable that such a position could be regarded as restructuring.

Therefore the position in Japan is that, until 2013, it looked as if it had almost achieved Marcks's criteria for price stability, primarily by way of the government assuming the responsibility for debts. This of course brought with it a mushrooming of governmental debt, which stood at 237 per cent of GDP in 2012[11]. Although this debt level ought to be unsustainable, sovereigns always have the ability to restructure debt and so Japan could at that point have stayed in the consolidation phase.

What is interesting is that Japan almost succeeded in entering the consolidation phase without experiencing any of the negative consequences that are more than likely to happen to comply with Marcks's three conditions – see below. Japan would have needed some further measures to secure the position – namely debt restructuring and rectifying government finances. However had it succeeded, it might have acted as a plan for other nations to follow.

Instead the false belief in the need for inflation resulted in the doctrine of Abenomics. This has more than likely pushed the country back into the inflationary wave, battling against the tide of its ageing population. Long-term the population dynamic will probably win, but short-term any number of outcomes is possible for Japan.

So, if Japan is not the blueprint for the world, what other scenarios might see it meet the criteria for the consolidation wave?

Scenario 1: a bond default crisis

One of the biggest challenges to the world economy currently is the ever-increasing amount of debt. The levels are becoming unsustainable. The short-term solution of creating more debt to deal with the existing debt is clearly not a long-term answer and risks a debt death spiral where even affording to pay the interest eventually becomes impossible.

Government debts in the developed world averaged 106 per cent of GDP in 2013. That level is higher than the theoretical threshold of 100 per cent that was proposed by Carmen Reinhart and Kenneth Rogoff[12] beyond which many nations frequently default. Indeed, many economists now think we are approaching levels where leverage is increasing so much that at some point things cannot continue without some form of restructuring. This is likely to be accompanied by a wider financial crisis. To quote the 2014 *Geneva Report on the World Economy* published by the International Center for Monetary and Banking Studies:

"Excessive level of debt poses both acute and chronic risks… if panic sets in, risk premia shoot up and the debt is no longer sustainable. In related fashion, a surge in risk premia will also be associated with a sell-off in asset markets, as investors fear that debtors may be forced into fire-sale disposals of assets if debts cannot be rolled over."

No one can tell what might trigger a debt crisis or what format it might take. It might even result from the 2014 commodity price decline. This has had a major impact on oil and other commodity producing countries such as Russia and Venezuela and still could trigger a world debt crisis.

The timing is also impossible to predict but, if this scenario is to happen, it could still be at least a decade away. Apparently unsustainable situations have a habit of persisting for far longer than many imagine possible. However, if it did happen, the results are possibly more predictable.

What we talking about is a situation where there is a major default on debt. This could set in train a cascade of events that creates a financial crash far worse than that witnessed in 2008. That is because this time the crash might well be centred around the government bond market, historically the safe-haven asset.

It is difficult to know where investors would go when they flee such bonds and their prices tumble. The system may even have insufficient cash to deal with such a mass exodus. Banks might crash again, but this time governments probably could not afford (or might not want) to bail out the speculative investors and might save only

THE TRANSITION PERIOD AND NEAR-TERM INFLATION

the small cash-holders. Stock prices would more than likely tumble as would those of all other assets, including housing, as margin investors sought to liquefy whatever they could in the turmoil.

The key aspect of this scenario is that counterparties to many debt contracts, from corporate bonds to mortgages, would either face default or be forced to restructure them. This would help restore the debt burden to a level more affordable for debt holders to service. This could meet condition 3.

That restructuring would in itself destroy the supply of money in proportion to the amount of debt written off. Further reduction of the money supply would probably occur due to knock-on effects such as bank failures. In order to comply with condition 2, there would have to be a reduction of the net money supply of at least 50 per cent. That is a staggering amount of worldwide money to be effectively destroyed at one time, but not inconceivable.

Implications of a bond market crisis

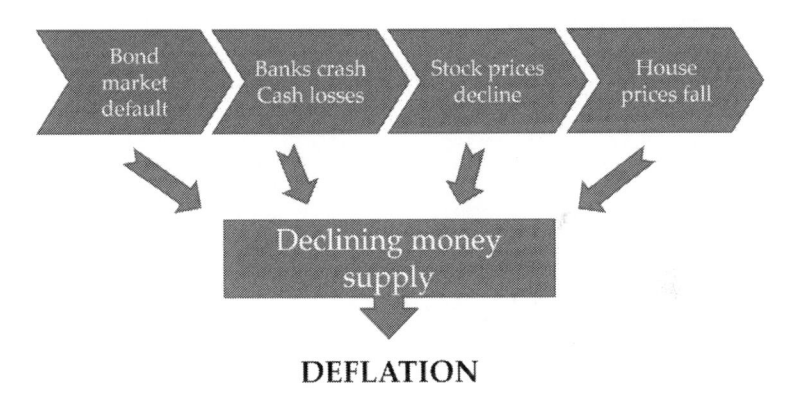

```
Bond market default → Banks crash Cash losses → Stock prices decline → House prices fall
          ↓              ↓              ↓              ↓
              Declining money supply
                      ↓
                  DEFLATION
```

This destruction of wealth would create a true worldwide depression. The velocity of money would also decline as people sought to retain whatever savings they could. The net effect would be deflation on the scale that typifies the historic wave crashes. Prices could easily halve within a few years. This would satisfy the final condition and create an environment where inflation could enter the consolidation period.

The above scenario of a bond crisis would likely be followed by major interventions by governments and central banks attempting to restore the economy. Again it is hard to predict what forms these might take. However, they could well involve Keynesian stimulus programmes and massive monetary stimulus. This would re-stoke inflation temporarily as such interventions are an imperfect science. Additional temporary inflation might occur if the depression ended up creating war and conflicts in a repeat of the 1930s scenario.

Scenario 2: The Chicago Plan

The banking crisis of the 1930s is the closest parallel of the above scenario that the world has witnessed. It resulted in much discussion over how such events could be avoided in the future. One such proposal by leading economists from the University of Chicago came to be known as the *Chicago Plan*. It has since come back into serious consideration following an IMF paper in 2012[13] when researchers looked at what would be the impact of adopting the policy on the IMF's model of the US economy.

The main idea behind the original Chicago Plan was that responsibility for creation of money in a country should move from private banks to a governmental body. Banks would be split into two organisations, one to collect savings and lend them out and the other to provide investment loans backed by collateral at the central bank. The existing power of banks to create money out of thin air would be removed.

Main theme of the Chicago Plan

> Responsibility for money creation moves from private banks to the state

In the somewhat complicated transition process that would then follow, the government would take over ownership of all household and existing government debt and write it off. Thereafter, the government would control the money supply. If new money was required for capital expenditure or to expand the economy, a governmental body would just create it and no longer have to go a private bank to create it for them.

In their analysis of the impact of such a plan, the IMF researchers concluded it would have a number of benefits for the world economy:

THE TRANSITION PERIOD AND NEAR-TERM INFLATION

- It would markedly reduce the impact of the boom and bust business cycle
- It would eliminate the possibility of bank runs
- It would grow the world economy by 10 per cent (mainly due to the one-off benefits in the reductions in taxes and efficiencies)
- It would reduce debt levels (and eliminate governmental ones)
- Inflation would tend towards zero.

The Chicago Plan would satisfy at least two, if not all three, of Marcks's conditions. Firstly it would provide a mechanism to stabilise the money supply, one far superior to the existing system where it is expanded at the whim of private bankers. Although some have argued that the governmental body in charge of the money supply might be open to influence, at least its actions would be open to public scrutiny and so abuse would be more visible. The Chicago Plan therefore satisfies condition 1.

The Chicago Plan would help deal with latent inflation during the transition phase as the effective writing off of governmental and many private debts would shrink the money supply whilst at the same time encouraging economic growth. Net money supply growth would therefore be strongly negative. Although normal economic theory might suggest this would lead to deflation, it might not in this unusual circumstance. The transition period may not cause a recession. Indeed in contrast, it could cause a mini boom. This could create a burst of inflation as consumers feel the impact of debt relief and the resulting increased competition for goods temporarily outstrips demand, before a new production equilibrium is reached. The combined effects of all the above could result in the satisfaction of condition 2.

It also provides a clear mechanism to restructure debt obligations. Governmental debt is written off effectively. In addition in the transition phase a large proportion of private debts would be forgiven too. The economic boost predicted should help corporates and financial organisations pay down debt and return to a more sustainable footing. The Chicago Plan therefore satisfies condition 3.

Overall, the Chicago Plan has a lot to recommend it and it is clearly a much more pleasant scenario for the world than a global bond crisis. The transition would be achieved positively and not negatively and it would not involve the immense misery and suffering that would result from a massive global financial crisis.

However, like so many utopian ideas, one fears that its chance of implementation would be low. Having said that, it would not be a difficult concept to sell to the electorate - offering to write off a large amount of private debt. Moreover, if global government debts continue to rise, the demands for some sort of managed solution will grow.

Might inflation come back before these scenarios?

Some economists have argued that inflation is due to return shortly. For example, on the basis of shorter term Kondratieff waves, Tony Plummer thinks that there might be an inflationary peak around 2024-27[14]. Given the amount of latent inflation, there has to be a possibility that this could happen before whatever scenario finally sees the transition phase begin.

Latent inflation data suggests that, in the UK, there is the possibility of prices doubling. Moreover, when prices and net money supply converge, they often overshoot in the other direction and so prices might rise even more than this.

Any number of conditions could cause this. A major rise in commodity prices following supply problems might be a trigger (as it was in the 1970s). This might seem a distant possibility at the moment, but so was the decline in energy prices witnessed in 2014 a mere year before. Alternatively it could be caused by further bouts of Quantitative Easing, especially if Europe finally decides to make this its main strategy.

A more likely change though is related to governmental policy or the general economic recovery. When the latter finally happens, it is not impossible that central banks would keep interest rates lower for longer than they need to. This could help foster another boom. Wages might start to rise (or even be forced up by governmental policy). Societal attitude towards risk and spending money could flip and the velocity of money might start to suddenly increase.

For example in the UK, the government is changing pension policy in 2015 to allow savers to withdraw all of their pension savings on retirement and removing the obligation to buy an annuity. This is likely to significantly increase money flows and in itself could create a mini-inflation boom in some categories.

Finally, it should be remembered that though there is strong correlation in inflation rates around the world they are not all the

THE TRANSITION PERIOD AND NEAR-TERM INFLATION

same. Although many developed consumer nations are seeing inflation rates head towards zero in the aftermath of the 2014 oil price crash, it is having the opposite effect in many producer nations. Countries such as Russia and Venezuela have seen their currencies decline and the price of imports soar. Inflation rose to over 50 per cent in Venezuela by the end of 2014.

What might cause inflation to return?

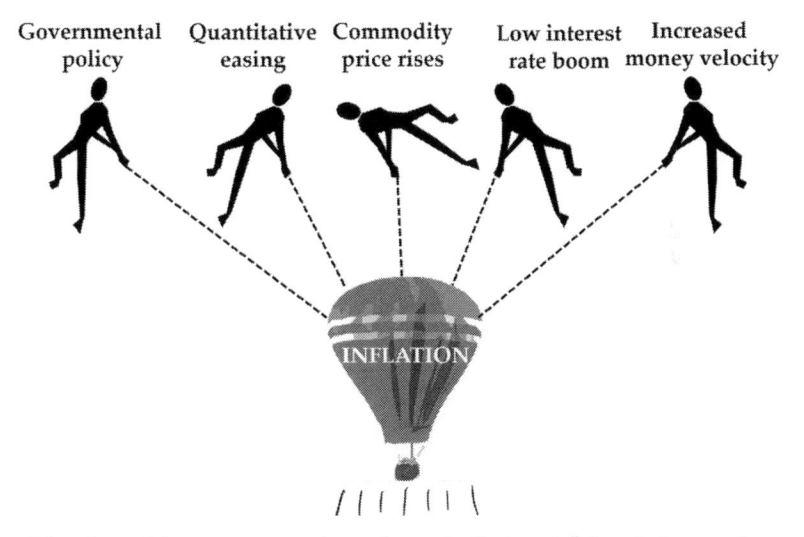

Governmental policy • Quantitative easing • Commodity price rises • Low interest rate boom • Increased money velocity

INFLATION

The key thing to remember about inflation is that it is partly an attitude of mind. It is also what is called pro-cyclical. If people see prices rise markedly, there can be an incentive to buy now before prices rise still further and the purchasing value of their money has been eroded. This demand pushes prices up in a vicious circle.

Therefore, though this higher inflation might go some way towards complying with two of Marcks's criteria—reducing latent inflation and helping to lower debt burdens—it would not create a system where the money supply stops growing. Indeed far from that, it would probably do the exact opposite and relight the fire of excess money printing. Therefore in itself this situation would not help the world into the transition phase. That said, it does not preclude it happening before the transition phase in some countries.

INFLATION MATTERS

KEY LEARNING POINTS:
- There are many deflationary forces supressing world prices largely as a result of the financial crisis and its aftermath which make the near-term outlook one of lowflation.
- The transition towards a near-zero inflation world may not be smooth and three conditions may need to be fulfilled: a stable money supply, no latent inflation in the system, and debt restructuring to a sustainable level. None of these conditions are currently met, even in Japan.
- Two scenarios that could cause them to be met are: (1) a future bond market crisis and (2) the Chicago Plan, i.e. a planned debt restructuring and reform of the banking system. Finally, it is not impossible that higher rates of inflation might return before a transition takes place.

QUIZ ANSWER:
C.

---

[1] Benes, J., and Kumhof, M., 2012, "The Chicago Plan Revisited", *IMF Working Paper*.

[2] Lowflation is a recent term first used by the IMF in early 2014. See: Moghadam, R., Teja, R. and Berkmen, P., 2014, "Euro Area –Deflation Versus Lowflation", *IMFdirect blog post*, March 2014.

[33] Parsson, J., 1974, "Dying of Money: Lessons of the Great German and American Inflations", *Wellspring Press*.

[4] This is because reductions in the money supply caused by a severe recession would more than likely reduce prices (therefore making the target reductions greater). Furthermore the key calculation related to latent inflation involves the net money supply having deducted GDP. If GDP went negative in a recession, it would increase net money supply and again make the reductions required to reach equilibrium even greater.

[5] Reddy, S., 2013, "Number of the Week: Total World Debt Load at 313% of GDP", *WSJ Blog*, 11 May 2013. (Original source was an *ING* report).

[6] Lane, P., Reichlin, L., Reinhart, V.,and Wyplosz, C., 2014, "Deleveraging? What Deleveraging? The 16th Geneva Report on the World Economy", *International Center For Monetary and Banking Studies*.

[7] ibid.

[8] ibid.

[9] Data source for debts: *Bank of England, ICMB, The Money Charity*. See: "The impact of current inflation" chapter for a breakdown.

[10] Source: *ONS* Family Spending Survey 2013.

[11] Gross debt - data source: *IMF* database, April 2014.

[12] Reinhart, C. and Rogoff, K., 2009, "This Time is Different: Eight Centuries of Financial Folly", *Princeton University Press*.

[13] Benes, J., and Kumhof, M., 2012, "The Chicago Plan Revisited", *IMF Working Paper*.

[14] Wilmot, S., 2014, "Waiting for the great inflation", *Investors Chronicle Blog*, 14 July 2014.

Q19. Who gains most from long-term stable prices?

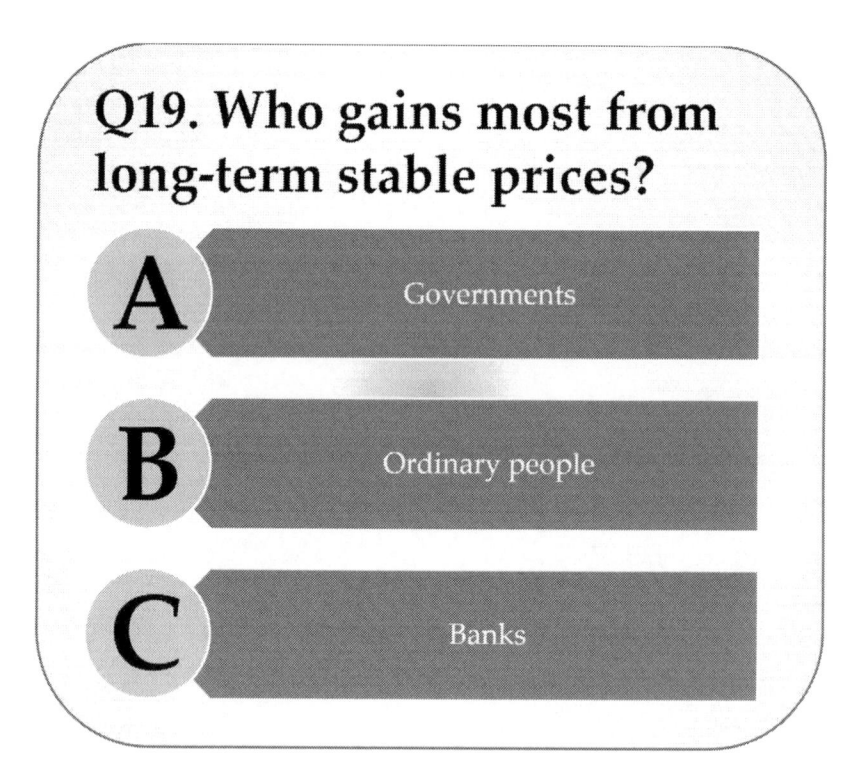

A Governments

B Ordinary people

C Banks

19

Price stability and the consolidation period

Following the transition phase, there could follow a period of relatively stable prices that could take the world into the 22nd Century. This could well be facilitated by major changes in the monetary system which would help maintain this stability. It would not mean that prices remain static. Instead over time and in aggregate they would stay around the same level and slightly decline due to technological and efficiency improvements.

There would be major implications for workers, who would be incentivised to improve productivity to gain a pay rise. The value of real wages would increase and this would be supported by the slight decline in prices overall. Inequality would therefore reduce. Business (though probably not the finance industry) would prosper. Governments would need to find new sources of taxation to replace the loss of inflation tax. Finally, increasing global prosperity in the late 21st Century might well lead to a rise in the population and a new inflationary wave would begin all over again.

A new monetary system: Chicago or bust

The transition period to the consolidation wave is likely to be a turbulent one for world finances. We've seen that historically the transition is often associated with some form of calamity and accompanied by prices declining by a half temporarily. Such an event, like the bond crisis scenario example, is likely to be accompanied by public demand for complete reform of the banking and monetary system to ensure such episodes do not happen again.

In addition, there may be such distrust of the existing financial order that any new innovations that appear to solve the problems would be examined very seriously.

A similar situation occurred in the 1930s and resulted in proposals such as the Chicago Plan. This sought to reform the banking system. A body was to be created to monitor the money supply and create just enough to cover the natural growth of the economy, thereby largely eliminating the boom and bust cycle. By definition, such a stable monetary world would have near-zero inflation over the long-term.

As we have seen, governments after World War II decided on a different policy of persistent inflation and the Chicago Plan was rejected. However the potential scale of the crisis this time could be so much larger than the 1930s and could affect so many people in so many countries that reform of some sort would be a very likely outcome. The format of that reform is impossible to predict. Its objective though might be to create a world where debt cannot spiral out of control for the benefit of certain individuals. A new trusted monetary system would be required that is transparent and independent of the influence of individuals, companies or governments.

The block chain world

One such solution to these new demands might be based on "block chain", the technology behind digital currencies like Bitcoin. The essence of this is that a public and transparent record is kept of all transactions that take place. The amount of money created would be regulated by some agreed formula and therefore not be open to easy abuse by individuals or governments. Concepts such as leverage, debt and derivatives do not exist with so-called cryptocurrencies based on block chain.

An existing cryptocurrency like Bitcoin is unlikely to be suitable for long-term global adoption. This is because Bitcoin was designed to have an increase in money supply over a period of just 20 years and that increase was linked to the speed of machines to mine bitcoins rather than being related to economic needs for money within an economy. It also has had unfortunate associations with asset bubbles and the criminal underworld.

However the technology behind it does have potential and could be used to facilitate a new monetary system for the world. This is because it could create a monetary system that complies with Marcks's three criteria[1] for stopping inflation. (See: "18-The transition period and near-term inflation.") These are:

1. It could provide a process to regulate and stop net money supply from rising.
2. It would encourage stable prices (as the value of money would not change) and so latent inflation could not build up.
3. Inventing money by borrowing would not be possible and so levels of debt would not increase again to unsustainable levels.

Inflation would never disappear

It is very important to understand that there would not be zero inflation in the consolidation wave. Periodic changes would never disappear, possibly as an effect of wars, shortages, commodity price rises or exchange rate changes. The Keynesian ideas of cost-pull and demand-push inflation would still have an impact on short-term inflation rates, as they always have. What would be different is that in most cases, after prices rises, overall prices would eventually decline back to their original levels as there would have been no change in the net money supply.

The prices of the individual 600+ items in a typical price index would also vary, sometimes substantially. The effects of supply and demand would not be extinguished and some items might consistently increase in price because of this. However there would be an overall drag of lower levels of prices from many items as the impact of technology or productivity improvements reduced their cost of production. In the digital world in which we increasingly live, the cost of producing many things is trending towards zero and the full impact of this would become more apparent. 3D printing for example could have a massive impact on the world economy when the technology fully evolves, possibly as much as the internet has had over recent decades.

INFLATION MATTERS

A final key factor is that we are talking here about average global inflation. There may still be a few countries that decide to organise themselves by increasing their money supply and printing money. Inflation would inevitably ensue. However it is likely that structural changes to the new financial order would make this more difficult and their overall impact on world inflation would be minimal. Remember there were no instances of hyperinflation anywhere in the world during the last three consolidation phases. (See: "8-World War I and learning about hyperinflation.")

Implications for pay and inequality

One of the key effects of the consolidation wave would be to instil in the world a different outlook with regard to inflation. Annual wage rises would become a distant memory. Instead workers would only get wage increases when they became more skilled or improved their productivity. Moreover the value of different jobs would become clearer as people came to know the rates over time and the picture was no longer confused by the impact of inflation.

Reasons inequality would decline

> Incentive to improve wages through higher productivity or reskilling/moving job

> Gradually lower prices for goods increasing purchasing power

> Wealth destruction during transition phase

The most likely effect of this change in attitude would be to act as a strong incentive for people to increase their wages either by improving their output in their current job or by reskilling to get a different more highly-paid job. Over time, people would be able to clearly see the effect of the changes they have made themselves on their salary and this should create a positive feedback loop. Contrast this to the current system, where most people receive annual pay rises whether they are doing a good job or not. Moreover evidence[2] shows that they erroneously attribute these rises to their own skill and not to inflation.

Combine this effect of slightly rising average wages with the overall gradual decline in prices of goods and services and the net spending power of the bulk of the population would rise. Inequality would therefore decline as it has done before in the consolidation wave. This would be reinforced by the fact that the wealthy would be unlikely to see the massive asset price gains they have seen over recent decades. Tight controls on the money supply would stop them. Moreover the rich would have more than likely suffered a sharp decline in their wealth during the transition period, which would already have levelled the inequality field significantly.

Implications for business

Contrary to the established dogma that business needs the subsidy of stealth inflation tax to survive, I believe the overall impact on business would be positive once we are through the transition period. There is a number of number of reasons for this.

Reasons business would flourish

- More stable economic environment
- More transparency in sales and profits
- Better decision making
- Less "shoe leather" costs
- Less competition from zombie companies
- More investment and less share buy backs

One of the key implications of near-zero inflation would be decreased costs for business because of the removal of the need to constantly change prices. Such "shoe leather" costs, as economists sometimes refer to them[3], mean that companies divert time and energy away from more productive activity. The removal of inflation as a variable from a company's sales also makes it much easier for stakeholders (both management and shareholders) to truly see what is happening to a business. For example food-price deflation recently in the UK has clearly exposed the lack of growth in major food retailers that was not obvious before.

In his book, *Less Than Zero*, Professor George Selgin put forward a number of arguments why a zero-inflation world would be better for business.[4] He thinks it would lead to greater macroeconomic stability with fewer booms and busts. He also thinks it would allow for prices and wages to change only in industries where there has been a change in productivity or costs. He also argues that businesses would make better decisions.

The other overriding impact on business would come from different credit conditions brought about by changes to the monetary system. The reduced credit facilities likely to result from removing banks' privilege to invent money would have a major impact. Far fewer companies would be able to massage their apparent profitability by leverage and schemes such as share buy backs. This would encourage companies instead to invest in an attempt to create genuine growth.

The cost of funding would also return to levels where there is a reasonable risk premium. This would discourage zombie companies and create a climate for more innovative new companies to evolve. Funding sources would also change and this would have implications for business. There is likely to be increased crowdfunding of new companies (that is, funding from retail investors) and funding by venture capitalists (funding from high net worth investors). Such investors are likely to seek greater transparency, which might lead to greater efficiency and more profitable companies.

A key difference to the current world would be that the financial sector would be much smaller. A combination of wealth destruction during the transition phase, regulation and a new monetary system would all significantly reduce the size of the global financial market. It would primarily be just an administrative function with regard to money. Investment banks would still exist but their ability to create opaque derivatives might well be more restrained, especially if the next major financial crisis was made worse by them.

Implications for government debt

The UK and many other developed nations including the US, Canada and Australia all have significant budget deficits. Their governmental spending has exceeded tax receipts for many decades and this has led to an accumulation of debt. The main way that they have dealt with this situation has been to use inflation tax to finance it. In this, the true value of those deficits and debts is eroded by inflation.

This system would no longer work in the consolidation wave. It seems unlikely that governmental expenditure would actually decline, as the ageing population would create higher demands on health, pensions and welfare. To make matters worse the declining working population would bring in lower tax receipts. Admittedly their real incomes would hopefully be rising gradually (see above), but that is unlikely to be enough to close the gap.

Possible substitutes for inflation tax

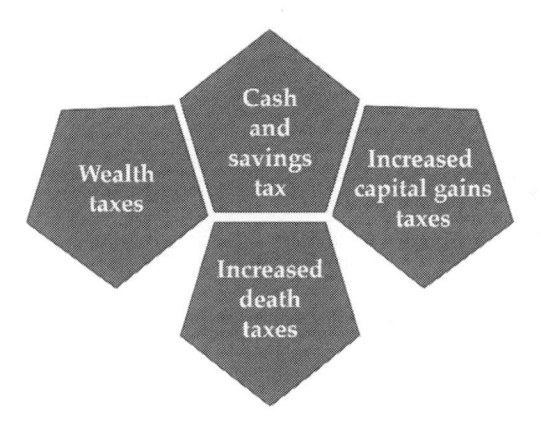

- Wealth taxes
- Cash and savings tax
- Increased capital gains taxes
- Increased death taxes

Some radical solution is going to be required to solve the revenue shortfall. Inflation tax is a capital tax and the most politically acceptable replacement is probably going to be some other form of capital tax. One option would be a direct replacement of inflation tax with governments levying a fixed rate of tax on all cash and savings. This would formalise the existing stealth tax into an overt tax. Governments might deduct say 2 per cent of the value of everyone's cash and savings accounts each year.

This would act as a strong incentive for consumers to spend and so could potentially boost the economy. However it could be argued that such a policy would run counter to the desire of most western governments to have their citizens fend for themselves and save for their own retirements. It is also likely to be strongly resisted by the population as witnessed by the protests in Greece in 2013.

Governments might even decide to extend the above scheme to levy an annual tax on all accumulated wealth. This would include housing, land and other investments. Again such a tax would be strongly resisted. It is possible that it could be implemented by a left-wing government with a sufficient majority – especially if it included some zero-rate bands to exempt the poorer majority of the population.

So, what other capital taxes might be sufficient to balance the missing inflation tax? One candidate is capital gains taxes. In many countries, these are currently set at advantageous levels compared to income taxes. For example in the UK, in 2015 there is a tax free allowance on the first £11,000 of gains in a year and then the remainder is taxed at either 18 per cent or a higher rate of 28 per cent. These rates are lower than the comparable income tax rates of 20 per cent and 40-45 per cent. The closing of this anomaly might help but is unlikely to be sufficient to bridge the gap.

Instead it seems the most likely candidate would be capital taxes on the accumulated estates of those who die. Again this is an emotive tax and often very unpopular. However it could be argued that the state provided the stable environment that the individual has exploited to create wealth during their lifetime and so the state probably has some moral claim on those gains. Furthermore relatively simple solutions such as making all income from estates subject to income tax does have the potential to raise significant revenue, probably enough to balance the loss from inflation tax.

In any event, the key conclusion of this analysis is that overt taxation would have to rise to make up for the loss of inflation tax when there is no inflation. In fact, this is already becoming a problem for governments in the disinflationary world in which we now live. Solutions may therefore have to be devised before we even start the consolidation wave.

The end of the cycle

The consolidation part of the wave would eventually end – probably at some point in the early 22nd Century if the approximately 80-year cycle repeats. The end would be marked by a gradual but consistent rise in the prices of certain goods until they break out of their previous range seen in the consolidation wave.

The ultimate trigger that starts the new inflationary wave would more than likely be related to demographics. The current ageing population of baby boomers in the post-war period would have long passed away. See, for example, the population pyramid from Japan below.

Age profile of Japan

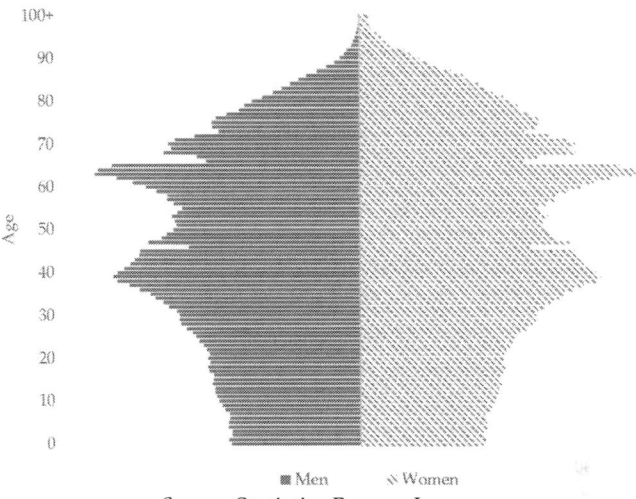

Source: Statistics Bureau Japan

By the second half of the 21st Century, most countries[5] could well have a more straight-sided profile with approximately equal numbers of all age groups (until illness finally reduces the numbers in the over 80s of course).

Indeed, once bulges from the 20th Century have finally died, there would start to be growing numbers in the working population relative to the total population in many countries. This would increase government tax takes and, overall, contribute to growing prosperity again towards the end of the 21st Century. If history repeats itself, the associated growing affluence of the average worker would more than likely create another baby boom. This new bulge in the population would be enough to form the basis for the start of the next great inflationary wave. Once started, man-made factors would again quickly take over as a whole new generation of speculators and governments discovered the benefits to be gained from having inflation.

KEY LEARNING POINTS:

- Stable prices may well be facilitated by major changes in the monetary system, potentially including the adoption of some form of cryptocurrency as the primary method of international exchange.
- Inequality would decline not only because of the destruction of

wealth during the transition phase but because of the incentive for workers to improve productivity and reskill as their only way to get a pay rise.
- Business would flourish in the more economically stable environment. However governments would need to find a substitute for inflation tax with new forms of transparent taxation.

QUIZ ANSWER:
B.

---

[1] Parsson, J., 1974, "Dying of Money: Lessons of the Great German and American Inflations", *Wellspring Press.*
[2] Katona, G., 1974, "Psychology and Consumer Economics", *Journal of Consumer Research,* 1(1).
[3] Mankiw, N.G., 2008. "Brief Principles of Macroeconomics", *Cengage Learning.*
[4] Selgin, G., 1997, "Less Than Zero: The Case for a Falling Price Level in a Growing Economy", *Institute of Economic Affairs.*
[5] The main exception will be many African nations.

Q20. Which is the best investing strategy for the next 50 years?

- **A** Buy and hold a portfolio of shares
- **B** Be aware of the inflation cycle and be prepared to switch asset allocations
- **C** Invest in government bonds

20
Managing wealth as we head towards near-zero inflation

This final chapter looks at the likely implications of future inflation patterns on wealth over the coming decades. More specifically it looks at the consequences for all types of wealth over the following three periods: near-term lowflation, a possible deflationary transitional period and a longer term near-zero inflation consolidation wave. Each phase would favour different assets. This has key implications for long-term investors.

DISCLAIMER: This chapter is based on logical deductions from the most likely scenarios portrayed in the previous chapters. However, as highlighted before, no one can predict the future accurately. Therefore this chapter should not be construed as advice to follow any particular investing strategy. Instead, it should be regarded as just another opinion to consider whilst making your own investment decisions. Please consult a professional for financial advice.

Overview of the implications for wealth

The implications for wealth are complicated because the likely pattern of future inflation is going to vary significantly with the economic conditions. The near-term outlook is most likely for a lowflation world. History suggests that the transition to the consolidation phase could well involve a marked decline of prices and asset prices. (See: "18-The transition period and near-term inflation.") Finally prices could well then remain largely stable or slightly declining over most of the remainder of the consolidation period. (See: "19-Price stability and the consolidation period.").

The following table illustrates that the impact of these periods on wealth would be very different. A traditional "buy and hold" strategy, or even a simple diversified portfolio, could lead to a significant loss of purchasing power over the coming decades.

Impact of likely future inflation on wealth

Wealth	Near term impact (lowflation)	Transition period (deflation)	Long term impact (zero inflation)
Shares	+	--	+
Government bonds	o	--	o (or n/a)
Corporate bonds	o	--	+
Precious metals	-	++	-
Other commodities	o	-	o
Property	+	--	o
Savings	-	+	+
Local currency cash	--	++	o
Digital currency	o	++	o

The following chapters look at each of these stages in more detail.

Near-term: central banks' attitudes are critical

The near-term prospects for wealth and asset prices are strongly influenced by central bank policy. There is an old adage in investing of *"Don't fight the Fed"*. Therefore, before we examine the impact of near-term inflation on wealth, it is worth briefly understanding this key issue.

It is in the current interests of central bankers and their governmental taskmasters to create positive inflation. Most central bankers' roles are defined in terms of fighting inflation. In simplistic terms, without inflation, they are in part redundant. Moreover, the armoury of techniques they employ to control the economy generally assumes there is positive inflation. Without inflation, they become more impotent. On the other side, their governmental directors seek positive inflation to help reduce the real size of their debt liabilities.

These are all strong forces on the future direction of inflation. It is therefore not surprising that the near-term prospects are for a lowflation world despite the many other strong deflationary factors that should be extinguishing inflation.

There may be a point in the coming decades when governments

decide (or are forced) to give up seeking positive inflation. It would result in assets that hitherto have produced good returns producing poor ones and vice versa. Until that point though, central banks' efforts to foster positive inflation would likely continue to increase the money supply and this would in turn support asset price growth.

Shares in a lowflation world

The current period, which could last a decade or more, is quite likely to be characterised by a lowflation world. This would be accompanied by low interest rates and periods of money printing and other stimuli from central banks. These so-called loose monetary conditions could well be very positive for companies who would find it cheap to borrow. Admittedly consumer demand would be subdued in the short-term, but this may well gradually recover over time as real wages stop declining so much in a world of low inflation rates.

This situation has the potential to bode well for shares, which should see dividends increase as the recovery eventually happens. Continued money printing by central banks would also support higher capital values for shares. Although some argue that some share indices are at all-time highs already and are relatively expensive, their arguments often ignore the impact of inflation.

For example by late 2014 the S&P 500 index in the US had grown just over 30 per cent since its highs in March 2000. But official inflation over that period was nearly 40 per cent, so it was lower in real terms (and even lower after actual inflation, without governmental manipulation – see: "6-Inflation measurement issues."). In the UK, the FTSE reached nearly 7000 in late 1999. It has still not risen above that level. During that time, even the official RPI has risen by over a half, so in real terms the FTSE is worth less than two thirds of what it was then.

There are also longer term cycles for shares that I described in my 2012 book, *Monkey with a Pin*. The graphic below taken from it shows the UK's bull and bear markets over the last century. The chart itself plots the FTSE All Share index, and the historic best estimate of it created by Barclays, adjusted for inflation and excluding dividends.

INFLATION MATTERS

UK Equity Index (adjusted for inflation)

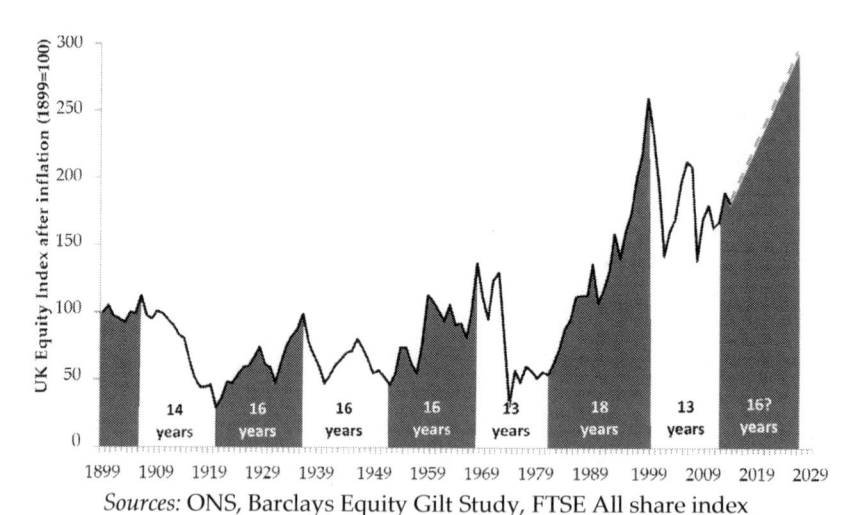

Sources: ONS, Barclays Equity Gilt Study, FTSE All share index

Assuming these secular cycles repeat, stock indices are due a period of at least a decade of broadly increasing prices from this point. The latest secular bear market probably ended in late 2012 following the announcement by the US Federal Reserve that it would embark on an enormous money printing programme nicknamed "QE-Infinity". Shortly after this in March 2013 the S&P Index broke into new highs. Such secular bull markets typically run for around 16 years, meaning towards around 2028.

Other wealth during the lowflation period

The other key asset that could benefit from continued cheap money is house prices. The overall picture for property and land prices ought to be supported by low interest rates. The key proviso would be that loans are not curtailed too heavily by regulations that would undoubtedly require higher capital ratios to be held by lenders. In addition, there may well be areas where prices might have reached affordability bounds, which would limit their increases from that point.

The converse to these winners from cheap money (shares and property) are people who are saving cash. Even though inflation may remain low, interest rates are more likely to remain even lower in the developed world during this period. Therefore savers would continue to see their money eroded by what inflation exists. This issue is bigger than it might at first seem as true inflation rates and prices rises are higher than implied by most officially published figures.

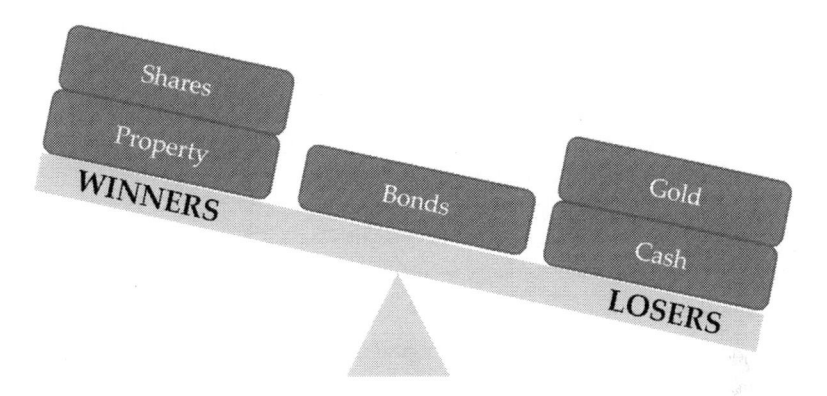

Wealth in the lowflation world

(Diagram: a balance scale tipping with WINNERS — Shares, Property — on the raised side, Bonds at the fulcrum, and LOSERS — Gold, Cash — on the lowered side.)

Commodity prices could well remain subdued during this period as world demand continues to suffer from deleveraging. But, balanced against this, the total world population would carry on growing and with it demand. Therefore overall commodity prices may even rise slightly. However the same may not be true for precious metals such as gold. These could decline as many perceive the asset to be an inflation hedge meaning that demand in a stable and lowflation world would be low – especially if shares generate good returns, as appears possible.

Finally, the outlook for bonds (both governmental and corporate) could well turn out to be less disastrous than many of the doomsayers predict, in the short-term at least. Governments in developed countries are adept at managing their debts and have the power to force parties to buy them (e.g. banks and pension funds) as well as the ability to effectively write them off by getting their central bank to print money to buy them. Another key factor in this area would be governments redeeming long-dated bond issues with high interest rates and replacing them with new bonds at lower rates. The UK has already started doing this. This process cuts government debt payments but at the same time reduces income for those who rely on it, such as pension funds.

Therefore although governmental debt is predicted to continue increasing, it may not lead immediately to large-scale abandonment of the asset. More likely is that real returns would be near zero for most of this period.

Everything changes in the transition period

All the above logic could change abruptly when the world enters the transition period in maybe a decade or more. The transition period would almost certainly be accompanied by a wide-scale restructuring of debt in some way in order to comply with Marcks's conditions for the end of inflation. (See: "18-The transition period and near-term inflation.")

It is impossible to predict the circumstances of this debt restructuring but the previously described scenario of a major bond crisis is not an impossible one. Restructuring of these debts would range from outright defaults to partial defaults and revised terms. The direct counterparties to corporate and government bonds would be the first affected. These are frequently pension and insurance companies who hold these assets as the savings of their clients or use them to pay out annuities. The value of these funds would be radically reduced and pensions would have to be scaled back accordingly.

Regulations have forced banks to become increasing holders of government debt in recent years. Because of the requirement to mark their assets to market values, many would quickly become insolvent and could be forced to close. More than likely this would create a domino effect that would cascade across financial institutions and other assets. It will be remembered that increases in the money supply first go into financial assets. The corollary is that those are the areas which suffer most when money supply contracts.

Implications for wealth in the transition period

The implication of the reduction of these asset prices and bank failures are numerous. Counterparties to banks would be affected. Savings held in banks might be lost where they exceed government guarantee thresholds (and possibly even below them). House prices would reduce, especially in areas where they have most been driven by leverage and speculation.

But one of the biggest implications would be with derivatives. The size of these has continued to grow even after the crisis and some estimate them now to be worth over $700 trillion[1]. This is seven times the size of global GDP. Any problem with these will have major implications for the world's finances.

Wealth in the transition period

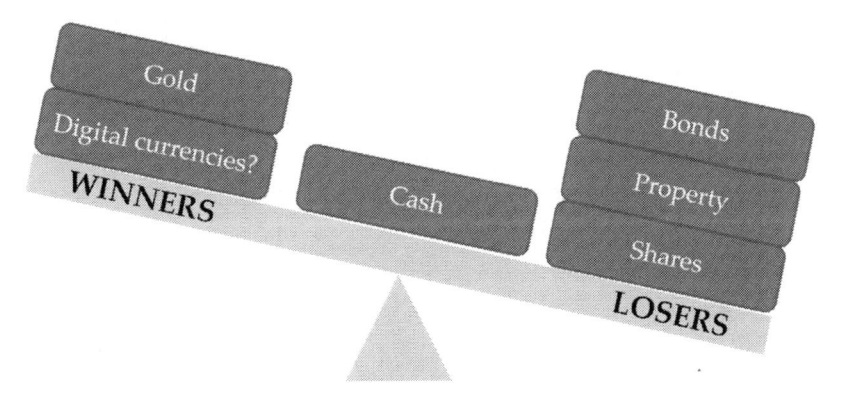

WINNERS: Gold, Digital currencies?

Cash (balance point)

LOSERS: Bonds, Property, Shares

One area where derivatives are particularly prevalent is as passive investment tools such as Exchange Traded Funds (ETFs). Although some of these put clients' money directly into physical investments, many these days are just synthetic swap contracts with other financial institutions based on promises to track an index. When a major crisis hits, these promise-based contracts could be particularly vulnerable. This could affect many private investors who have switched their savings into such funds because of their lower charges from what might turn out to have been the relative security of traditional unit trust funds (which have to buy physical assets or shares).

More broadly, stockmarket prices would probably tumble to generational lows in the height of the crisis. However any stimulus programs implemented afterwards to aid economic recovery might well cause a sharp rebound in prices. Thereafter and longer term during the consolidation period, prices may not increase much, once a new equilibrium level has been established. Indeed it has been argued that what has been driving stock prices higher during the last century was primarily increasing money supply effects[2].

Commodity prices would also be heavily affected by the crisis. Demand would fall globally for many commodities and contribute in large part to the fall in retail prices that would accompany the crisis. Commodities might be affected even more than other assets as most are traded as options and are not physically backed. They are therefore particularly vulnerable to credit drying up and counterparty failures.

The winners during the transition period?

That being said, precious metals would probably be the only commodity to rise in value. The gold price is strongly correlated to financial anxiety and, being seen as a safe-haven, can rise during crises. However there are effectively two gold markets: one based on physical ownership of bullion and the other based on options and synthetic paper contracts (many precious metal ETFs are not physically backed). It would not be surprising if this crisis finally saw the divergence between these two classes, with gold (and silver) bullion rising in price and the options and contracts falling along with the other commodities.

Precious metals would not be the only refuge. Digital currencies might come to the fore during this period if they have become a trusted store of wealth by that time. Indeed, this might be a turning point for their adoption and could even lead to them becoming part of a new world currency system. (See: "19-Price stability and the consolidation period.")

The final wealth category is that of cash. In theory holders of cash should be net beneficiaries of a steep decline in prices. Their purchasing power could even double. However there are a number of factors that in practice mean that cash-holders' outcomes may not be so good. Many financial institutions hold their cash in very short dated government debt. This might be devalued as bonds are rerated.

Private savers in theory should be protected up to a certain level by government backed insurance schemes. However, given the wide scale size of the crisis, it is not impossible that such agreements would be reneged upon[3]. In addition, there would be savers who have savings over the compensation limits who would be severely penalised as was seen in Cyprus in 2013. Even traditionally safe banks operated by governments may fail as safe-havens on this occasion as their owners seek to spread the costs of the crisis with anyone who holds any wealth.

The net effect of this scenario would be to reduce private wealth substantially. It would affect pretty much all portfolios no matter how they try to spread their risk across different asset types. It would impact those with the most money the greatest and have little impact on the wealth of the poorest. It would help redistribute wealth and so contribute to redressing the current inequality between rich and poor.

Investing in the consolidation wave

After the turbulence of the transition period, the world would more than likely enter a more stable period where prices vary less and over time remain stable and even start to decline.

Wealth in the consolidation wave

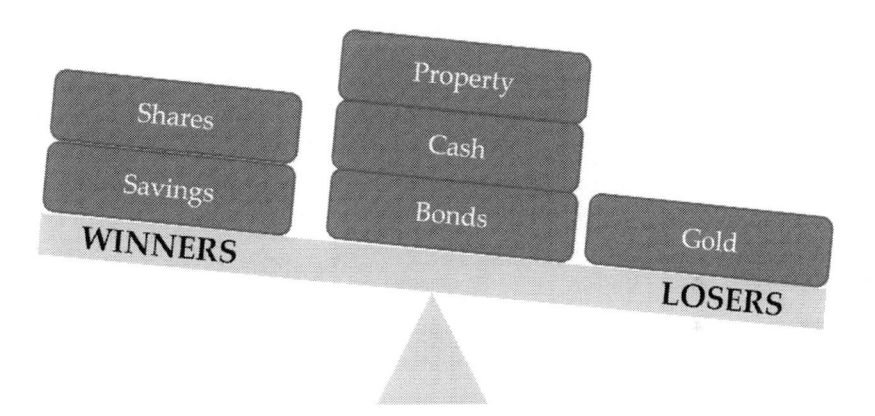

WINNERS: Shares, Savings, Property, Cash, Bonds
LOSERS: Gold

A key aspect of this period would probably be the reform of the remit of central banks. No longer would they be tasked with creating inflation. At the same time, a risk lending premium would return to savers and investors. This would mean that those with cash who were willing to tie it up for a period of time would probably receive a positive rate of interest again.

Owners of shares would also see positive returns. However, although there might there be a sharp rebound in prices during the transition period, the longer-term increases might well be more subdued. The key difference between the consolidation period and current times is that the long-term return may be lower, as it would not be flattered by inflation in subtle ways. In particular capital growth would be found only in growing companies.

Moreover borrowing would be more restrained during this period and companies would not benefit so much from leverage as they used to. Added to this, companies would face lower consumer demand. This would be partly due to demographics. The ageing and declining population would simply consume less. In addition, those that borrow would have lower consumption as they would need to set aside more to cover capital repayments as they could no longer rely on inflation to effectively pay the capital back for them.

In the 20th Century, the historical real return rate for shares (including dividends and deducting inflation) has been estimated at around 5 per cent a year[4]. It is likely that this figure would be lower during the consolidation wave – maybe even as low as 3 per cent (in actual and inflation adjusted terms). The return would primarily be that of dividends.

There would be a different attitude towards shares after the transition period and this would impact on money invested in them. So many people would have lost so much money during the transition bust that the asset class could be shunned for a generation at least. This would be exacerbated by the deleveraging of the baby-boomer generation, which would be selling shares to pay for healthcare and retirement.

There would also be positive risk returns again for lending to business. This might be via corporate bonds. However the bond crisis may have resulted in such loss of confidence in this market that alternative forms of business finance might take over, for instance peer-to-peer lending and crowdsourcing.

The same applies to government bonds. It is not impossible that the concept might not even exist in the consolidation wave. Alternative forms of government finance may have been implemented following the transition period. However, should they exist, the returns might be low given the safety guarantee that would probably be demanded following the crisis.

Stable prices = stable wealth

Low returns would probably be a key theme of wealth during the consolidation wave. There would be no free lunch anymore. Currently certain assets look like free lunches, but the gains they offer are in fact being paid for by others using the subtle effects of the inflation conveyor belt. (See: "16-The impact of current inflation.")

There would be no long-term return on zero-risk assets such as cash, gold and digital currencies. Having said that, the prospects for gold specifically may be poor during the initial decade of the consolidation wave. Its price may have risen strongly during the crisis of the transition period beyond any measure of real value. This would need to unwind and come down. Thereafter it would resemble other zero-risk assets and have a near-zero return.

Assets that used to rely heavily on appreciation related to the money supply, such as property and commodities, would be more stable in price and mainly influenced by supply and demand factors. The recent period of massive house price rises was an unusual one in history and may not to be repeated for a long time.

Concluding thoughts

The key theme of the consolidation wave is that money returns to its original purpose: it becomes largely just a method of exchange and a store of value over time. The perversion of being able to create money from nothing would be largely extinguished. Instead those who wish to get more money would either have to work directly to get it or be prepared to risk their capital to invest in real businesses that might provide a better return.

The world that accompanies these changes would be a more equitable place. The transition period would have removed a lot of the wealth that has created the rising inequality of recent decades. Instead the poor would have seen marked increases in their purchasing power as the prices of many things reverted to close to their true value. In particular, younger people would be able to afford to buy houses and might be less dependent on the older generation.

However the resulting new world would unfortunately one day sow the seeds of its own destruction and the 22nd Century would at some point undoubtedly usher in a new wave of inflation and the cycle would start all over again.

KEY LEARNING POINTS:

- In the near-term world of lowflation, central banks' determination to maintain positive inflation will support the prices of shares and property. The key losers will probably be cash-holders, savers and those with precious metals.
- The transition period is likely to be accompanied by restructuring of debt in some way. This means a significant reduction of wealth to the holders of such debts. This will likely be accompanied by widespread wealth destruction across shares, property, commodities and cash (when not protected by guarantees). Holders of gold (and possibly digital currencies) will probably be the temporary winners.
- The consolidation phase will mark an era when money returns to being more a method of exchange and a store of value. Gains from wealth will be much lower but still positive for shares and cash savings. Gold will likely quickly decline in value.

QUIZ ANSWER:
B.

---

[1] Carney, J. and Reilly, D., 2014, "Bank Regulators Roar at $700-Trillion Market", *WSJ*, 6 August 2014.

[2] Parsson, J., 1974, "Dying of Money: Lessons of the Great German and American Inflations", *Wellspring Press*.

[3] It could be argued that the Bank of England has already stated that it may renege on the guarantee system in such a crisis. See: "Resolving Globally Active, Systemically Important, Financial Institutions", *Federal Deposit Insurance Corporation and Bank of England*, 12 December 2012.

[4] Dimson, E., Marsh, P. and Staunton, M., 2002, "Triumph of the Optimists: 101 Years of Global Investment Returns ", *Princeton University Press*.

EPILOGUE

I have become very much a determinist in my views. By this I mean that I believe the world's broad destiny is largely determined by powerful forces and the way that humans typically react to those challenges. Human behaviour has a habit of repeating itself, or more precisely as Mark Twain supposedly said, it rhymes.

If you look back into history, you can see that the current inflationary trend is highly unlikely to continue forever. There will be something that causes it to end at some point. Nobody can say for sure when that will be or what will cause it. Demographics are clearly against inflation over the coming century. In addition, I suspect that the world's increasing debt is likely to influence it in some way. If it does, the transition period may not be pretty.

The world could choose now to avert that pain by reforming the way that money is created and by restructuring debts before they collapse. The Chicago Plan is a blueprint for how to do that which has existed for over 80 years. But history also shows that large bodies of humans rarely agree to come together and take such rational decisions for the common good. This is an example of an economic theory called "collective action" where a solution might benefit the wider group but implementation costs to individuals make it unlikely.

Although we cannot predict or change our fate we can at least have a perspective on the higher level forces that are shaping it, I hope this book has provided you with some of that context. Forearmed with that knowledge, you can perhaps arrange your life in a way that maximises its potential within those constraints.

I hope you will now agree: *Inflation Matters*.

inflationmatters.com
#inflationmatters
@petecomley

GLOSSARY OF TERMS

Block chain. A block chain is a public ledger of all digital currency transactions that have ever been executed. See Cryptocurrency.

Bretton Woods Agreement. A system of monetary management created in 1944 that established the rules for commercial and financial relations among the world's major industrial states. As well as founding the World Bank and the IMF, it linked the value of the pound to the US dollar from 1946–1971.

Central bank. A public institution that manages a country's currency, money supply and interest rates. Central banks usually also oversee the commercial banking system of a country (e.g. the Bank of England).

CPI. Consumer Price Index (formerly the "Harmonised Index of Consumer Prices" in the UK). This is the UK government's preferred measure of inflation. It excludes many housing expenses and is typically lower than RPI, due mainly to the way it goes about calculating mean scores.

Cryptocurrency. A medium of exchange using cryptography to secure the transactions and to control the creation of new units. They typically have a public ledger (such as block chain) to store a record of the transactions. Digital currencies such as Bitcoin are an example.

Deficit. The size of the difference between a government's expenditure and revenue from taxes, when expenditure is higher. In the opposite case, it creates a surplus. It differs from the country's debt, which is the total of all previous deficits (less surpluses).

Deflation. Deflation occurs when the general prices of goods and services are falling in nominal terms.

Deflator. A measure used when calculating GDP to decrease nominal prices to see what the real growth has been.

Disinflation. A period when price increases are slowing down (e.g. when inflation goes from 3 per cent to 2 per cent). It is different from deflation, when prices are lower than the previous period.

Fiat currency. A currency that a government has declared to be legal tender, despite the fact that it has no intrinsic value and is not backed by reserves (e.g. gold) or linked to a currency that is so backed. Most currencies nowadays are fiat currencies.

GLOSSARY OF TERMS

Financial repression. Any measures that governments employ to channel funds to themselves. Typically, it means supressing interest rates and creating inflation to relieve the burden of debts.

GDP. Gross domestic product is the market value of all goods and services produced within a country in a given period of time. It is often quoted as a percentage change versus the previous quarter (having first allowed for inflation using a deflator).

Geometric mean. A specific type of mean score used when the numbers you want to average all have a specific linked relationship with each other. It is sometimes incorrectly used in price indices.

Gross public debt. The total value of all government debt issued. It contrasts to net public debt, which has a reduction to allow for governments assets. This measure is used most for international comparisons.

Hedonic pricing. A statistical process involving regression to identify the value of different quality components of a product.

Inflation. A rise in the general level of prices of goods and services in an economy over a period of time.

Keynesians. People who believe in the thinking of John Maynard Keynes.

Lowflation. A term first created in 2014 by researchers at the IMF to describe the situation of very low inflation rates near to zero levels.

Monetarist. An economist who believes that the economy's performance is determined almost entirely by changes in the money supply. In particular they think that inflation is caused when the money supply increases faster than economic growth.

Net public debt. The total value of all government debt issued, less a reduction to allow for governments assets (e.g. gold). This is the preferred UK government measure of debt.

Nominal. In the context of this book, it means a number that has not been adjusted for inflation. The opposite is called "real".

Quantitative Easing (QE). A process whereby a central bank (e.g. the Bank of England) creates money to buy some asset. In the UK, most of the money so created has been used to buy government debt.

RPI. Retail Price Index. The original cost of living index in the UK. This has a wider coverage of items than CPI and results in higher prices due to using normal mean scores to calculate average prices.

Yield (in the context of bonds). The amount of annual interest expressed as a percentage of its current face value (as opposed to its value when first issued).

INDEX

1

1970s inflation · 5, 4, 21, 72, 101, 106, 109, 110, 111, 112, 113, 120, 133, 144, 151, 204

A

Asset price inflation · 5, 15, 38, 74

B

Bank of England · 13, 14, 15, 17, 38, 81, 87, 103, 113, 133, 137, 140, 143, 145, 147, 153, 156, 157, 165, 167, 170, 172, 178, 187, 196, 197, 207, 232, 236, 237
Bernanke, Ben · 38, 41, 95, 96, 157, 158, 159
Bitcoin, Cryptocurrency · 210, 236
Block chain · 236
Bretton Woods Currency Agreement · 103, 104, 110, 111, 113, 133, 150, 151, 236

C

Chicago Plan · 189, 194, 202, 203, 206, 207, 210, 235
China · 36, 80, 119, 121, 122, 123, 134, 155, 182, 183, 184, 191
Copernicus, Nicolaus · 10, 11
Core inflation · 5
CPI (Consumer Prices Index) · 3, 5, 31, 38, 43, 44, 45, 46, 47, 48, 52, 53, 54, 55, 57, 58, 61, 62, 63, 64, 65, 119, 137, 142, 143, 156, 165, 170, 171, 173, 236, 237
 History · 44
 Underestimation of inflation · 62

D

Dalton, Hugh · 103, 105, 139, 147
Definitions of inflation · 79
Deflation: · 5, 27, 29, 30, 33, 35, 36, 39, 40, 41, 70, 91, 93, 97, 129, 206, 236
 Bad deflation · 31
 Central banks · 37
 Debtors · 33
 Economic argument · 32
 Effects on companies · 35
 Effects on spending · 36
 Good deflation · 31, 40
Demographics · 235
Dent, Harry · 25
Disinflation · 236
Douglas, Roger · 151

F

Federal Reserve Bank · 5, 92, 94, 95, 96, 103, 112, 114, 120, 121, 150, 155, 157, 159, 183, 191, 224

G

GDP deflator · 47, 135, 143, 146, 147, 237
Governments
 Benefits of inflation · 141
 Inflation tax · 48, 140, 146, 147, 215
 Inflation-friendly polices · 145
 Switzerland · 137
Great depression (1930s) · 5, 29, 30, 33, 72, 82, 88, 91, 92, 93, 95, 96,

150, 202, 210
Great Moderation · 5, 119, 120, 124, 155
Great Recession · 5, 21, 119, 120, 122, 123, 124, 128, 155, 164, 171, 183, 184, 195

H

HICP (Harmonised Index of Consumer Prices) · 44, 45, 48, 58
Historical inflation
   Ancient Greece/Rome · 70
   Babylonia · 70, 76
   World War I · 5, vi, 12, 21, 43, 48, 73, 74, 79, 81, 82, 87, 94, 99, 101, 102, 106, 107, 110, 127, 137, 139, 144, 150, 159, 169, 210, 212
   World War II · 5, vi, 21, 79, 87, 94, 99, 102, 106, 110, 127, 137, 139, 144, 150, 159, 210
Hyperinflation · 86, 87, 88
   Causes · 80
   Weimar Republic · 12, 79, 82, 84, 85, 86, 87

I

Inequality · 209, 213, 217
Inflation prediction · 177
Inflation targeting · 149, 158, 159
   Detailed process · 37, 154
   Higher targets · 6, 153, 156, 159
   Origins · 151
   Targets by country · 152
Inflationary Wave Theory · 69-76, 132, 179, 180, 195
   Crest of the wave · 183

J

Japan · 5, 23, 30, 31, 33, 40, 58, 86, 123, 127, 128, 129, 130, 131, 132, 133, 134, 135, 137, 144, 146, 155, 181, 182, 183, 187, 189, 190, 192, 194, 195, 197, 198, 199, 206, 216, 217
Exchange rate · 127, 133, 134, 135, 198

K

Keynes, John Maynard · 19, 20, 21, 22, 23, 26, 27, 84, 85, 88, 100, 102, 103, 104, 105, 107, 138, 147, 150, 152, 159, 237

L

Latent inflation · 26, 195, 204
Lowflation · 206, 237

M

Maastricht Treaty · 44, 48, 81, 88
Malthus, Reverend (Thomas) Robert · 19, 23, 24, 26, 27, 72, 77
Man-made inflation · vii
Marcks, Ronald · 84, 112, 193, 194, 195, 198, 199, 203, 205, 211, 226
Mean scores
   Carli · 55, 56, 57, 58, 64
   Dutot · 55, 56, 57, 58
   Jevons (See · 47, 56, 57, 58
Measurement issues · 5, 3, 46, 51, 135, 142, 156, 223
   calculation · 55
   coverage · 53, 54
   Geometric means · 56, 237
   quality adjustments · 60, 65, 143, 170
   substitution · 59
Monetarist · 5, 22, 237
Money creation · 15
Money supply · 13, 14, 15, 195, 196

N

Near-zero inflation · 183

O

ONS (Office of National Statistics) · 13, 14, 15, 17, 25, 26, 45, 47, 48, 52, 54, 55, 57, 58, 59, 60, 61, 62, 63, 64, 71, 102, 106, 109, 140, 147, 165, 166, 181, 196, 197, 207, 224
Other UK inflation measures
  CPIH · 47, 54
  PPI · 47
  RPIJ · 47
  TPI · 47

P

Piketty, Thomas · vii, viii
Population · 25, 27, 54, 77, 181, 186

Q

QE (Quantitative Easing) · 30, 86, 87, 123, 140, 144, 167, 192, 204, 224, 237
Quantity theory of money · 11

R

Return of inflation · 204
RPI (Retail Prices Index) · 14, 15, 17, 31, 43, 44, 45, 46, 47, 48, 53, 54, 55, 57, 58, 60, 63, 64, 65, 123, 130, 142, 143, 145, 147, 156, 165, 168, 169, 170, 171, 172, 173, 223, 236, 237

S

Selgin, George · 40, 213, 218

V

Velocity of money · 12, 13, 17, 31, 36, 37, 81, 93, 195, 199, 201, 204
Volcker, Paul · 112, 113, 114, 120

W

Wage inflation · 5
Wealth
  Consolidation period · 229
  FTSE cycles · 15, 223, 224
  Gold · 10, 70, 80, 81, 82, 87, 94, 102, 103, 110, 113, 150, 225, 228, 230, 231, 236, 237
  implications of inflation · 5, vii, 10, 16, 35, 36, 79, 85, 86, 87, 91, 93, 106, 157, 158, 161, 162, 164, 166, 167, 168, 170, 172, 183, 201, 213, 214, 215, 216, 218, 221, 222, 224, 226, 228, 230, 231
  property · 32, 56, 92, 113, 127, 224, 230, 231
  Transition period · 226
Wicksell, Knut · 149, 150, 152, 158
Winners and losers with inflation · 39, 161, 162, 163, 164, 172, 224, 228, 231

Y

Yellen, Janet · 191

ABOUT THE AUTHOR

Pete's first book, *Monkey with a Pin*, was published in 2012. It exposed how most private investors' returns are much worse in real life than the theoretical returns promoted by the finance industry. It went viral and was downloaded by over 10,000 people. His second book, *Inflation Tax: The Plan To Deal With The Debts* was published in 2013.

You might describe Pete as an author with an inquiring mind. He is not one to blindly accept the orthodoxy and conventional wisdom. Instead, he forms his opinions by painstakingly re-evaluating the facts – and by joining the dots sometimes coming to different conclusions.

He has a degree in psychology and has worked for most of his career in market research. He's well known within the industry as a conference speaker and also an innovator. He was the first person to run commercial online surveys in the UK in the mid-1990s. He founded the first UK online market research agency in 1998. The company is now called Join the Dots and has its head office in Manchester.

Pete's interests include gardening, and he recently created allotments in his local village for 150 people. He is in the process of walking the entire coast of England and Wales with his wife, Trish.

Pete can be contacted on twitter: @petecomley or by email: pete.comley@inflationmatters.com.

ACKNOWLEDGEMENTS

Can I thank all of the people who have helped me write this book and for all their feedback. Specifically, I'd like to thank my wife Trish Comley, my son David Comley, Jon Fewtrell, Neil Glass, James Paton and Kate Rhodes (cover designer).

Your inputs have been invaluable in making this book so much better than I could ever have achieved on my own.

Printed in Great Britain
by Amazon.co.uk, Ltd.,
Marston Gate.